Connected Mathematics™

Accentuate the Negative

Integers

Teacher's Guide

Glenda Lappan
James T. Fey
William M. Fitzgerald
Susan N. Friel
Elizabeth Difanis Phillips

PEARSON
Prentice Hall

Glenview, Illinois
Needham, Massachusetts
Upper Saddle River, New Jersey

Connected Mathematics™ was developed at Michigan State University with financial support from the Michigan State University Office of the Provost, Computing and Technology, and the College of Natural Science.

This material is based upon work supported by the National Science Foundation under Grant No. MDR 9150217.

This project was supported, in part, by the
National Science Foundation
Opinions expressed are those of the authors and not necessarily those of the Foundation

The Michigan State University authors and administration have agreed that all MSU royalties arising from this publication will be devoted to purposes supported by the Department of Mathematics and the MSU Mathematics Education Enrichment Fund.

Photo Acknowledgements: 14 © Esbin-Anderson/The Image Works; 29 © Mike Douglas/The Image Works; 30 Michael Dwyer/Stock, Boston; 34 © Peter Menzel/Stock, Boston; 46 © Alan Carey/The Image Works; 50 © Superstock, Inc.; 63 © Superstock, Inc.; 65 © Barbara Van Cleve/Tony Stone Images

PEARSON
Prentice Hall

ISBN 0-13-180791-9
1 2 3 4 5 6 7 8 9 10   07 06 05 04 03

The Connected Mathematics Project Staff

Project Directors

James T. Fey
University of Maryland

William M. Fitzgerald
Michigan State University

Susan N. Friel
University of North Carolina at Chapel Hill

Glenda Lappan
Michigan State University

Elizabeth Difanis Phillips
Michigan State University

Project Manager

Kathy Burgis
Michigan State University

Technical Coordinator

Judith Martus Miller
Michigan State University

Collaborating Teachers/Writers

Mary K. Bouck
Portland, Michigan

Jacqueline Stewart
Okemos, Michigan

Curriculum Development Consultants

David Ben-Chaim
Weizmann Institute

Alex Friedlander
Weizmann Institute

Eleanor Geiger
University of Maryland

Jane Mitchell
University of North Carolina at Chapel Hill

Anthony D. Rickard
Alma College

Evaluation Team

Mark Hoover
Michigan State University

Diane V. Lambdin
Indiana University

Sandra K. Wilcox
Michigan State University

Judith S. Zawojewski
National-Louis University

Graduate Assistants

Scott J. Baldridge
Michigan State University

Angie S. Eshelman
Michigan State University

M. Faaiz Gierdien
Michigan State University

Jane M. Keiser
Indiana University

Angela S. Krebs
Michigan State University

James M. Larson
Michigan State University

Ronald Preston
Indiana University

Tat Ming Sze
Michigan State University

Sarah Theule-Lubienski
Michigan State University

Jeffrey J. Wanko
Michigan State University

Field Test Production Team

Katherine Oesterle
Michigan State University

Stacey L. Otto
University of North Carolina at Chapel Hill

Teacher/Assessment Team

Kathy Booth
Waverly, Michigan

Anita Clark
Marshall, Michigan

Julie Faulkner
Traverse City, Michigan

Theodore Gardella
Bloomfield Hills, Michigan

Yvonne Grant
Portland, Michigan

Linda R. Lobue
Vista, California

Suzanne McGrath
Chula Vista, California

Nancy McIntyre
Troy, Michigan

Mary Beth Schmitt
Traverse City, Michigan

Linda Walker
Tallahassee, Florida

Software Developer

Richard Burgis
East Lansing, Michigan

Development Center Directors

Nicholas Branca
San Diego State University

Dianne Briars
Pittsburgh Public Schools

Frances R. Curcio
New York University

Perry Lanier
Michigan State University

J. Michael Shaughnessy
Portland State University

Charles Vonder Embse
Central Michigan University

Field Test Coordinators

Michelle Bohan
Queens, New York

Melanie Branca
San Diego, California

Alecia Devantier
Shepherd, Michigan

Jenny Jorgensen
Flint, Michigan

Sandra Kralovec
Portland, Oregon

Sonia Marsalis
Flint, Michigan

William Schaeffer
Pittsburgh, Pennsylvania

Karma Vince
Toledo, Ohio

Virginia Wolf
Pittsburgh, Pennsylvania

Shirel Yaloz
Queens, New York

Student Assistants

Laura Hammond
David Roche
Courtney Stoner
Jovan Trpovski
Julie Valicenti
Michigan State University

Advisory Board

Joseph Adney
Michigan State University (Emeritus)

Charles Allan
Michigan Department of Education

Mary K. Bouck
Portland Public Schools
Portland, Michigan

C. Stuart Brewster
Palo Alto, California

Anita Clark
Marshall Public Schools
Marshall, Michigan

David Doherty
GMI Engineering and Management Institute
Flint, Michigan

Kay Gilliland
EQUALS
Berkeley, California

David Green
GMI Engineering and Management Institute
Flint, Michigan

Henry Heikkinen
University of Northern Colorado
Greeley, Colorado

Anita Johnston
Jackson Community College
Jackson, Michigan

Elizabeth M. Jones
Lansing School District
Lansing, Michigan

Jim Landwehr
AT&T Bell Laboratories
Murray Hill, New Jersey

Peter Lappan
Michigan State University

Steven Leinwand
Connecticut Department of Education

Nancy McIntyre
Troy Public Schools
Troy, Michigan

Valerie Mills
Ypsilanti Public Schools
Ypsilanti, Michigan

David S. Moore
Purdue University
West Lafayette, Indiana

Ralph Oliva
Texas Instruments
Dallas, Texas

Richard Phillips
Michigan State University

Jacob Plotkin
Michigan State University

Dawn Pysarchik
Michigan State University

Rheta N. Rubenstein
University of Windsor
Windsor, Ontario, Canada

Susan Jo Russell
TERC
Cambridge, Massachusetts

Marjorie Senechal
Smith College
Northampton, Massachusetts

Sharon Senk
Michigan State University

Jacqueline Stewart
Okemos School District
Okemos, Michigan

Uri Treisman
University of Texas
Austin, Texas

Irvin E. Vance
Michigan State University

Linda Walker
Tallahassee Public Schools
Tallahassee, Florida

Gail Weeks
Northville Public Schools
Northville, Michigan

Pilot Teachers

California

National City

Laura Chavez
National City Middle School

Ruth Ann Duncan
National City Middle School

Sonia Nolla
National City Middle School

San Diego

James Ciolli
Los Altos Elementary School

Chula Vista

Agatha Graney
Hilltop Middle School

Suzanne McGrath
Eastlake Elementary School

Toni Miller
Hilltop Middle School

Lakeside

Eva Hollister
Tierra del Sol Middle School

Vista

Linda LoBue
Washington Middle School

Illinois

Evanston

Marlene Robinson
Baker Demonstration School

Michigan

Bloomfield Hills

Roxanne Cleveland
Bloomfield Hills Middle School

Constance Kelly
Bloomfield Hills Middle School

Tim Loula
Bloomfield Hills Middle School

Audrey Marsalese
Bloomfield Hills Middle School

Kara Reid
Bloomfield Hills Middle School

Joann Schultz
Bloomfield Hills Middle School

Flint

Joshua Coty
Holmes Middle School

Brenda Duckett-Jones
Brownell Elementary School

Lisa Earl
Holmes Middle School

Anne Heidel
Holmes Middle School

Chad Meyers
Brownell Elementary School

Greg Mickelson
Holmes Middle School

Rebecca Ray
Holmes Middle School

Patricia Wagner
Holmes Middle School

Greg Williams
Gundry Elementary School

Lansing

Susan Bissonette
Waverly Middle School

Kathy Booth
Waverly East Intermediate School

Carole Campbell
Waverly East Intermediate School

Gary Gillespie
Waverly East Intermediate School

Denise Kehren
Waverly Middle School

Virginia Larson
Waverly East Intermediate School

Kelly Martin
Waverly Middle School

Laurie Metevier
Waverly East Intermediate School

Craig Paksi
Waverly East Intermediate School

Tony Pecoraro
Waverly Middle School

Helene Rewa
Waverly East Intermediate School

Arnold Stiefel
Waverly Middle School

Portland

Bill Carlton
Portland Middle School

Kathy Dole
Portland Middle School

Debby Flate
Portland Middle School

Yvonne Grant
Portland Middle School

Terry Keusch
Portland Middle School

John Manzini
Portland Middle School

Mary Parker
Portland Middle School

Scott Sandborn
Portland Middle School

Shepherd

Steve Brant
Shepherd Middle School

Marty Brock
Shepherd Middle School

Cathy Church
Shepherd Middle School

Ginny Crandall
Shepherd Middle School

Craig Ericksen
Shepherd Middle School

Natalie Hackney
Shepherd Middle School

Bill Hamilton
Shepherd Middle School

Julie Salisbury
Shepherd Middle School

Sturgis

Sandra Allen
Eastwood Elementary School

Margaret Baker
Eastwood Elementary School

Steven Baker
Eastwood Elementary School

Keith Barnes
Sturgis Middle School

Wilodean Beckwith
Eastwood Elementary School

Darcy Bird
Eastwood Elementary School

Bill Dickey
Sturgis Middle School

Ellen Eisele
Sturgis Middle School

James Hoelscher
Sturgis Middle School

Richard Nolan
Sturgis Middle School

J. Hunter Raiford
Sturgis Middle School

Cindy Sprowl
Eastwood Elementary School

Leslie Stewart
Eastwood Elementary School

Connie Sutton
Eastwood Elementary School

Traverse City

Maureen Bauer
Interlochen Elementary School

Ivanka Berskshire
East Junior High School

Sarah Boehm
Courtade Elementary School

Marilyn Conklin
Interlochen Elementary School

Nancy Crandall
Blair Elementary School

Fran Cullen
Courtade Elementary School

Eric Dreier
Old Mission Elementary School

Lisa Dzierwa
Cherry Knoll Elementary School

Ray Fouch
West Junior High School

Ed Hargis
Willow Hill Elementary School

Richard Henry
West Junior High School

Dessie Hughes
Cherry Knoll Elementary School

Ruthanne Kladder
Oak Park Elementary School

Bonnie Knapp
West Junior High School

Sue Laisure
Sabin Elementary School

Stan Malaski
Oak Park Elementary School

Jody Meyers
Sabin Elementary School

Marsha Myles
East Junior High School

Mary Beth O'Neil
Traverse Heights Elementary School

Jan Palkowski
East Junior High School

Karen Richardson
Old Mission Elementary School

Kristin Sak
Bertha Vos Elementary School

Mary Beth Schmitt
East Junior High School

Mike Schrotenboer
Norris Elementary School

Gail Smith
Willow Hill Elementary School

Karrie Tufts
Eastern Elementary School

Mike Wilson
East Junior High School

Tom Wilson
West Junior High School

Minnesota

Minneapolis

Betsy Ford
Northeast Middle School

New York

East Elmhurst

Allison Clark
Louis Armstrong Middle School

Dorothy Hershey
Louis Armstrong Middle School

J. Lewis McNeece
Louis Armstrong Middle School

Rossana Perez
Louis Armstrong Middle School

Merna Porter
Louis Armstrong Middle School

Marie Turini
Louis Armstrong Middle School

North Carolina

Durham

Everly Broadway
Durham Public Schools

Thomas Carson
Duke School for Children

Mary Hebrank
Duke School for Children

Bill O'Connor
Duke School for Children

Ruth Pershing
Duke School for Children

Peter Reichert
Duke School for Children

Elizabeth City

Rita Banks
Elizabeth City Middle School

Beth Chaundry
Elizabeth City Middle School

Amy Cuthbertson
Elizabeth City Middle School

Deni Dennison
Elizabeth City Middle School

Jean Gray
Elizabeth City Middle School

John McMenamin
Elizabeth City Middle School

Nicollette Nixon
Elizabeth City Middle School

Malinda Norfleet
Elizabeth City Middle School

Joyce O'Neal
Elizabeth City Middle School

Clevie Sawyer
Elizabeth City Middle School

Juanita Shannon
Elizabeth City Middle School

Terry Thorne
Elizabeth City Middle School

Rebecca Wardour
Elizabeth City Middle School

Leora Winslow
Elizabeth City Middle School

Franklinton

Susan Haywood
Franklinton Elementary School

Clyde Melton
Franklinton Elementary School

Louisburg

Lisa Anderson
Terrell Lane Middle School

Jackie Frazier
Terrell Lane Middle School

Pam Harris
Terrell Lane Middle School

Ohio

Toledo

Bonnie Bias
Hawkins Elementary School

Marsha Jackish
Hawkins Elementary School

Lee Jagodzinski
DeVeaux Junior High School

Norma J. King
Old Orchard Elementary School

Margaret McCready
Old Orchard Elementary School

Carmella Morton
DeVeaux Junior High School

Karen C. Rohrs
Hawkins Elementary School

Marie Sahloff
DeVeaux Junior High School

L. Michael Vince
McTigue Junior High School

Brenda D. Watkins
Old Orchard Elementary School

Oregon

Canby

Sandra Kralovec
Ackerman Middle School

Portland

Roberta Cohen
Catlin Gabel School

David Ellenberg
Catlin Gabel School

Sara Normington
Catlin Gabel School

Karen Scholte-Arce
Catlin Gabel School

West Linn

Marge Burack
Wood Middle School

Tracy Wygant
Athey Creek Middle School

Pennsylvania

Pittsburgh

Sheryl Adams
Reizenstein Middle School

Sue Barie
Frick International Studies Academy

Suzie Berry
Frick International Studies Academy

Richard Delgrosso
Frick International Studies Academy

Janet Falkowski
Frick International Studies Academy

Joanne George
Reizenstein Middle School

Harriet Hopper
Reizenstein Middle School

Chuck Jessen
Reizenstein Middle School

Ken Labuskes
Reizenstein Middle School

Barbara Lewis
Reizenstein Middle School

Sharon Mihalich
Reizenstein Middle School

Marianne O'Connor
Frick International Studies Academy

Mark Sammartino
Reizenstein Middle School

Washington

Seattle

Chris Johnson
University Preparatory Academy

Rick Purn
University Preparatory Academy

Contents

Overview

In the middle grades, students are introduced to fractions and decimals. The next major hurdle is building an understanding of positive and negative numbers, and in particular, integers. These kinds of numbers have been experienced by students informally in their everyday world—as temperatures in the winter drop below zero, as sports teams are said to be ahead or behind by so much. Students have intuitively used operations on integers to make sense of these situations. This unit explores situations that require representation with integers and that suggest more formal ways to add, subtract, multiply, and divide positive and negative numbers.

To introduce students to work with integers, the context of winning points (represented by positive integers) and losing points (represented by negative integers) in a game is used. The game provides an entry point for discussing order and the comparing of integers as well as for developing the concepts of opposites, distances on a number line, and absolute value. The number line is used throughout the unit to model strategies for adding, subtracting, and multiplying integers. A board with chips of two colors is a second model students will use for addition and subtraction.

The inverse relationships between addition and subtraction and between multiplication and division are investigated to help students generalize rules for these four operations. Looking at number patterns that are familiar and extending them to operations on integers is another way to attach operations on these new numbers to ideas students already have.

The Mathematics in *Accentuate the Negative*

Most of your students can add, subtract, multiply, and divide whole numbers and decimals. However, most have not been asked to think about what the operations mean and what kinds of situations call for which operation. Without the development of the disposition to seek ways of making sense of mathematical ideas and skills, students may end up with technical skills but without ways of deciding when and how those skills can be used to solve problems.

One good way to work toward creating the desire to make sense of these ideas is to model such thinking in rich classroom conversation. Asking questions about meaning, about what makes sense, as a regular, expected part of classroom discourse helps focus students on making connections. Exploring new aspects of number in a way that builds on and connects to what they already know is likely to have two good effects. First, students will deepen their understanding of familiar numbers and operations on them. Second, the new numbers—in this case, integers—will be more deeply integrated into students' own mathematical knowledge and resources.

Students find several things difficult about integers and operations on integers.

- The fact that $^{-}27$ is less than $^{-}12$ is contrary to students' experience with (positive) whole numbers. This understanding requires building mental images and models that allow students to visualize these new comparisons and relationships.

- The operation of subtraction, and especially subtracting a negative, is difficult for students to make sense of. In this unit, students will have several opportunities to think about what makes sense and why, and they will encounter several representations and models that will help them think more deeply about subtraction.
- The idea that subtracting a negative number gives the same result as adding the opposite of the negative number (adding a positive) is difficult for many students. This understanding must develop over time as students make observations and comparisons between subtraction and addition. Recognizing that these are inverse operations and that addition sentences are related to subtraction sentences helps students to expand their understanding of this concept.
- Multiplying two negatives and getting a positive seems like magic to most students. In fact, the usual ways of giving meaning to multiplication—such as accumulating an amount over and over (repeated addition)—seem of no help in making sense of $^-12 \times {}^-5$.

In the unit, we approach these difficult concepts through the use of two basic models and the observation of patterns. The accumulation of evidence from the models is more powerful than that from a single model. In addition, a particular model may be more useful for making sense of parts of the picture, but not the whole picture.

Modeling Addition of Integers

In this unit, students will use the number line to find a strategy for adding integers. Adding positive integers is interpreted as "going to the right"; adding negative numbers is interpreted as "going to the left." To add $^+5$ and $^-7$, for example, the strategy is to start at the point marked 0, go right 5 units to the point labeled 5, and then go left 7 units, which puts you at the point labeled $^-2$. Thus, $5 + {}^-7 = {}^-2$.

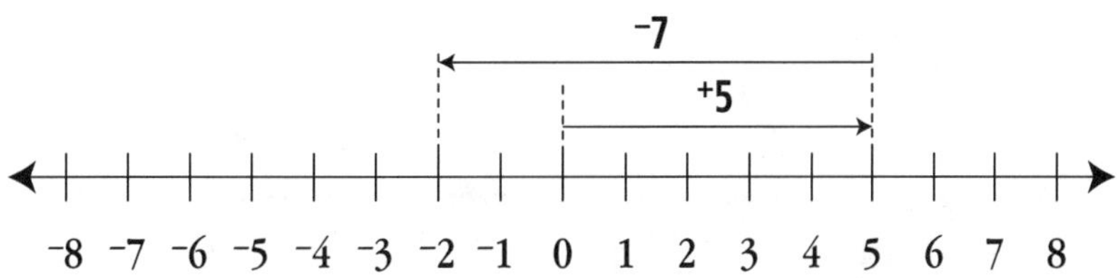

Colored chips can also be used to develop a strategy for adding integers. Using this model requires an understanding of opposites. Two colors of chips are used, one color (such as black) to represent positive numbers and another (such as red) to represent negative numbers. To add $^+8 + {}^-5$, the strategy is to first put 8 black chips on the chip board. Since the problem involves addition, which means to combine, 5 red chips are added to the board to represent the $^-5$.

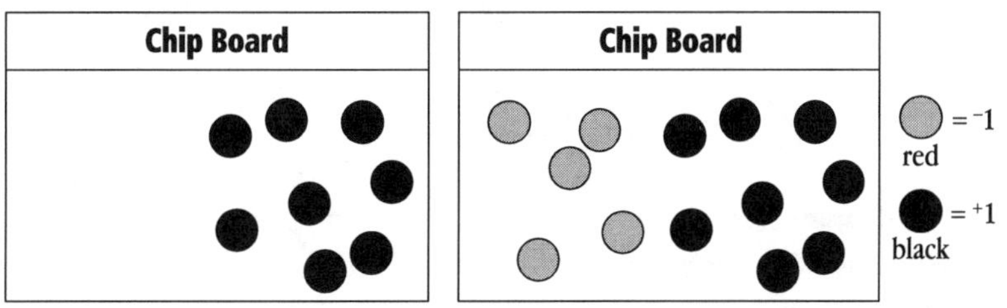

Because each chip represents 1 unit, either positive or negative, a black and red chip are thought of as opposites. Two opposite chips make 0 ($^+1 + {}^-1 = 0$). In this problem, 5 chips of each color can be paired to make zeros. After the paired chips are removed, 3 black chips remain—which represent $^+3$, the sum.

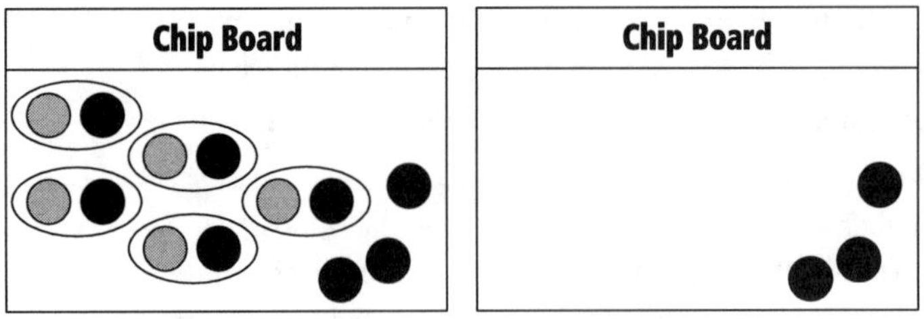

Modeling Subtraction of Integers

Since addition and subtraction are inverse, or opposite, operations, subtraction can be represented as doing the inverse of addition. To calculate $^{+}7 - {}^{+}5$, the strategy is to start at 0 and go to the right 7 units to $^{+}7$ (the same as in the addition strategy). Then, because the operation is subtraction, the direction of the $^{+}5$ move is reversed (this may also be thought of as going in the opposite direction), going to the left 5 units to $^{+}2$. Thus, $^{+}7 - {}^{+}5 = {}^{+}2$.

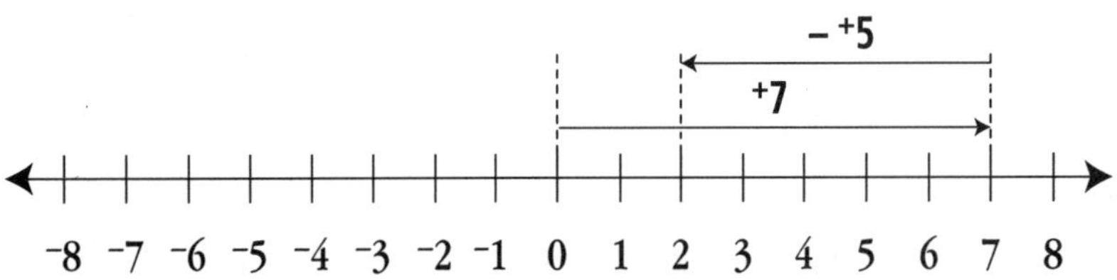

Examining the number line model for subtraction often leads students to observe that the subtraction expression is equivalent to an addition expression ($^{+}7 + {}^{-}5$) and to recognize that the strategy of subtracting an integer is equivalent to adding the opposite of the integer ($^{+}7 - {}^{+}5 = {}^{+}7 + {}^{-}5$). Students will need several experiences with subtraction before they notice these patterns.

On a chip board, subtraction involves removing the number of chips (of the correct color) by the amount indicated after the subtraction sign. To calculate $^{+}7 - {}^{+}5$, the strategy is to first add 7 black chips to the board (the same as in the addition strategy). Since the problem involves subtraction, 5 black chips are removed, leaving 2 black chips (which represent $^{+}2$). Removing chips is the opposite of the procedure for addition, in which the amount of the number after the operation sign is added to the board. Thus, $^{+}7 - {}^{+}5 = {}^{+}2$.

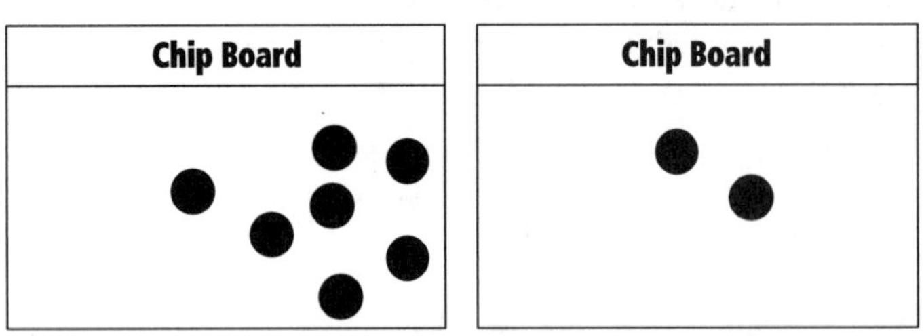

A more complex problem is $^{+}7 - {}^{-}5$. To do this problem on a chip board, 7 black chips are added to the board. Then, because the operation is subtraction, 5 red chips need to be removed ($^{-}5$). Since there are no red chips on the board, zeros—in the form of black-red pairs of chips—must be added to the board. In this problem, 5 red chips and 5 black chips must be added. Once there are 5 red chips on the board, they can be removed, leaving 12 black chips. Thus, $^{+}7 - {}^{-}5 = {}^{+}12$.

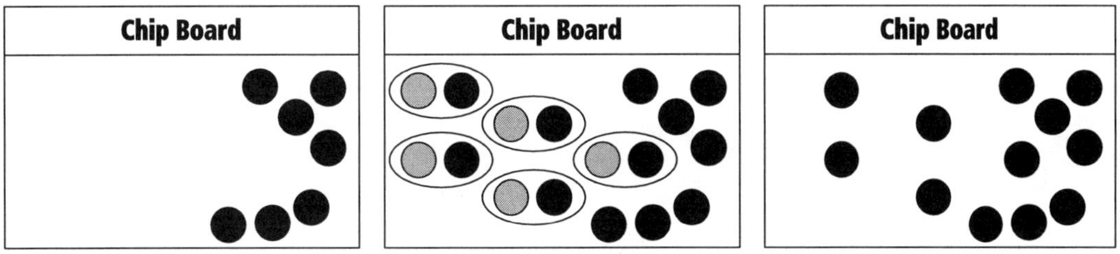

Modeling Multiplication of Integers

Movement right and left (or up and down) on a number line can be used to model multiplication of integers, but it can be difficult to follow. Consider this example: The temperature at midnight is 0°C. If the temperature drops an average of 3° per hour, what is the temperature at 2:00 A.M.?

This problem is asking what the temperature will be 2 hours after midnight if the temperature drops 3° each hour, or $2 \times {}^{-}3$. This can be represented on a thermometer, or on a number line as shown below, to demonstrate that ${}^{-}3 + {}^{-}3 = 2 \times {}^{-}3 = {}^{-}6$.

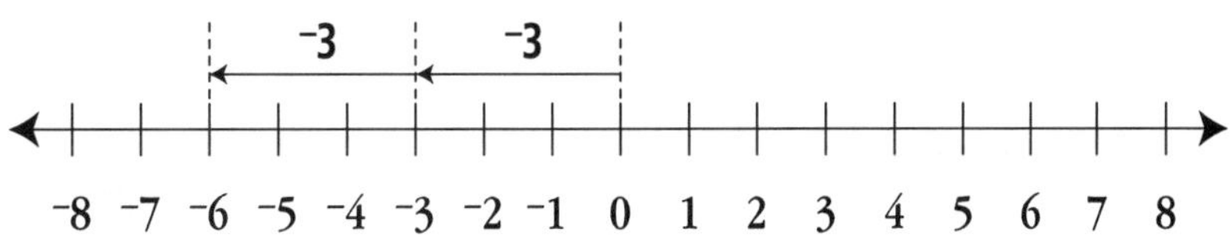

Making sense of a negative integer times a negative integer is difficult to do with models, but looking at patterns and understanding positive and negative integers can help students to make sense of this concept. For example, consider the following list of number sentences, which asks what the pattern suggests for the product of ${}^{-}5$ and ${}^{-}1$, and so on.

$${}^{-}5 \times 3 = {}^{-}15$$
$${}^{-}5 \times 2 = {}^{-}10$$
$${}^{-}5 \times 1 = {}^{-}5$$
$${}^{-}5 \times 0 = 0$$
$${}^{-}5 \times {}^{-}1 = ?$$
$${}^{-}5 \times {}^{-}2 = ?$$
$${}^{-}5 \times {}^{-}3 = ?$$

Division of Integers

Division of integers is developed by relating division to multiplication. Multiplication sentences yield related division sentences and can tell students about the sign of a division problem involving these new kinds of numbers. For example, since we know that

$$5 \times {}^{-}1 = {}^{-}5$$
$$5 \times {}^{-}2 = {}^{-}10$$
$$5 \times {}^{-}3 = {}^{-}15$$

we can write related division sentences:

$5 = {}^-5 \div {}^-1$ or ${}^-1 = {}^-5 \div 5$
$5 = {}^-10 \div {}^-2$ or ${}^-2 = {}^-10 \div 5$
$5 = {}^-15 \div {}^-3$ or ${}^-3 = {}^-15 \div 5$

From these kinds of experiences, students can generalize rules for handling the sign of the quotient in a division problem.

Connections to Other Units

The ideas in *Accentuate the Negative* build on and connect to several big ideas in other Connected Mathematics™ units.

Big Idea	Prior Work	Future Work
defining and developing understanding of negative integers	developing understanding of whole numbers and rational numbers (*Prime Time*; *Bits and Pieces II*)	interpreting and applying positive and negative slopes of lines and positive and negative coefficients in equations (*Moving Straight Ahead*; *Thinking with Mathematical Models*; *Say It with Symbols*)
exploring relationships between positive and negative integers (e.g., interpreting positive integers as a loss and negative integers as a gain)	using models to develop understanding of mathematical concepts (*Covering and Surrounding*; *Ruins of Montarek*; *Stretching and Shrinking*)	understanding relationships between positive and negative coefficients in equations (*Thinking with Mathematical Models*; *Say It with Symbols*); using positive and negative integers to communicate directions in two dimensions (*Kaleidoscopes, Hubcaps, and Mirrors*)
developing understanding of arithmetic operations with positive and negative integers	understanding and applying arithmetic operations with rational numbers (*Bits and Pieces II*; *Comparing and Scaling*)	evaluating algebraic expressions involving positive and negative coefficients or values for variables (*Moving Straight Ahead*; *Thinking with Mathematical Models*; *Frogs, Fleas, and Painted Cubes*; *Say It with Symbols*; *Clever Counting*); interpreting isometries in the plane given in symbolic form (*Kaleidoscopes, Hubcaps, and Mirrors*)
extending the coordinate grid to include negative coordinates	using a coordinate grid with positive coordinates (*Data About Us*; *Covering and Surrounding*; *Variables and Patterns*; *Stretching and Shrinking*)	graphing equations on coordinate grids (*Moving Straight Ahead*; *Thinking with Mathematical Models*; *Growing, Growing, Growing*; *Frogs, Fleas, and Painted Cubes*; *Say It with Symbols*; *Kaleidoscopes, Hubcaps, and Mirrors*)

Mathematical and Problem-Solving Goals

***Accentuate the Negative* was created to help students**

- Develop strategies for adding, subtracting, multiplying, and dividing integers
- Determine whether one integer is greater than, less than, or equal to another integer
- Represent integers on a number line
- Model situations with integers
- Use integers to solve problems
- Explore the use of integers in real-world applications
- Compare integers using the symbols =, >, and <
- Understand that an integer and its inverse are called opposites
- Graph in four quadrants
- Set up a coordinate grid on a graphing calculator by naming the scale and maximum and minimum values of x and y
- Graph linear equations using a graphing calculator
- Informally observe the effects of opposite coefficients and adding a constant to $y = ax$
- Answer questions using equations, tables, and graphs

The overall goal of the Connected Mathematics curriculum is to help students develop sound mathematical habits. Through their work in this and other number units, students learn important questions to ask themselves about any situation that can be represented and modeled mathematically, such as: *What situations in daily life can be represented by positive or negative numbers? How can a meaning be found for operations on negative numbers? Where can such operations be modeled? Is it possible to use "less than" or "greater than" concepts with integers? How are the integers different from ordinary whole numbers? How are these two sets of numbers alike? Can the coordinate grid be expanded to include negative numbers? Is it possible to make graphs on such grids using a graphing calculator? What patterns will occur in these graphs? How can these patterns be used to find and understand other patterns?*

Summary of Investigations

Investigation 1: Extending the Number Line

Students are introduced to and build on their intuitive sense of integers. They compare, order, and solve simple problems involving integers. (Operation rules are not the focus of this investigation.) A game in which points are won (+) and lost (–) introduces integers and provides an entry point for comparing integers, discussing order, and working with opposites. The representation of integers on a number line is introduced by having students examine temperature changes on a thermometer (a vertical number line). The number line is used throughout the unit to model strategies for adding, subtracting, and multiplying integers.

Investigation 2: Adding Integers

Students develop rules for adding integers. They explore two models—a number line and a board with chips of two colors, one to represent $^{+}1$ and the other to represent $^{-}1$—as ways to represent, solve, and explain addition problems involving positive and negative integers.

Investigation 3: Subtracting Integers

Students develop an understanding of subtraction as well as rules for subtracting integers. Number lines and chip boards are used to model the subtraction of positive and negative integers. Subtraction, interpreted as the opposite of addition, is modeled on a chip board as "taking away" chips and on a number line as reversing the direction of the arrow representing the second integer in a subtraction expression. Students look for patterns and find rules for subtracting positive and negative integers.

Investigation 4: Multiplying and Dividing Integers

Students develop rules for multiplying and dividing integers. As it is difficult to model multiplying or dividing a negative integer by a negative integer, students look for patterns and further develop their understanding of integers and of the operations of multiplication and division as a means for developing rules with integers. Students use a thermometer (a kind of vertical number line) to show, for example, that $3 \times {}^{-}2$ is the same as ${}^{-}2 + {}^{-}2 + {}^{-}2$. They continue to investigate the multiplication of integers by examining series of related equations and looking for patterns. They play a game with products in which the factors include positive and negative integers. Finally, they look at the relationship between multiplication and division and derive rules for dividing integers.

Investigation 5: Coordinate Grids

In previous units, students graphed in the first quadrant of a coordinate grid. In this investigation, the use of integers facilitates the introduction of the complete coordinate grid with all four quadrants. Students have used a number line to represent integers; here, the axes for coordinate grids are described as two perpendicular number lines representing both positive and negative integers. As part of their work in this unit, students spend time getting familiar with how to set up a coordinate grid and display one or more graphs on the grid using graphing calculators.

Materials

For students

- Labsheets
- Chips or tiles in two colors (about 15–25 of each color per pair of students; student edition refers to red and black)
- Chip boards (optional; provided as blackline masters, or students can simply label sheets of paper)
- Colored pens, markers, or pencils (optional)
- Graphing calculators (with the capacity to display a function as a table)
- Number lines (provided as a blackline master)
- Coordinate grids (provided as a blackline master)
- Graphing calculator grids (provided as a blackline master)
- Grid paper (provided as a blackline master)
- Paper clips

For the teacher

- Transparencies and transparency markers (optional)
- Transparencies of number lines, chip boards, coordinate grids, and graphing calculator grids (optional; provided as blackline masters)
- Transparency of Labsheet 4.3 (optional)
- Transparent chips or tiles in two colors
- Overhead display model of the students' graphing calculator (optional)

Technology

Connected Mathematics was developed with the belief that calculators should always be available and that students should decide when to use them. For this reason, we do not designate specific problems as "calculator problems." The calculations in *Accentuate the Negative* involve arithmetic with integers, so nonscientific calculators are adequate.

Investigation 5 requires a graphing calculator. This tool allows students to explore many examples quickly and to observe patterns and make conjectures. In the teaching notes, examples using the Texas Instruments TI-80 and TI-82 graphing calculators show teachers how to help students use the calculators. If other types of graphing calculators are used, see the reference manuals for instruction. If your calculators cannot generate tables, have students create tables for some of the problems by hand. It is important for them to make connections between the tables and the graphs.

Pacing Chart

This pacing chart gives estimates of the class time required for each investigation and assessment piece. Shaded rows indicate opportunities for assessment.

Investigations and Assessments	Class Time
1 Extending the Number Line	3 days
2 Adding Integers	3 days
Check-Up 1	$\frac{1}{2}$ day
3 Subtracting Integers	5 days
Check-Up 2	$\frac{1}{2}$ day
4 Multiplying and Dividing Integers	5 days
5 Coordinate Grids	5 days
Self-Assessment	Take home
Unit Test	1 day

Accentuate the Negative Vocabulary

The following words and concepts are used in *Accentuate the Negative.* Concepts in the left column are those essential for student understanding of this and future units. The Descriptive Glossary gives descriptions of many of these words.

Essential terms developed in this unit
absolute value
integer
negative integer, negative number
number sentence
opposites
positive integer, positive number

Nonessential terms
coordinates
inverse operations
quadrant

Other terms students should know
difference
expense, loss
income, profit
operations
product
sum

Assessment Summary

Embedded Assessment

Opportunities for informal assessment of student progress are embedded throughout *Accentuate the Negative* in the problems, ACE questions, and Mathematical Reflections. Suggestions for observing as students explore and discover mathematical ideas, for probing to guide their progress in developing concepts and skills, and for questioning to determine their level of understanding can be found in the Launch, Explore, or Summarize sections of all investigation problems. Some examples:

- Investigation 3, Problem 3.1 *Launch* (page 52a) suggests ways to assess your students' understanding of the operation of subtraction.
- Investigation 5, Problem 5.5 *Explore* (page 82g) suggests how you might help students choose window settings on a graphing calculator that will allow them to view the part of a graph in which they are interested.
- Investigation 4, Problem 4.1 *Summarize* (page 66a) suggests questions you can ask to assess your students' understanding of multiplication with positive and negative integers.

ACE Assignments

An ACE (Applications–Connections–Extensions) section appears at the end of each investigation. To help you assign ACE questions, a list of assignment choices is given in the margin next to the reduced student page for each problem. Each list indicates the ACE questions that students should be able to answer after they complete the problem.

Check-Ups

Two check-ups, which may be given after Investigations 2 and 3, are provided for use as quick quizzes or warm-up activities. Check-ups are designed for students to complete individually. You will find the check-ups and their answer keys in the Assessment Resources section.

Question Bank

A Question Bank provides questions you can use for homework, reviews, or quizzes. You will find the Question Bank and its answer key in the Assessment Resources section.

Notebook/Journal

Students should have notebooks to record and organize their work. Notebooks should include student journals and sections for vocabulary, homework, and check-ups. In their journals, students can take notes, solve investigation problems, and record their ideas about Mathematical Reflections questions. Journals should be assessed for completeness rather than correctness; they should be seen as "safe" places where students can try out their thinking. A Notebook Checklist and a Self-Assessment are provided in the Assessment Resources section. The Notebook Checklist helps students organize their notebooks. The Self-Assessment guides students as they review their notebooks to determine which ideas they have mastered and which ideas they still need to work on.

Unit Test

The final assessment for *Accentuate the Negative* is a unit test, which focuses on using and making sense of integers.

Introducing Your Students to *Accentuate the Negative*

In this unit, students work with positive and negative integers and build on their intuitive understanding of these numbers. They are asked to order, compare, and perform arithmetic operations on positive and negative integers.

Introduce the unit to your students by explaining that this is a unit about using positive and negative integers. Read through the introduction, and discuss the three questions posed on the opening page of the student edition. Ask students to add to the two real-world examples—temperature changes and yards gained or lost in football—other situations that involve positive and negative numbers. For each situation, talk about what the positive and negative signs mean. Explain that their work in this unit will enable them to answer these questions and others like them.

Accentuate the Negative

On Tuesday, a cold front passed through, causing the temperature to change $^{-}2$°F per hour from noon until 10:00 A.M. the next morning. The temperature at noon on Tuesday was 75°F. What was the temperature at 4:00 P.M. Tuesday?

If a negative number is subtracted from a negative number, then the difference is a negative number. *Decide whether this statement is always true, sometimes true, or always false. Give examples to illustrate your thinking.*

In the first quarter of the big game, the Littleton Lions gain 5 yards on every play. They are now on their own 25-yard line. On what yard line were the Lions three plays ago?

Most of the numbers you have worked with in math class this year have been greater than or equal to 0. However, many times numbers less than 0 can provide important information. Winter temperatures in many places fall below 0°. Businesses that lose money report profits less than \$0. Scores for professional golfers are often reported as numbers less than 0, indicating the number of strokes under par.

Numbers greater than 0 are called **positive numbers**, and numbers less than 0 are called **negative numbers**. In *Accentuate the Negative*, you will work with both positive and negative numbers. In particular, you will study a set of numbers called the integers, and you will explore models that help you think about adding, subtracting, multiplying, and dividing positive and negative integers.

As you work through the investigations in this unit, you will solve problems like those on the opposite page.

Mathematical Highlights

The Mathematical Highlights page provides information for students and for parents and other family members. It gives students a preview of the activities and problems in *Accentuate the Negative.* As they work through the unit, students can refer back to the Mathematical Highlights page to review what they have learned and to preview what is still to come. This page also tells students' families what mathematical ideas and activities will be covered as the class works through *Accentuate the Negative.*

Mathematical Highlights

In *Accentuate the Negative* you will develop understanding of and algorithms for operations with integers. The unit should help you to:

- Compare and order integers;
- Represent integers on a number line;
- Understand the relationship between an integer and its inverse and the absolute value of numbers;
- Develop ways to model sums, differences, and products of integers, including number line models and chip models;
- Develop strategies and algorithms for adding, subtracting, multiplying, and dividing integers;
- Model situations and solve problems using integers;
- Graph in four quadrants; and
- Graph linear equations using a graphing calculator to observe the effects of changing a coefficient to its inverse or adding a constant to $y = ax$.

As you work the problems in this unit, make it a habit to ask yourself questions about situations that involve integers: *What quantities in the problem can be represented with positive and negative numbers? How can you tell which of two integers is the greater? What models or diagrams might help decide which operation is useful in solving a problem? What is the approximate answer to the computation?*

The Investigations

The teaching materials for each investigation consist of three parts: an overview, student pages with teaching outlines, and detailed notes for teaching the investigation.

The overview of each investigation includes brief descriptions of the problems, the mathematical and problem-solving goals of the investigation, and a list of necessary materials.

Essential information for teaching the investigation is provided in the margins around the student pages. The "At a Glance" overviews are brief outlines of the Launch, Explore, and Summarize phases of each problem for reference as you work with the class. To help you assign homework, a list of "Assignment Choices" is provided next to each problem. Wherever space permits, answers to problems, follow-ups, ACE questions, and Mathematical Reflections appear next to the appropriate student pages.

The Teaching the Investigation section follows the student pages and is the heart of the Connected Mathematics curriculum. This section describes in detail the Launch, Explore, and Summarize phases for each problem. It includes all the information needed for teaching, along with suggestions for what you might say at key points in the teaching. Use this section to prepare lessons and as a guide for teaching investigations.

Assessment Resources

The Assessment Resources section contains blackline masters and answer keys for the check-ups, the Question Bank, and the Unit Test. Blackline masters for the Notebook Checklist and the Self-Assessment are given. These instruments support student self-evaluation, an important aspect of assessment in the Connected Mathematics curriculum. A discussion of how one teacher uses the vocabulary for the unit is included, along with a sample page from the vocabulary section of one student's mathematics journal.

Blackline Masters

The Blackline Masters section includes masters for all labsheets and transparencies. Blackline masters of number lines, chip boards, coordinate grids, graphing calculator grids, and grid paper are also provided.

Additional Practice

Practice pages for each investigation offer additional problems for students who need more practice with the basic concepts developed in the investigations as well as some continual review of earlier concepts.

Descriptive Glossary

The Descriptive Glossary provides descriptions and examples of the key concepts in *Accentuate the Negative.* These descriptions are not intended to be formal definitions but are meant to give you an idea of how students might make sense of these important concepts.

INVESTIGATION 1

Extending the Number Line

This investigation introduces students to the study of integers.

In Problems 1.1 and 1.2, a game similar to the television show *Jeopardy!®* is used to introduce the topic of integers. In Problem 1.1, Playing MathMania, students focus on the meaning of integers and informally compare and add them. In Problem 1.2, Winning the Game, they continue to investigate relationships among integers by comparing and ordering them. Students use the idea of being ahead or behind in the MathMania game to decide whether one integer is less than or greater than another: if one team has a score of $^{-}200$ and another has a score of $^{-}300$, the team with the score of $^{-}300$ is trailing ($^{-}300 < {}^{-}200$). From this experience, students move on to arrange sets of integers from least to greatest. Problem 1.3, Measuring Temperature, introduces the extended number line (one that includes negative numbers) in the context of temperature. The thermometer records changes in temperature, and ideas of inequality are reinforced as students compare, order, add, and subtract integers representing temperatures. The concept of opposites is introduced in the follow-up to this problem.

Mathematical and Problem-Solving Goals

- *To explore the use of integers in applied settings*
- *To compare integers using the symbols =, >, and <*
- *To represent integers on a number line*
- *To understand that an integer and its inverse are called opposites*

Materials

Problem	For students	For the teacher
All		Transparencies 1.1A to 1.3 (optional)

Student Pages 5–17 | Teaching the Investigation 17a–17f

INVESTIGATION 1

Extending the Number Line

In math class this year, you have worked with numbers greater than or equal to 0. Numbers greater than 0 are called *positive numbers.* You can write a positive number with a plus sign, as in +150, with a raised plus sign, as in $^{+}150$, or without a plus sign, as in 150. For example, a temperature of 10 degrees above zero can be written +10°, $^{+}10°$, or 10°.

Often we need to talk about numbers less than 0. For example, on a very cold day, the temperature might drop below 0°. A company may spend more money than it earns and report a profit less than $0. Numbers less than 0 are called **negative numbers.** You can write a negative number with a minus sign, as in –150, or with a raised minus sign, as in $^{-}150$. For example, a temperature of 10 degrees below zero can be written –10° or $^{-}10°$.

Did you know?

You have probably seen golf scores reported with negative numbers. A golf hole is assigned a value called par. *Par* is the number of strokes a skilled golfer might take to reach the hole. For example, a skilled golfer should be able to complete a par-4 hole in four strokes. If a golfer completes a par-4 hole in six strokes, then her score for the hole could be reported as $^{+}2$, or "two over par." If a golfer completes a par-4 hole in two strokes, her score for the hole could be reported as $^{-}2$, or "two under par." Some scores for a hole are given special names. A score of $^{+}1$ is a *bogey,* a score of $^{-}1$ is a *birdie,* and a score of $^{-}2$ is an *eagle.* A player's score for a round of golf can be reported as the total number of strokes she is above or below par for the entire course.

Tips for the Linguistically Diverse Classroom

Enactment The Enactment technique is described in detail in *Getting to Know Connected Mathematics.* Students act out mini-scenes, using props, to make information comprehensible. Example: For the information in the "Did you know?" feature, ask students to play the role of golfers trying to put an imaginary ball into an imaginary hole. The first golfer makes six strokes to get the ball in a par-4 hole; the class counts each time the golfer swings and advances toward the hole. When the sixth stroke puts the ball in the hole, the teachers writes $^{+}2$ on the board. The second golfer completes a par-4 hole in five strokes, and so on. A sign reading Par 4, a paper cup on its side, and a meterstick can serve as props.

1.1

Playing MathMania

At a Glance

Grouping: whole class

Launch

- Talk with the class about the *Jeopardy!*® game show.
- Read the introduction to the MathMania game.
- As a class, discuss parts A and C.

Explore

- As pairs work on the problem and follow-up, remind them to explain their solutions.
- Ask extension questions of pairs who finish early.

Summarize

- Have pairs share their solutions and the strategies they used in the problem and follow-up.

Assignment Choices

ACE questions 1–7 and 27

1.1 Playing MathMania

Ms. Bernoski's third-period class is playing MathMania, a game similar to the *Jeopardy!*® game show. The game board is shown below. The top row gives six math categories. Below each category name are five cards. The front of each card shows a point value, and the back of each card has a question related to the category. Cards with higher point values have more difficult questions.

Operations with fractions	Similarity	Probability	Area and perimeter	Tiling the plane	Factors and multiples
50	50	50	50	50	50
100	100	100	100	100	100
150	150	150	150	150	150
200	200	200	200	200	200
250	250	250	250	250	250

The game is played by teams. One team starts the game by choosing a category and a point value. The teacher asks the question on the back of the corresponding card. The first team to answer the question correctly gets the point value on the card, and the card is removed from the board. If a team misses the question, the point value is subtracted from their score. The team that answers correctly gets to choose the next category and point value.

At one point in the game, the scores for Ms. Bernoski's class are as follows:

There are several ways each team could have reached their score. For example, to earn their 150 points, the Rocket Scientists may have answered a 100-point question and a 50-point question correctly, or they may have answered a 200-point question correctly and then missed a 50-point question.

Problem 1.1

A. Which team has the highest score? Which team has the lowest score? Explain how you know your answers are correct.

B. How many points separate the highest score and the lowest score?

C. The discussion above describes two possible ways the Rocket Scientists may have reached their score. Describe another possible way. For each of the other two teams, give one possible way the team could have reached their score.

After achieving the scores shown above, the teams continue to play the game. Here is what happens:

- The SuperBrains answer a 200-point question correctly, a 150-point question incorrectly, a 50-point question correctly, and another 50-point question correctly.
- The Rocket Scientists answer a 50-point question incorrectly, a 200-point question incorrectly, a 100-point question correctly, and a 150-point question incorrectly.
- The Know-It-Alls answer a 100-point question incorrectly, a 200-point question correctly, a 150-point question correctly, and a 50-point question incorrectly.

D. What is each team's score now?

E. Which team is in last place? How far behind each of the other two teams is this team?

Problem 1.1 Follow-Up

In Ms. Bernoski's fifth-period class, the Smarties have $^{-}300$ points, and the Brain Surgeons have $^{-}150$ points. After answering the next four questions, the Smarties are tied with the Brain Surgeons. Give two possible ways the Smarties could have done this.

Answers to Problem 1.1

See page 17e.

Answer to Problem 1.1 Follow-Up

The Smarties had to have answered at least one question incorrectly. For example, the Smarties could have gotten a 150-point question correct, a 100-point question correct, a 50-point question incorrect, and a 50-point question incorrect. Or, the Smarties could have gotten a 200-point question correct, a 100-point question correct, a 100-point question incorrect, and a 50-point question incorrect.

1.2 Winning the Game

At a Glance

Grouping:* *pairs

Launch

- Read the introduction and the problem with the class.

Explore

- As pairs work on the problem, remind them to be ready to explain their solutions.
- Have pairs work on the follow-up.

Summarize

- Review the answers to the questions.
- Offer another set of scores, and ask questions about them. *(optional)*
- Discuss the follow-up questions.

1.2 Winning the Game

At the end of the MathMania game, the scoreboard looks like this:

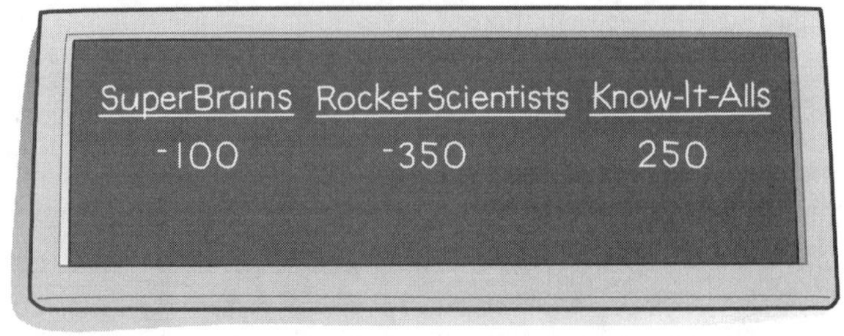

The Know-It-Alls are the winners because they have the highest score. The Rocket Scientists are in last place because they have the lowest score. The SuperBrains are in second place because they have a lower score than the Know-It-Alls but did not lose as many points as the Rocket Scientists. You can write this as

-350 is less than -100, which is less than 250.

Or, you can use symbols to write

$$-350 < -100 < 250$$

Problem 1.2

Mr. Hazan plays MathMania with his class. He divides the class into five teams. At the end of the game, the scores are as follows:

Team A: 200 Team B: -250 Team C: -400 Team D: 350 Team E: -100

A. Order the teams by score, from first place through fifth place.

B. By how many points is the first-place team ahead of the second-place team?

C. By how many points is the first-place team ahead of the third-place team?

D. By how many points is the second-place team ahead of the fourth-place team?

E. By how many points is the third-place team ahead of the fifth-place team?

Assignment Choices

ACE questions 9–14, 26, and unassigned choices from earlier problems

Answers to Problem 1.2

A. First place: Team D, 350
Second place: Team A, 200
Third place: Team E, -100
Fourth place: Team B, -250
Fifth place: Team C, -400

B. 150 points

C. 450 points

D. 450 points

E. 300 points

Problem 1.2 Follow-Up

1. Copy each pair of numbers below, inserting > or < to make a true statement.
   a. 53 35 **b.** -50 0 **c.** -30 15 **d.** -70 -90

2. Order the numbers below from least to greatest.

   25, 2, 5, -3, 15, -7, -25, 12, 1, -4, 0

1.3 Measuring Temperature

You have used the number line to help you think about whole numbers and fractions and decimals greater than 0. These are all examples of positive numbers. The number line can be extended to the left of 0 to include negative numbers.

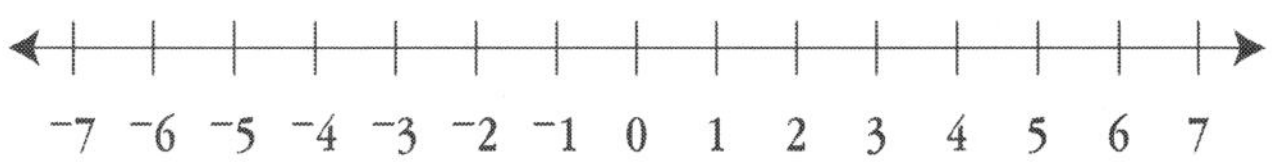

A thermometer can be thought of as a vertical number line with the positive numbers above 0 and the negative numbers below 0. The temperature in many places falls below 0° during the winter months. The thermometer below shows a temperature reading of -4°F.

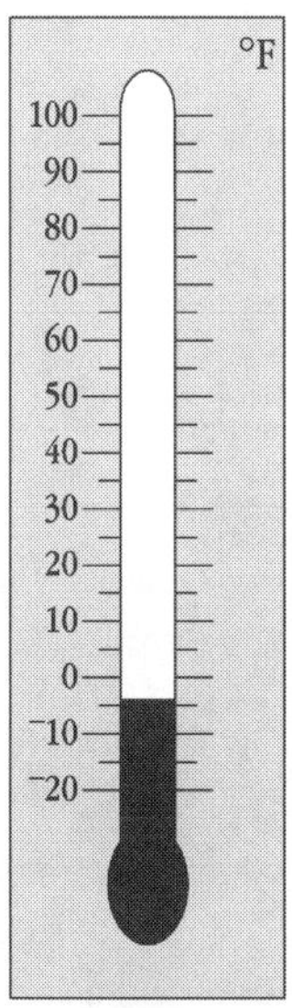

1.3 Measuring Temperature

At a Glance

Grouping: individuals or pairs

Launch

- Read through the problem with the class.
- Have students work on the problem individually or in pairs.

Explore

- As you circulate, ask students to explain how they are finding their solutions.

Summarize

- Discuss students' solutions to the problem.
- Ask a few questions about the integers on thermometers and number lines.
- Have students work on the follow-up and share their answers.

Answers to Problem 1.2 Follow-Up

1. a. 53 > 35
   b. -50 < 0
   c. -30 < 15
   d. -70 > -90
2. -25, -7, -4, -3, 0, 1, 2, 5, 12, 15, 25

Assignment Choices

ACE questions 8, 15–25, 28, 29, and unassigned choices from earlier problems

Problem 1.3

A. Arrange the following temperatures in order from lowest to highest:

−8°, 4°, 12°, −2°, 0°, −15°

B. The temperature reading on a thermometer is 5°F. Tell what the new reading will be if the temperature

1. rises 10° **2.** falls 2° **3.** falls 10° **4.** rises 7°

C. The temperature reading on a thermometer is −5°F. Tell what the new reading will be if the temperature

1. falls 3° **2.** rises 3° **3.** falls 10° **4.** rises 10°

D. In 1–6, give the temperature halfway between the two given temperatures.

1. 0° and 10° **2.** −5° and 15° **3.** 5° and −15°
4. 0° and −20° **5.** −8° and 8° **6.** −6° and −16°

E. In 1–4, tell which temperature reading is farther from −2°.

1. −6° or 6° **2.** −7° or 3° **3.** 2° or −5° **4.** −10° or 5°

F. Explain how you determined your answer for part 4 of question E.

Problem 1.3 Follow-Up

The numbers −3 and 3 are represented on the number line below.

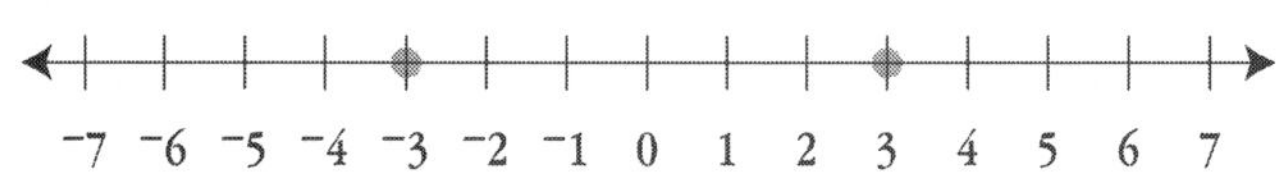

Notice that both numbers are 3 units from 0, but 3 is to the right of 0, and −3 is to the left of 0.

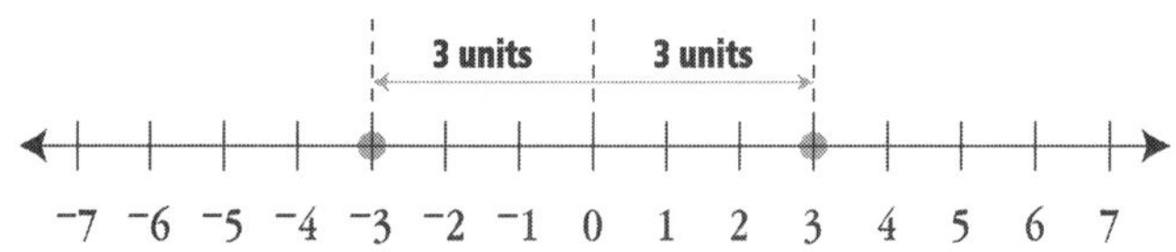

The numbers −3 and 3 are called opposites. **Opposites** are numbers that are the same distance from 0 but on different sides of 0. If you folded the number line at 0, each number would match up with its opposite.

Answers to Problem 1.3

A. −15°, −8°, −2°, 0°, 4°, 12°

B. 1. 15°F 2. 3°F 3. −5°F 4. 12°F

C. 1. −8°F 2. −2°F 3. −15°F 4. 5°F

D. 1. 5° 2. 5° 3. −5° 4. −10° 5. 0° 6. −11°

E. 1. 6° 2. Both readings are 5 units from −2. 3. 2° 4. −10°

F. Possible answer: I counted the number of degrees on the thermometer from −2° to each of the other temperatures. It is 8 degrees from −2° to −10° and 7 degrees from −2° to 5°.

Answers to Problem 1.3 Follow-Up

1. a. 7 b. −18 c. 42 d. 0

If a team playing the MathMania game starts with 0 points and then answers a 50-point question correctly, they will have +50 points. If they miss the question, they will have −50 points. The numbers +50 and −50 are opposites: they are the same distance from 0 on the number line, but in different directions. The sign of a number tells its direction from 0.

1. Give the opposite of each number.
a. −7 **b.** 18 **c.** −42 **d.** 0

2. Name two numbers on the number line that are the same distance from −2. Are these numbers opposites?

At the end of Mr. Hazan's MathMania game, the scores of the five teams are as follows:
Team A: −50 Team B: 150 Team C: −300 Team D: 0 Team E: 100

3. Order the teams from first place through fifth place.

4. Draw a number line. Mark and label each team's score. Label the point for each team with both the team letter and the score.

5. On the number line, what is the distance between the scores of Team A and Team B?

6. On the number line, what is the distance between the scores of Team C and Team A?

7. On the number line, what is the distance between the scores of Team D and Team E?

8. Tell how each team, by answering one question, could change their score to 0. Give the point value of the question, and tell whether the team must answer the question correctly or incorrectly. If this is not possible for a particular team, explain why.

2. Possible answer: −1 and −3, which are both 1 unit from −2. They are not opposites. (Note: An infinite number of pairs are possible, and none will be opposites, as opposites are the same distance from 0, not from −2.)

3. First place: Team B, 150
Second place: Team E, 100
Third place: Team D, 0
Fourth place: Team A, −50
Fifth place: Team C, −300

4.

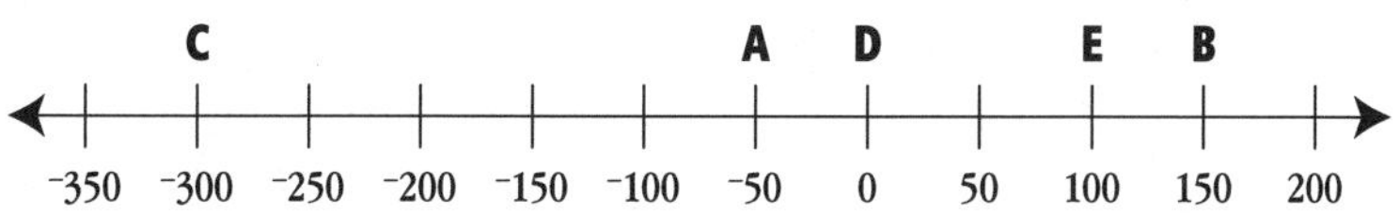

5. 200 points 6. 250 points 7. 100 points 8. See page 17e.

ACE

Answers

Applications

1. $^{+}250 + 100 + 200 - 150 - 200 = {}^{+}200$ points

2. $^{-}200 + 50 + 250 - 150 - 50 = {}^{-}100$ points

3. $^{-}50 - 200 + 100 + 200 - 150 = {}^{-}100$ points

4. Possible answer: win 100, lose 250, win 200, win 150, win 100

5. Possible answer: lose 50, win 250, lose 150, lose 200, lose 50

6. Possible answer: win 100, lose 250, win 150, lose 50, lose 200

7. Possible answer: win 250, lose 150, lose 50, lose 150, win 100

8a. See below right.

8b. $^{-}18$

8c. $^{+}10$

8d. Possible answers: $^{-}1$, 0, 3, $^{-}4.9$

8e. Possible answers: $^{-}15.1$, $^{-}100$

8f. $^{-}8$ and 4

Applications • Connections • Extensions

As you work on these ACE questions, use your calculator whenever you need it.

Applications

In 1–3, tell what the MathMania team's score would be after the events described. Assume the team starts with 0 points.

1. The Protons answer a 250-point question correctly, a 100-point question correctly, a 200-point question correctly, a 150-point question incorrectly, and a 200-point question incorrectly.

2. The Neutrons answer a 200-point question incorrectly, a 50-point question correctly, a 250-point question correctly, a 150-point question incorrectly, and a 50-point question incorrectly.

3. The Electrons answer a 50-point question incorrectly, a 200-point question incorrectly, a 100-point question correctly, a 200-point question correctly, and a 150-point question incorrectly.

In 4–7, a MathMania score is given. Describe a sequence of five events that would produce the score.

4. 300 **5.** $^{-}200$ **6.** $^{-}250$ **7.** 0

8. **a.** Draw a number line, and mark and label points for the following numbers:

$^{-}10, {}^{-}15, 18, {}^{-}5, 8, 0, 15, {}^{-}1$

Use your number line to help you with parts b–f.

b. What is the opposite of 18?

c. What is the opposite of $^{-}10$?

d. Find a number greater than $^{-}5$.

e. Find a number less than $^{-}15$.

f. Which numbers are 6 units from $^{-}2$?

8a.

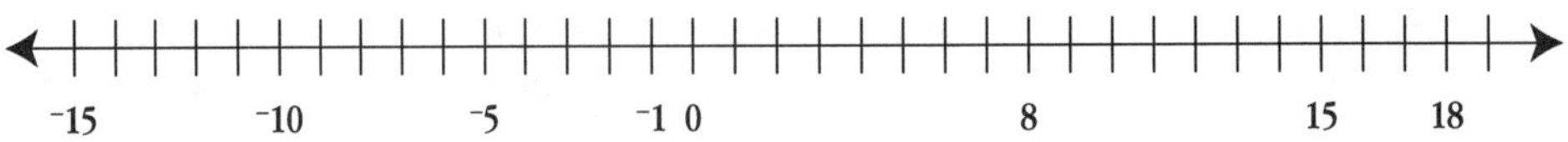

In 9–14, copy the pair of numbers, inserting > or < to make a true statement.

9. 3 0

10. $^-23$ 25

11. 46 $^-79$

12. $^-75$ $^-90$

13. $^-300$ 100

14. $^-1000$ $^-999$

In 15–17, give the distance between the two numbers on the number line.

15. 53 and 35

16. $^-50$ and $^-90$

17. $^-30$ and 15

In 18–20, use the thermometer shown to help you answer the questions. The thermometer shows temperatures on the Celsius temperature scale. On this scale, 0°C is the freezing point of water.

18. What is the temperature change from $^-12$°C to $^+13$°C?

19. What is the temperature change from $^+32$°C to $^+12$°C?

20. What is the temperature change from $^+8$°C to $^-7$°C?

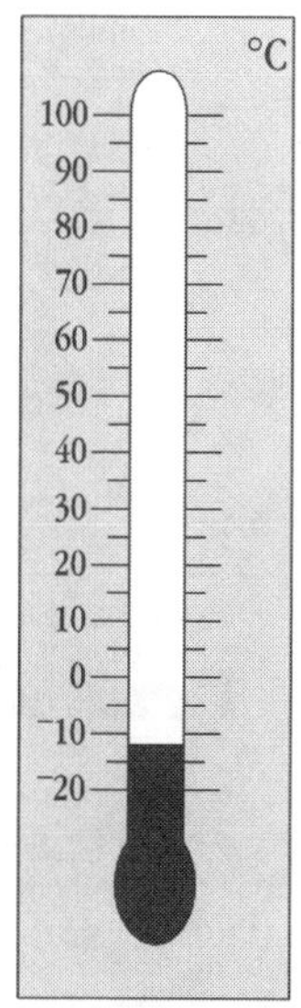

9. $3 > 0$

10. $^-23 < 25$

11. $46 > {^-79}$

12. $^-75 > {^-90}$

13. $^-300 < 100$

14. $^-1000 < {^-999}$

15. 18 units

16. 40 units

17. 45 units

18. $^+25$°C

19. $^-20$°C

20. $^-15$°C

21. See below right.

22a. 118.9°C

22b. 214°F

Connections

23. Possible answer: gaining and then losing 5 yards in football, losing $10 and then finding $10, buying a $25 item and then returning it

21. Copy the table below. Study the first two rows, and then complete the table.

Temperature at 9:00 A.M.	Temperature at 9:00 P.M.	Change in temperature from 9:00 A.M. to 9:00 P.M.
−3°	5°	8°
5°	−3°	−8°
−10°	3°	
−2°	−10°	
−13°	−5°	
2°	−12°	
−10°		−7°
	6°	15°
−2°		−10°

22. The highest temperature ever recorded in the United States was 56.7°C (about 134°F) in Death Valley, California, on July 10, 1913. The lowest recorded U.S. temperature was −62.2°C (about −80°F) in Prospect Creek, Alaska, on January 23, 1971.

a. In Celsius degrees, what is the difference between the record high and record low temperatures?

b. In Fahrenheit degrees, what is the difference between the record high and record low temperatures?

Connections

23. In MathMania, winning 100 points and then losing 100 points have the effect of "undoing" each other. In other words, since they are opposites, 100 and −100 combine to give 0. Describe three real-life situations in which two events undo each other.

21.

Temperature at 9:00 A.M.	Temperature at 9:00 P.M.	Change in temperature from 9:00 A.M. to 9:00 P.M.
−3°	5°	8°
5°	−3°	−8°
−10°	3°	**+13°**
−2°	−10°	**−8°**
−13°	−5°	**+8°**
2°	−12°	**−14°**
−10°	**−17°**	−7°
−9°	6°	15°
−2°	**−12°**	−10°

In 24 and 25, copy the number line below. Mark and label the number line to show the approximate locations of the numbers given.

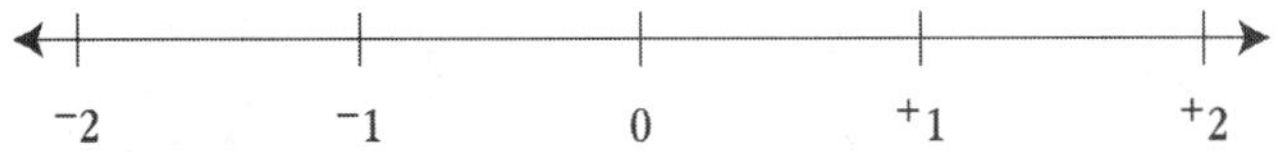

24. $^{-}\frac{2}{3}, ^{+}\frac{2}{5}, ^{-}1.5, ^{+}1\frac{3}{4}$

25. $^{-}1.25, ^{-}\frac{1}{3}, ^{+}1.5, ^{-}\frac{1}{6}$

26. The list below gives average temperatures (in °C) for Fairbanks, Alaska, for each month of the year from January through December.

$^{-}25, ^{-}20, ^{-}13, ^{-}2, ^{+}9, ^{+}15, ^{+}17, ^{+}14, ^{+}7, ^{-}4, ^{-}16, ^{-}23$

a. What is the median of these monthly temperatures?

b. What is the range of these monthly temperatures (lowest to highest)?

Extensions

Extending the Number Line

27. At the start of December, Shareef has a balance of $595.50 in his checking account. The following is a list of transactions he makes during the month.

Date	Transaction	Balance
December 1		$595.50
December 5	Writes a check for $19.95	
December 12	Writes a check for $280.88	
December 15	Deposits $257.00	
December 17	Writes a check for $58.12	
December 21	Withdraws $50	
December 24	Writes checks for $17.50, $41.37, and $65.15	
December 26	Deposits $100	
December 31	Withdraws $50	

a. What is Shareef's balance at the end of December?

b. On what day is his balance greatest? On what day is his balance least?

27a.

Date	Transaction	Balance
December 1		$595.50
December 5	Writes a check for $19.95	$575.55
December 12	Writes a check for $280.88	$294.67
December 15	Deposits $257.00	$551.67
December 17	Writes a check for $58.12	$493.55
December 21	Withdraws $50	$443.55
December 24	Writes checks for $17.50, $41.37, and $65.15	$319.53
December 26	Deposits $100	$419.53
December 31	Withdraws $50	**$369.53**

24. See page 17f.

25. See page 17f.

26a. In order, the temperatures are $^{-}25, ^{-}23, ^{-}20, ^{-}16, ^{-}13, ^{-}4, ^{-}2, ^{+}7, ^{+}9, ^{+}14, ^{+}15, ^{+}17$. The median is between $^{-}4$ and $^{-}2$, or $^{-}3$.

26b. The range is from $^{-}25$ to $^{+}17$, which is a spread of 42 degrees.

Extensions

27a. See below left.

27b. His balance is greatest on December 1 ($595.50). His balance is least on December 12 ($294.67).

28a. In three plays, the Lions gained $3 \times 5 = 15$ yards. Three plays ago they were on the $25 - 15 =$ 10-yard line.

28b. In two plays, they will gain $2 \times 5 = 10$ yards and will be on the $25 + 10 = 35$-yard line.

29a. In two plays, the Lions have lost $2 \times 5 = 10$ yards. Two plays ago they were on the $25 + 10 =$ 35-yard line.

29b. In two plays, they will lose $2 \times 5 = 10$ yards, putting them on the $25 - 10 = 15$-yard line.

28. In the first quarter of the big game, the Littleton Lions gain 5 yards on every play. They are now on their own 25-yard line.

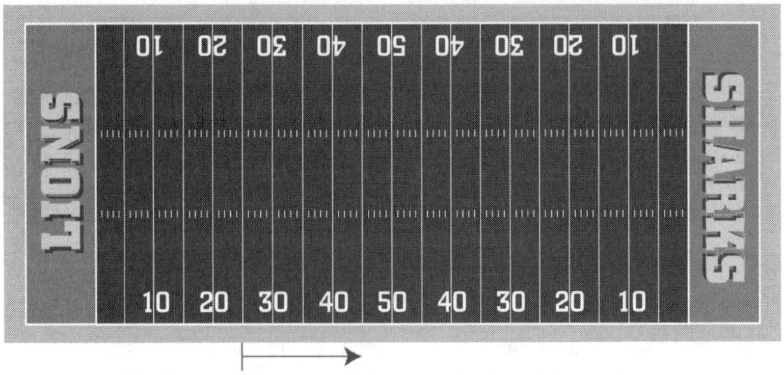

The Lions are here now and are moving from left to right—that is, they move right when they gain yards.

a. On what yard line were the Lions three plays ago?

b. On what yard line will they be after the next two plays?

29. In the last quarter of the big game, the Littleton Lions (see question 28) lose 5 yards on every play. They are now on their own 25-yard line. They move left when they lose yards.

a. On what yard line were the Lions two plays ago?

b. On what yard line will they be after the next two plays?

Mathematical Reflections

In this investigation, you worked with positive and negative numbers. You analyzed sequences of events in the MathMania game, looked at temperature, and extended the number line to represent numbers less than 0. You also learned how to decide whether one number is less than or greater than another number. These questions will help you summarize what you have learned:

1. Describe what positive numbers, negative numbers, and 0 mean in terms of
   - **a.** keeping score in MathMania.
   - **b.** temperature readings.
2. Describe how you can compare the following types of numbers to decide which is greater. Use examples to illustrate your thinking.
   - **a.** two positive numbers
   - **b.** two negative numbers
   - **c.** a positive number and a negative number
3. Describe how to locate numbers on a number line. Use examples to illustrate your thinking. Be sure to include positive and negative numbers as well as fractions and decimals in your examples.

Think about your answers to these questions, discuss your ideas with other students and your teacher, and then write a summary of your findings in your journal.

Tips for the Linguistically Diverse Classroom

Diagram Code The Diagram Code technique is described in detail in *Getting to Know Connected Mathematics*. Students use a minimal number of words and drawings, diagrams, or symbols to respond to questions that require writing. Example: Question 3—A student might answer this question by drawing a number line from $^-5$ to $^+5$. Beneath it, the student might write *4: + or – ?* Under this, the student might write *if +, then right; if –, then left; 4 is +, so right 4 spaces*. The student would use this approach to show how to locate negative numbers, fractions, and decimals as well.

Possible Answers

1a. Positive numbers represent winning points and increasing the score, negative numbers represent losing points and decreasing the score, and 0 means you have no points.

1b. Positive numbers represent temperatures above 0°, negative numbers represent temperatures below 0°, and 0 is a specific temperature reading on a thermometer.

2a. If you are comparing two positive numbers, the number with the greater value is the greater number. For 35 and 50, for example, 50 has the greater value, so it is the greater number.

2b. If you are comparing two negative numbers, the greater negative number (the greater number when the negative signs are ignored) has the smaller value. For $^-49$ and $^-56$, $^-49$ is greater than $^-56$. Or, since $^-56$ is more in the hole than $^-49$, $^-56$ is smaller. (Note: Because students do not yet know the concept of absolute value they may struggle to explain this idea.)

2c. If you are comparing a positive and a negative number, the positive number is always greater. For example, 9 is greater than $^-111$.

3. See 17f.

1.1 • Playing MathMania

The *Jeopardy!*® game show is familiar to many students. MathMania, a similar game, is an easy and engaging way to begin students' work with integers.

You can introduce the context by asking students to describe the game of *Jeopardy!*® and how it is played. Make sure the class discusses how points are earned. When a contestant answers a question correctly, he or she receives the points (money) assigned to that question. When a contestant misses a question, the points for that question are deducted from his or her score. Some students may observe that the current game show's board has amounts greater than those on the MathMania board.

Launch

Read through the introduction to the MathMania game with your students. You may want to display Transparency 1.1A, or put the three scores on the board, and discuss parts A and C as a class.

> Who has the highest score? *(the Rocket Scientists)* Who has the lowest score? *(the Know-It-Alls)* How did you decide? *(The Rocket Scientists is the only team with a positive score, which is a score greater than 0. The Know-It-Alls have the lowest score, because their score of $^-500$ is further in the hole than the SuperBrains' score of $^-300$.)*

If students are struggling with part C, which asks about different ways each team could have arrived at their score, discuss the example about the Rocket Scientists that precedes the problem. Then, ask the class for a sequence of events that would produce one of the given scores.

> Describe a sequence of events that would produce the SuperBrains' score. *(One possibility is that they answered a 200-point question and a 100-point question incorrectly.)*

Thinking about these ideas should give the class a good understanding of the context and help them to work through the remaining questions. Have students work in pairs on the rest of the problem and on the follow-up.

Explore

Remind students that, in addition to giving a solution for each question, they will need to explain why they believe their solutions make sense.

You might ask the following extension questions of pairs who finish early.

> What is the fewest number of questions that each team could have attempted to answer to get their current score? *(SuperBrains—two questions, Rocket Scientists—one question, Know-It-Alls—two questions)*

If the Rocket Scientists arrived at their score after answering ten questions, what is a possible sequence of questions they could have answered? Is that the only sequence?

Summarize

Go over the questions as a class. For part B, ask the class how they found the difference between the highest and lowest scores. Here are some explanations students have given.

- Jonna: "We added 500 and 150. The Know-It-Alls are 500 points below 0, and it would take that many points just to get back to 0. The Rocket Scientists are 150 points above 0, so it would take 650 points in all to get from the Know-It-Alls' score to the Rocket Scientists' score."
- Ty: "The Know-It-Alls are 500 points in the hole, so they need 500 points to get to 0 and another 150 points to tie the Rocket Scientists."

There are many ways each team could have arrived at their score. Have several pairs share their answers to part C for each team.

You may want to project Transparency 1.1B to discuss parts D and E. Ask pairs to explain how they found each team's new score. Here are two explanations students have given.

- CeCe: "The SuperBrains had a score of $^-300$. When they got the 200-point question, their score changed to $^-100$. Then they missed a 150-point question, so their score changed to $^-250$. Next they got a 50-point question, so they went up to $^-200$ points. Then they got another 50-point question, so their score went up again, to $^-150$."
- André: "We made a table to show what happened to the scores after each question."

	Score	Event	Score	Event	Score	Event	Score	Event	Final score
SuperBrains	$^-300$	win 200	$^-100$	lose 150	$^-250$	win 50	$^-200$	win 50	$^-150$
Rocket Scientists	150	lose 50	100	lose 200	$^-100$	win 100	0	lose 150	$^-150$
Know-It-Alls	$^-500$	lose 100	$^-600$	win 200	$^-400$	win 150	$^-250$	lose 50	$^-300$

Once the class agrees on the final scores, discuss part E.

Which team is the furthest behind now? *(the Know-It-Alls)* How much behind the SuperBrains and the Rocket Scientists are the Know-It-Alls? *(They are 150 points behind each of them.)* How did you find that amount? *(They are all in the hole, so we can think about the difference between 300 and 150, which is 150.)*

Ask a few pairs to share their ideas about the follow-up. Various sequences of questions answered correctly and incorrectly could tie the Smarties and the Brain Surgeons. (Note that the question implies that the Brain Surgeons answered no questions during this time.)

1.2 • Winning the Game

This problem is a continuation of the MathMania game from Problem 1.1 and should not need an extensive launch. Students order sets of integers and find the number of points between two scores. Although the difference between scores can easily be found by subtracting, the intent of this problem is not to discuss subtraction of integers but to continue to work with the mathematical ideas on an intuitive level, exploring integers and what they mean.

Launch

Read the introduction and the problem with the class. Have students again work in pairs on the problem and the follow-up questions.

Explore

As pairs work on the questions, remind them to be prepared to describe how they decided on their solutions. When they finish with the problem, have them answer the follow-up questions.

Summarize

As the class discusses the problem, try to elicit strategies for determining the order of two or more integers and for finding the difference between two integers. If some students are struggling with ordering integers or finding the amount between two integers, put another set of scores on the board and ask the class to order them. Ask several questions that involve finding the amount between two integers.

Suppose these were the scores in a MathMania game:

Order these scores from first place through fourth place. *($^{+}250$, $^{+}200$, $^{-}150$, $^{-}250$)*

How much ahead of the second-place team is the first-place team? *(50 points)* How did you determine this? *(subtracted 200 from 250)*

How much ahead of the third-place team is the first-place team? *(400 points)* How did you determine this? *(For the third-place team to catch up to the first-place team, they would need to make 150 points to get to 0 and then another 250 points, which is a total of 400 points.)*

The follow-up questions ask students to work with integers independent of a context. Be sure to ask pairs to explain their solutions. If students answered these questions with little difficulty, ask them to describe any rules they have found for ordering positive and negative numbers. Also ask for any rules they can use to compare any two positive numbers, any two negative numbers, or a positive number and a negative number. Here are some strategies that students in one class offered.

- Diane: "When I compare a negative number and a positive number, I know the negative number is always less because it is less than 0 and any positive number is always bigger than 0."
- Carroll: "If I compare two positive numbers, the larger number is always bigger."
- Sandra: "When I compare two negative numbers, the smaller number is always the one farther from 0 because you are more in the hole, and that means having less."

1.3 • Measuring Temperature

This problem continues the concept of negative numbers by using one of its most familiar applications: temperatures below 0 on the thermometer.

Launch

Read through the problem with your students. If students are making sense of integers, have them work on this problem individually. If they appear to still be struggling to understand the concepts, especially with informally combining integers or finding the difference between two integers, have them work with a partner.

Explore

As you circulate, ask students how they are determining their solutions.

The follow-up questions introduce the concept of opposites. Leave these questions until the summary, and then discuss them as a class.

Summarize

Discuss the students' solutions and strategies for the problem. For parts B and C, display Transparency 1.3 or draw a thermometer on the board for students to use to demonstrate what happens as the temperature rises and falls. For part D, some students may talk about finding the distance between the numbers and taking half of that distance. Others may use the thermometer and count in equal units from the endpoints until they meet. Both are reasonable strategies at this point, and if they are not presented by students in the class conversation, present them yourself for students to consider. In parts E and F, students may subtract to find the answers, but they should not be expected to use subtraction; counting is a reasonable strategy at this time.

After reviewing the problem, ask some additional questions about thermometers and number lines.

> On a regular horizontal number line, where are the positive numbers in relation to 0? *(to the right of the 0 mark)* Where are the negative numbers? *(to the left of the 0 mark)*
>
> We can think of this kind of thermometer as a vertical number line. On this thermometer, where are the positive numbers located in relation to 0? *(above the 0 mark)* Where are the negative numbers located in relation to 0? *(below the 0 mark)*

Suppose the temperature is ⁺5°. Where is ⁺5 located on this vertical number line in relation to 0? *(5 units above the 0 mark)* Suppose the temperature is ⁻5°. Where is ⁻5 located on this vertical number line in relation to 0? *(5 units below the 0 mark)*

Name two other numbers on our vertical number line that are the same distance from 0, with one number above 0 and the other below 0.

Name two other numbers that are the same distance from 0 on the horizontal number line, with one number to the left of 0 and the other to the right of 0.

Numbers that are the same distance from 0 but in opposite directions from 0 are called *opposites.* What is the opposite of 12? *(⁻12)* What is the opposite of ⁻9? *(9)*

Read through the follow-up with the class. Give students a few minutes to write answers to the questions, then ask them to share their responses. Additional discussion about why 0 is its own opposite may be needed.

Additional Answers

Answers to Problem 1.1

A. The Rocket Scientists have the highest score (150), and the Know-It-Alls have the lowest score (⁻500). Possible explanation: The 150 is the only positive score, and ⁻500 represents more points lost than ⁻300 does.

B. The Know-It-Alls and the Rocket Scientists are separated by 650 points.

C. Possible answer: The Rocket Scientists could have answered one 150-point question correctly. The SuperBrains could have missed two 150-point questions. The Know-It-Alls could have missed two 250-point questions.

D. The SuperBrains have ⁻150, the Rocket Scientists have ⁻150, and the Know-It-Alls have ⁻300. (Two possible ways to arrive at these answers are given in the Summarize section.)

E. The Know-It-Alls have the lowest score (⁻300). Since the Rocket Scientists and the SuperBrains are tied at ⁻150, 150 points separate the Know-It-Alls from the other two teams.

Answers to Problem 1.3 Follow-Up

8. Team A could answer a 50-point question correctly, Team B could answer a 150-point question incorrectly, and Team E could answer a 100-point question incorrectly. Team D's score is 0 already, so answering any single question—correctly or incorrectly—would give that team a score other than 0. Team C needs 300 points to reach 0, and the greatest score possible for answering a question correctly is only 250, so Team C cannot reach 0 by answering one question.

ACE Answers

Connections

24.

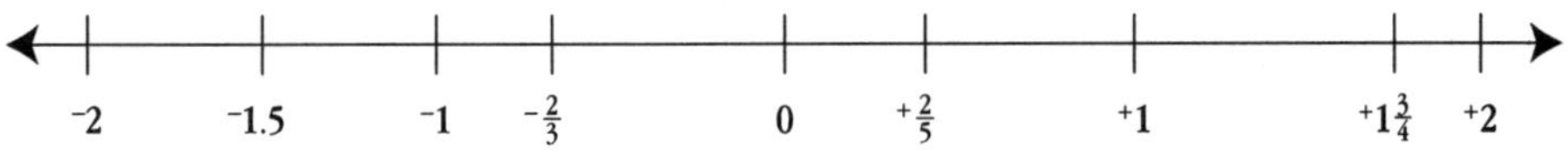

25.

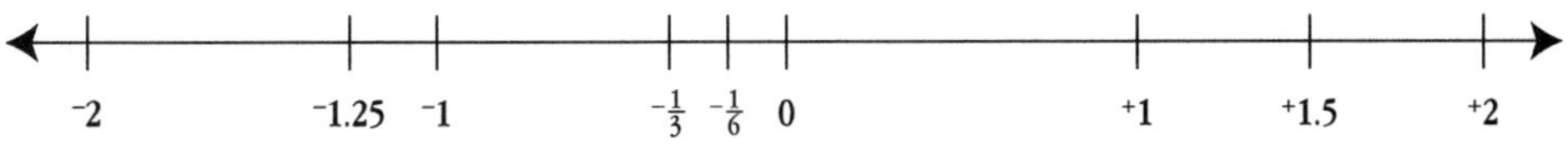

Mathematical Reflections

3. To locate a number on a number line, first check to see whether the number is positive or negative. If it is positive, it will be to the right of 0. If it is negative, it will be to the left of 0. For example, 50 is 50 units to the right of (or above) 0, and $^{-}50$ is 50 units to the left of (or below) 0. The same is true for fractions and decimals. They are to the right or left (or above or below) depending on whether they are positive or negative.

INVESTIGATION 2

Adding Integers

In this investigation, students develop rules for adding with integers.

Problem 2.1, Adding on a Number Line, incorporates the number line as a tool to help students explore the addition of positive and negative integers. Students relate addition sentences to movements along a number line. In Problem 2.2, Inventing a New Model, students explore another method of modeling the addition of integers. The chip board model employs two colors of chips, one representing $^{+}1$ and the other representing $^{-}1$. Students use the chip board to concretely represent the addition of integers.

Mathematical and Problem-Solving Goals

- *To explore addition of integers using two models (a number line and a chip board)*
- *To develop strategies for adding integers*
- *To recognize and solve problems involving addition of integers*

Materials

Problem	For students	For the teacher
All	Graphing calculators	Transparencies 2.1 and 2.2 (optional)
2.1	Number lines (provided as a blackline master)	Transparency of number lines (optional)
2.2	Chip boards (optional; provided as blackline masters, or students can simply label sheets of paper), chips or tiles in two colors (about 15–25 of each color per pair of students; student edition refers to red and black)	Transparency of chip boards (optional), transparent chips or tiles in two colors
ACE	Number lines and chip boards (optional)	

Student Pages 18–33 Teaching the Investigation 33a–33l

INVESTIGATION 2

Adding Integers

The numbers 0, 1, 2, 3, 4, . . . are *whole numbers.* These numbers are labeled on the number line below.

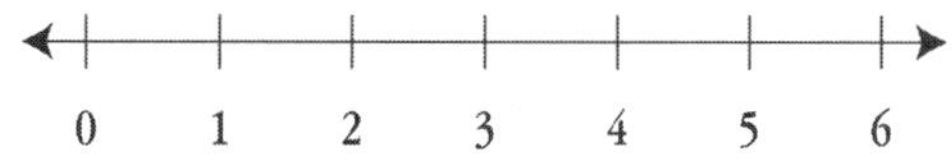

If we extend this pattern to the left of 0, we get . . . , $^{-}4$, $^{-}3$, $^{-}2$, $^{-}1$, 0, 1, 2, 3, 4, ...

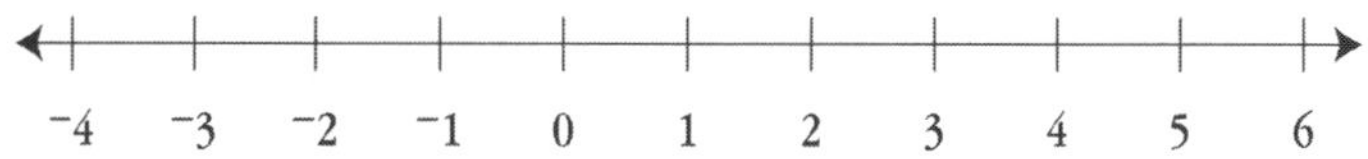

This larger set of numbers is called the **integers**. The numbers 1, 2, 3, 4, . . . are *positive integers,* and the numbers . . . , $^{-}4$, $^{-}3$, $^{-}2$, $^{-}1$ are *negative integers.* The number 0 is neither positive nor negative.

In many situations, you need to combine integers to find a sum. In this investigation, you will use two models that will help you think about how to add positive and negative integers.

Did you know?

The Hindus were the first to use negative numbers. The Hindu mathematician Brahmagupta used negative numbers as early as A.D. 628, and even stated the rules for adding, subtracting, multiplying, and dividing with negative numbers. Many European mathematicians of the sixteenth and seventeenth centuries did not accept the idea of negative numbers, referring to them as "absurd" and "fictitious." Mathematicians of that time who did accept negative numbers often had strange beliefs about them. For example, John Wallis believed that negative numbers were greater than infinity!

2.1 Adding on a Number Line

Monique and Ethan were thinking about how to show addition of integers on a number line. They decided to start by working with whole numbers. Monique came up with the following method for representing the **number sentence** $3 + 2 = 5$:

> Start at 0, and move 3 units to the right. To show the addition of 2, move 2 more units to the right. You end up at 5, so $3 + 2 = 5$.

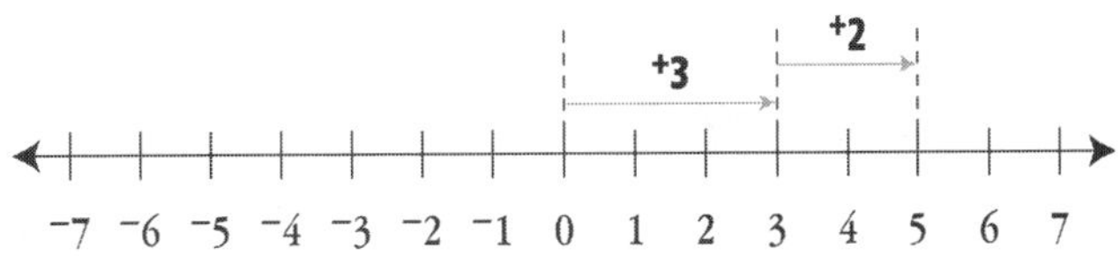

Ethan thought a similar method would work for adding negative integers. He came up with the following plan for finding $^-3 + {}^-2$:

> Start at 0, and move 3 units to the left (the negative direction) to represent the $^-3$. To show the addition of $^-2$, move 2 more units to the left. You end up at $^-5$, so $^-3 + {}^-2 = {}^-5$.

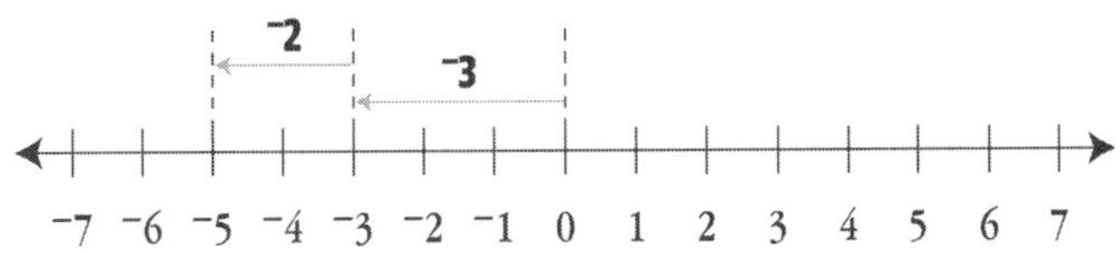

When Ethan wrote $^-3 + {}^-2 = {}^-5$, he used raised negative symbols to help him separate the sign of the integer from the operation sign for addition.

Then, Ethan wanted to try adding a negative integer and a positive integer on a number line. He followed these steps to find $^-3 + {}^+2$:

> Start at 0, and move 3 units to the left (the negative direction) to represent $^-3$. To show the addition of $^+2$, move two units to the right (the positive direction). You end up at $^-1$, so $^-3 + {}^+2 = {}^-1$.

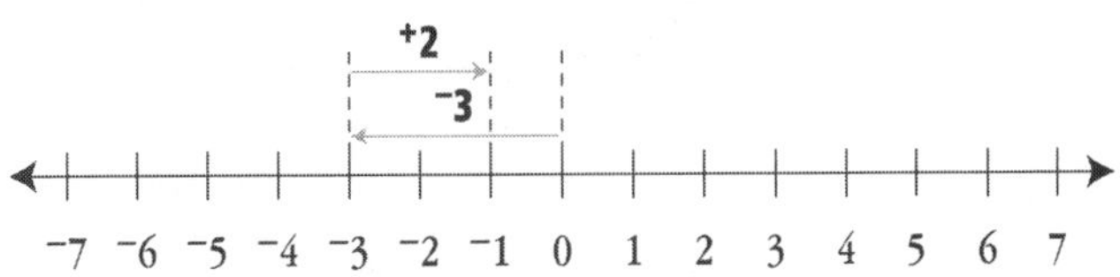

2.1 Adding on a Number Line

At a Glance

***Grouping:* pairs**

Launch

- Talk with the class about integers, extending the number line, and the meaning of addition.
- Have pairs search for a way to show addition on a number line.
- Discuss the various representations that students propose.

Explore

- As pairs work on the problem, check for those who are writing expressions rather than complete number sentences.

Summarize

- Have pairs share their addition sentences.
- Discuss parts B and C of the problem.
- Have students answer the follow-up.

Assignment Choices

ACE questions 1–7, 29, and unassigned choices from earlier problems

Monique asked Ethan what he thought they would get if they used a number line to find $^{+}2 + ^{-}3$. What do you think?

Problem 2.1

A. Write the addition sentence illustrated by each figure.

1.

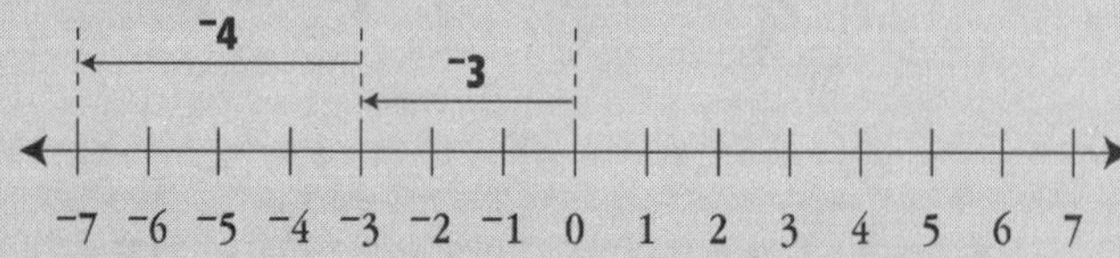

2.

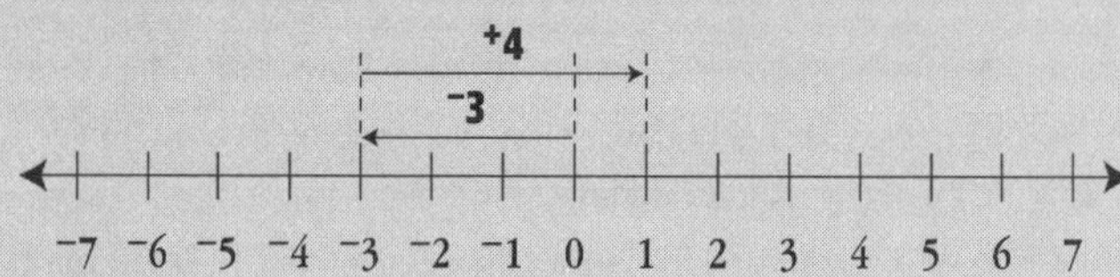

3.

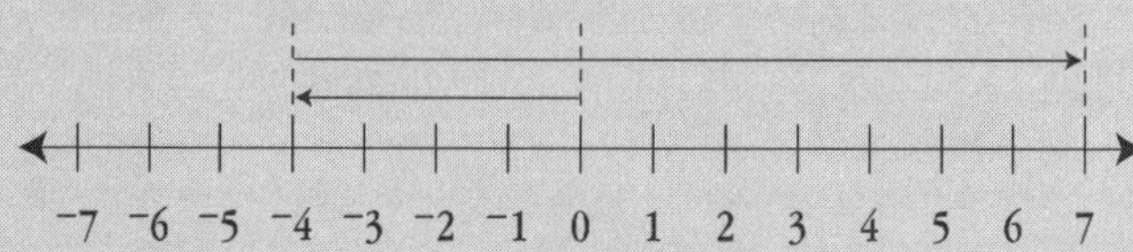

4.

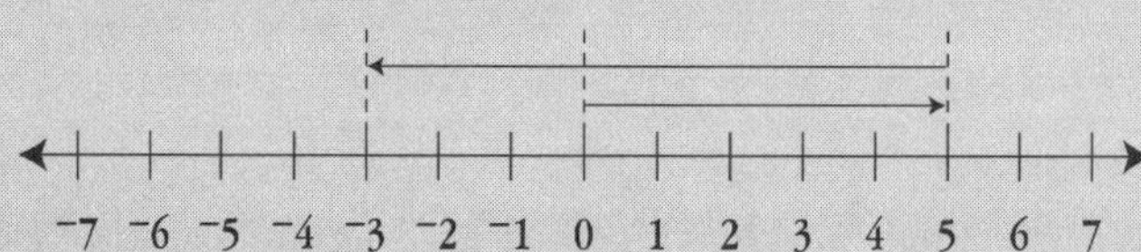

B. Illustrate each addition problem on a number line, and give the answer.

1. $^{-}5 + ^{+}8$ **2.** $^{-}4 + ^{-}3$ **3.** $^{-}2 + ^{-}3 + ^{+}10$

C. When you add two integers, does the order of the numbers make a difference? Illustrate your answer by showing each of these pairs of sums on a number line.

1. $^{-}5 + ^{+}10$ and $^{+}10 + ^{-}5$ **2.** $^{-}4 + ^{-}6$ and $^{-}6 + ^{-}4$

3. $^{+}8 + ^{-}8$ and $^{-}8 + ^{+}8$ **4.** $^{+}6 + ^{-}7$ and $^{-}7 + ^{+}6$

Answers to Problem 2.1

A. 1. $^{-}3 + ^{-}4 = ^{-}7$

2. $^{-}3 + ^{+}4 = ^{+}1$

3. $^{-}4 + ^{+}11 = ^{+}7$

4. $^{+}5 + ^{-}8 = ^{-}3$

B. See page 33g.

C. See page 33h.

Problem 2.1 Follow-Up

1. You can think of the scoring in MathMania as follows: When a team answers a question correctly, a positive integer is added to their score. When a team answers a question incorrectly, a negative integer is added to their score. For each of the following situations, write an addition sentence that will give the team's score. Assume each team starts with 0 points.
   a. The Brainiacs answer a 200-point question correctly and a 150-point question incorrectly.
   b. The Aliens answer a 100-point question correctly and a 100-point question incorrectly.
   c. The Prodigies answer a 50-point question incorrectly, a 100-point question incorrectly, and a 250-point question correctly.
2. Illustrate each addition problem on a number line and give the answer.
   a. $^{-}2 + {}^{+}2$ b. $^{+}8 + {}^{-}8$ c. $^{-}1 + {}^{+}1$
3. What happens when you add opposites? Explain how you know your answer is correct.

2.2 Inventing a New Model

In the last problem, you used the number line to help you think about adding integers. In this problem, you will explore another way to model the addition of integers.

Amber's mother is an accountant. One day, Amber heard her mother talking to a client on the phone. During the conversation, her mother used the phrases "in the red" and "in the black."

That evening at dinner, Amber asked her mother what these terms meant. Her mother said:

"When people in business talk about income and expenses, they often use colors to describe the numbers they are dealing with. Black refers to profits (or income); red refers to losses (or expenses). A company that is making money, or has money, is 'in the black'; a company that is losing money, or owes money, is 'in the red.'"

2.2 Inventing a New Model

At a Glance

Grouping:* *pairs

Launch

- Talk with the class about any patterns they have noticed about adding positive and negative integers.
- Read the story setting with the class, and introduce the chip board model.

Explore

- Circulate as pairs work, suggesting that those having trouble consider the number line model to help make sense of the chip board model.

Summarize

- Review the problem as a class.
- Ask students to generalize the patterns they have discovered.
- Do and discuss the follow-up questions.

Answers to Problem 2.1 Follow-Up

1. a. $^{+}200 + {}^{-}150 = {}^{+}50$
   b. $^{+}100 + {}^{-}100 = 0$
   c. $^{-}50 + {}^{-}100 + {}^{+}250 = {}^{+}100$
2. See page 33i.
3. When you add opposites, the sum is 0. Possible explanation: I know this is correct, because the two numbers cancel each other out. This can be seen on the number lines for question 2.

Assignment Choices

ACE questions 8–28, 30–37, and unassigned choices from earlier problems

Assessment

It is appropriate to use Check-Up 1 after this problem.

Amber was studying integers in her math class and thought she could use these ideas of "in the black" and "in the red" to model the addition of positive and negative integers. Her model uses a chip board and black and red chips. Each black chip represents $^{+}1$, and each red chip represents $^{-}1$.

For example, this chip board shows a value of $^{+}5$:

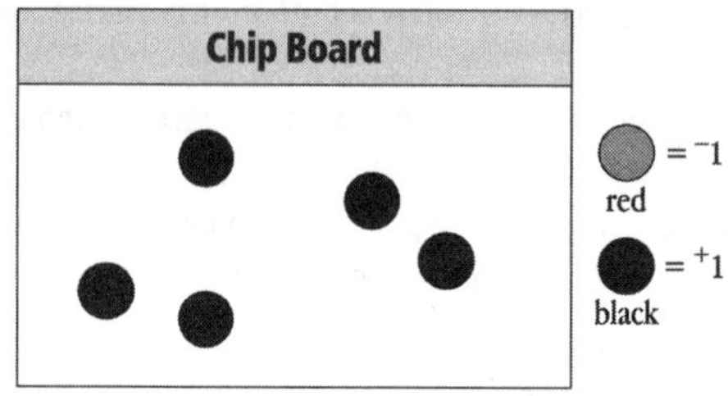

This chip board shows a value of $^{-}5$:

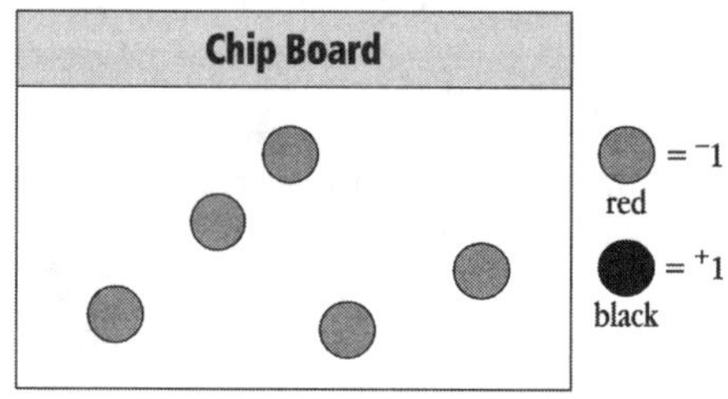

To represent $^{-}4 + {}^{-}3$, Amber started with an empty chip board. She represented $^{-}4$ by putting four red chips on the board.

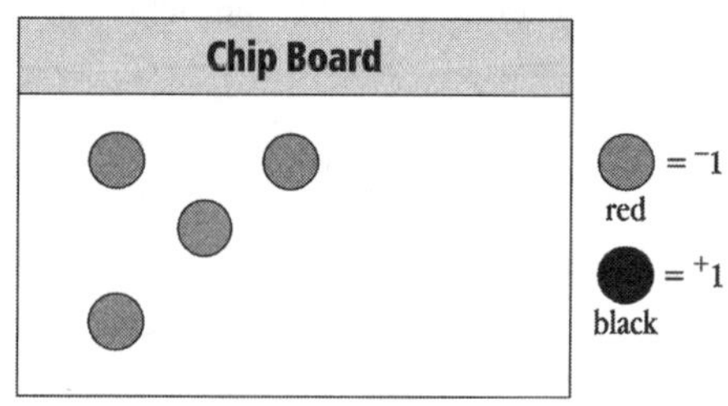

To represent the addition of $^-3$, she put three more red chips on the board.

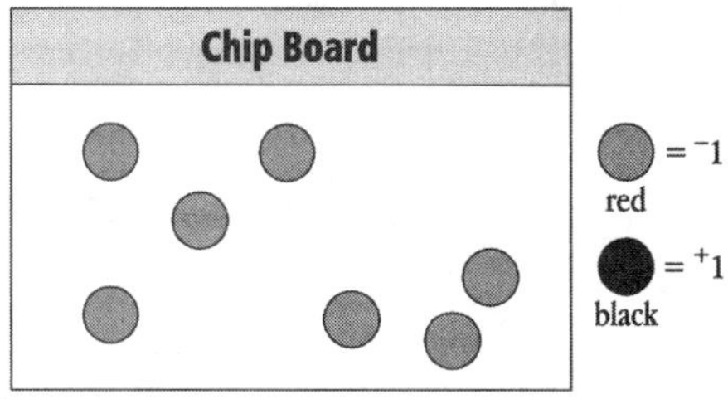

Since there were seven red chips on the board, Amber concluded that the sum of $^-4$ and $^-3$ is $^-7$. She wrote the number sentence $^-4 + ^-3 = ^-7$ to represent what she did on the chip board.

Amber showed her idea to her friend Adil. Adil liked Amber's model, but he wasn't sure how to use it to add a negative integer and a positive integer. Amber explained by modeling $^-4 + ^+5$. She started by clearing the board. She then put four red chips on the board to represent $^-4$.

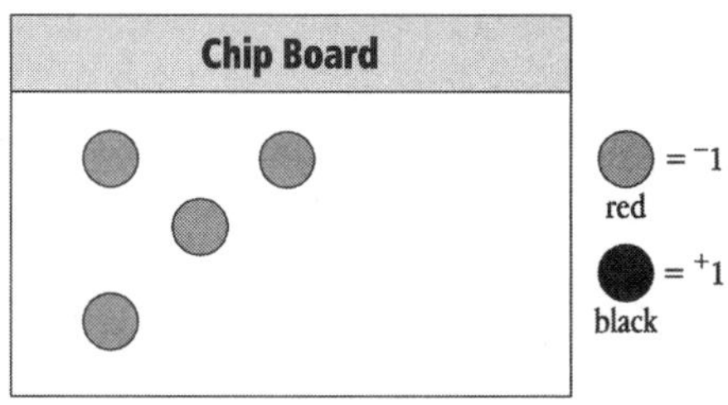

To add +5, Amber added five black chips to the board.

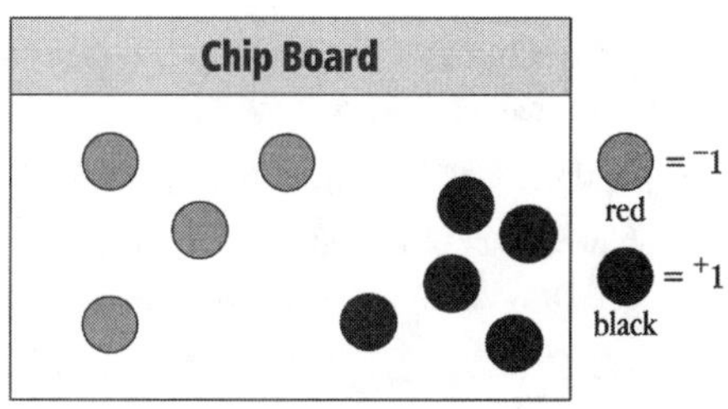

Amber said that next she had to simplify the board so that the answer would be easier to read. She reminded Adil that since $^{+}1$ and $^{-}1$ are opposites, they add to 0. So, a pair consisting of one black chip ($^{+}1$) and one red chip ($^{-}1$) represents 0. Amber formed as many black-red pairs as she could.

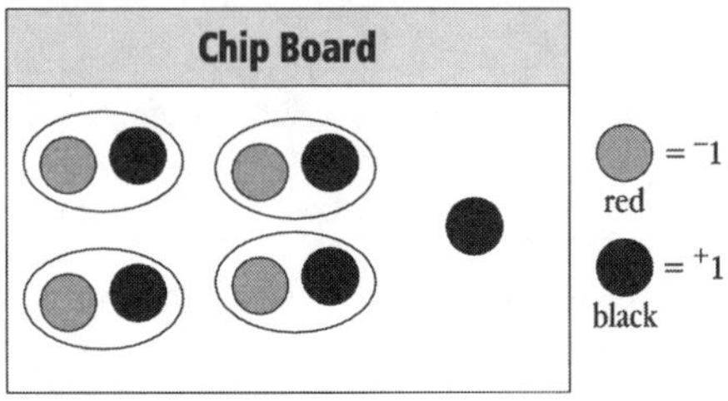

Since each black-red pair represents 0, all the black-red pairs can be removed from the board without changing the total value on the board. After Amber removed these "zeros" from the board, only one black chip remained, representing a sum of $^{+}1$.

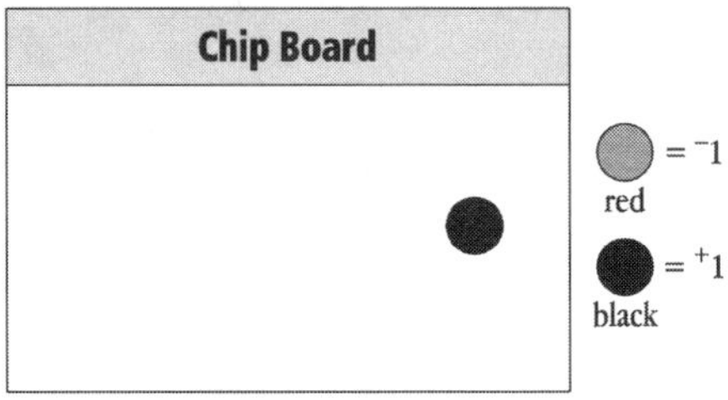

Adil wrote $^{-}4 + {}^{+}5 = {}^{+}1$ to represent the problem Amber had modeled.

Problem 2.2

A. Use a chip board and black and red chips to find each sum. Draw a series of chip boards to illustrate your work.

1. $^{-}8 + {}^{-}7$ **2.** $^{-}8 + {}^{+}7$ **3.** $^{+}8 + {}^{-}7$ **4.** $^{+}8 + {}^{+}7$

B. Find two combinations of black and red chips that will simplify to represent the given integer. Draw a series of chip boards to prove that each combination works.

1. $^{-}3$ **2.** $^{+}5$

C. Write each combination you found in part B as an addition sentence.

Answers to Problem 2.2

See page 33i.

Problem 2.2 Follow-Up

1. What integer added to $^{-}8$ gives a sum of $^{-}4$?

2. Give two integers with a sum that is less than either of the two integers.

3. Give two integers with a sum that is greater than either of the two integers.

Conrado was adding the integers $^{-}5$ and $^{+}8$ on a chip board. First, he represented $^{-}5$ and $^{+}8$.

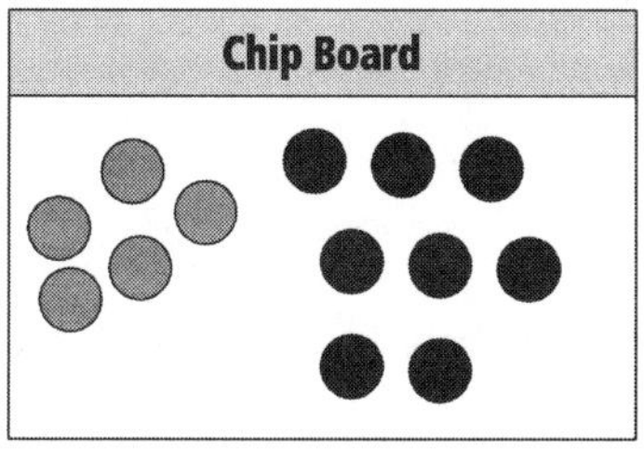

He then rearranged the chips to form a group of five red chips (representing $^{-}5$) and a group of five black chips (representing $^{+}5$). Since the two groups add to 0, he removed them from the board.

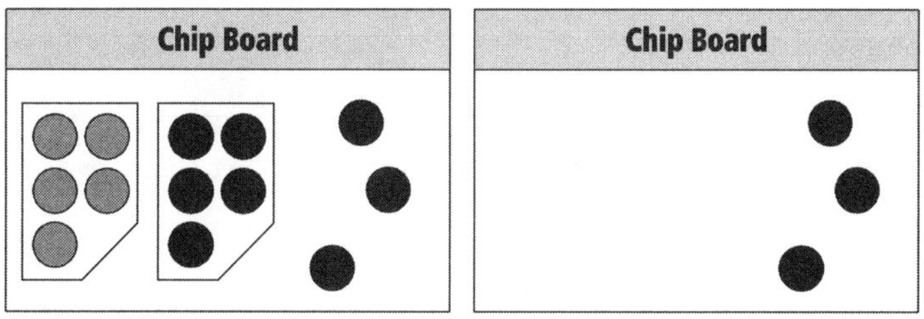

He wrote a series of equations to represent what he had done on the chip board.

$$\begin{aligned} {}^{-}5 + {}^{+}8 &= {}^{-}5 + {}^{+}5 + {}^{+}3 \\ &= ({}^{-}5 + {}^{+}5) + {}^{+}3 \\ &= 0 + {}^{+}3 \\ &= {}^{+}3 \end{aligned}$$

Conrado thought that this method of regrouping to find numbers with a sum of 0 would be a good way to compute sums in his head.

4. Use Conrado's method to compute the following sums in your head.

a. $^{+}9 + {}^{-}7$ **b.** $^{-}80 + {}^{+}50$ **c.** $^{+}35 + {}^{-}27$ **d.** $^{-}8 + {}^{-}5$

Answers to Problem 2.2 Follow-Up

1. $^{+}4$
2. Possible answer: $^{-}2 + {}^{-}3 = {}^{-}5$ (The sum will be less than the two addends when they are both negative numbers.)
3. Possible answer: 2 + 3 = 5 (The sum will be greater than the two addends when they are both positive numbers.)
4. (Students are to try to compute these mentally using Conrado's strategy; see the Summarize section.)

   a. $^{+}2$ b. $^{-}30$ c. $^{+}8$ d. $^{-}13$

ACE

Answers

Applications

1. See below right.
2. See below right.
3. See page 33k.
4. $^-6 + 5 = {^-1}$
5. $7 + {^-7} = 0$
6. $^-4 + {^-2} = {^-6}$
7. $^-6 + 4 = {^-2}$

Applications • Connections • Extensions

As you work on these ACE questions, use your calculator whenever you need it.

Applications

In 1–3, illustrate the addition problem on a number line, and give the answer.

1. $6 + {^-6}$

2. $^-4 + {^-3} + {^-8}$

3. $^+8 + {^-11} + {^-9}$

In 4–7, write the addition sentence illustrated by the figure.

4.

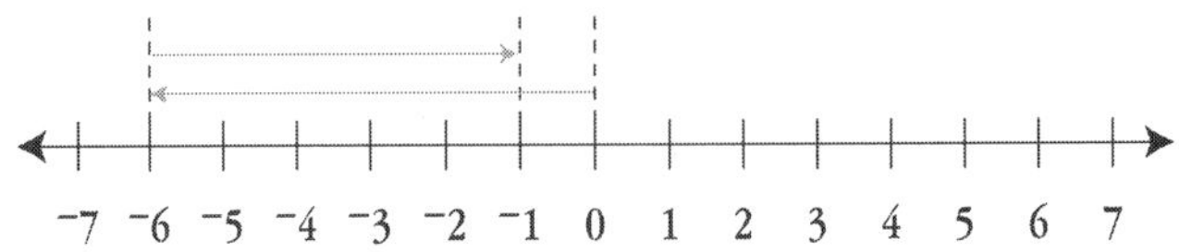

5.

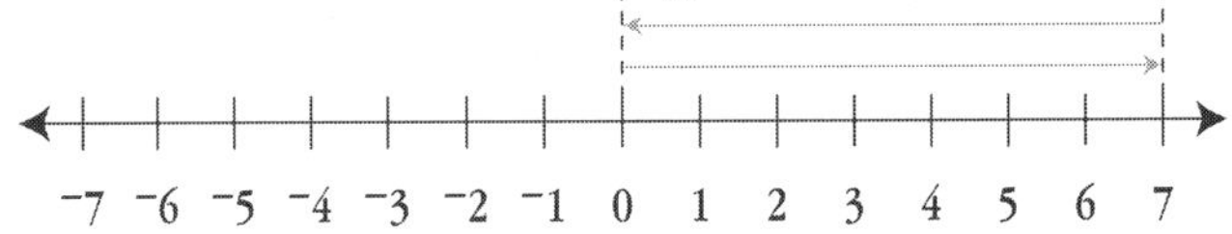

6.

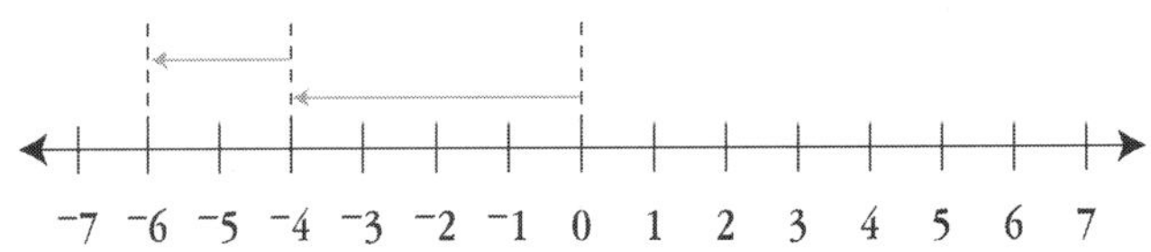

7.

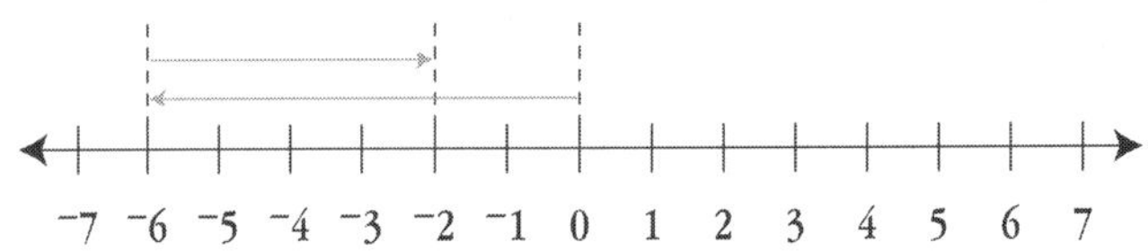

1. $6 + {^-6} = 0$

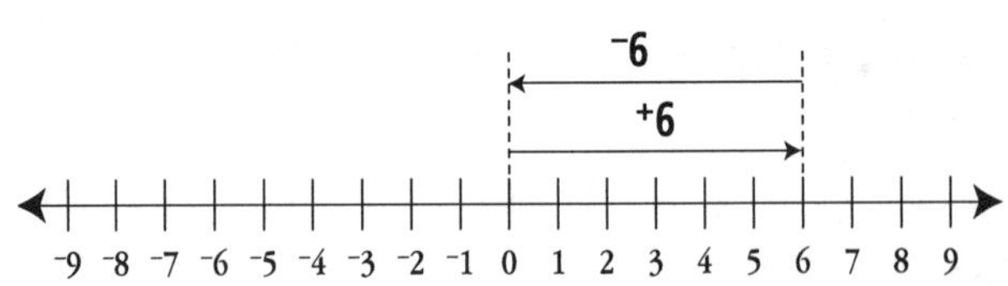

2. $^-4 + {^-3} + {^-8} = {^-15}$

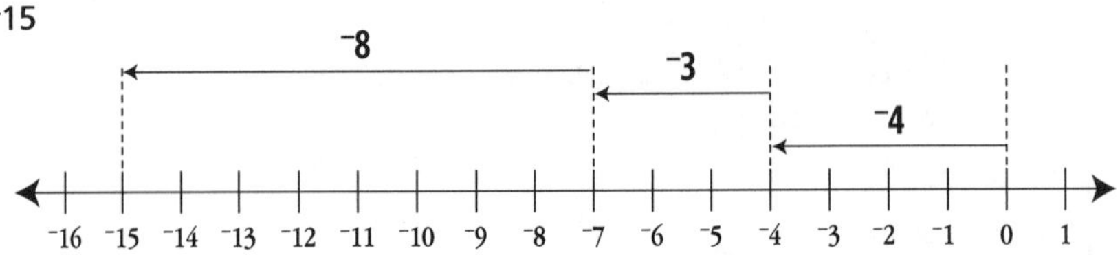

ACE

In 8 and 9, use the chip board below.

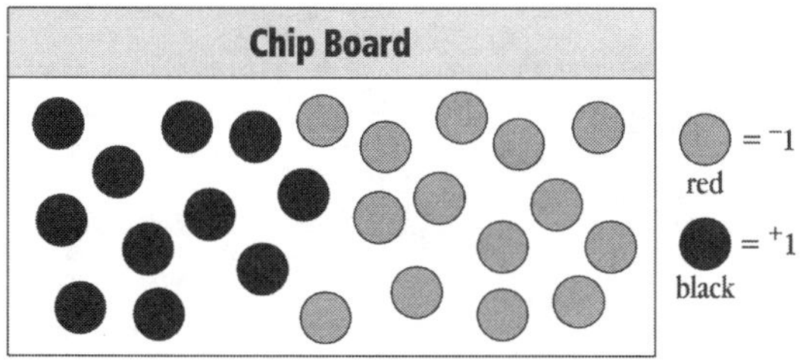

8. **a.** After you simplify the board by removing zeros (black-red pairs), what chips would remain? What integer do these chips represent?

b. Give another combination of black and red chips that would simplify to give the same result you got in part a.

9. Starting with the board as shown above, the following series of actions takes place. Write an addition sentence to describe each action. (A correct addition sentence will show the previous value represented by the board, the value of the chips that are added, and the new value represented by the board.)

a. Seven black chips are added.

b. Three more black chips are added.

c. Three red chips are added.

10. **a.** Find two combinations of black and red chips that simplify to represent $^{-}11$.

b. Draw a chip board to represent each combination from part a.

c. Write an addition sentence to represent each combination from part a.

11. **a.** Find two combinations of black and red chips that simplify to represent $^{+}7$.

b. Draw a chip board to represent each combination from part a.

c. Write an addition sentence to represent each combination from part a.

8a. This board has 14 red chips and 11 black chips, so 3 red chips would remain, which represents $^{-}3$.

8b. Possible answer: 4 red chips and 1 black chip (Any representation with 3 more red chips than black chips would represent $^{-}3$.)

9a. $^{-}3 + {}^{+}7 = {}^{+}4$

9b. $^{+}4 + {}^{+}3 = {}^{+}7$

9c. $^{+}7 + {}^{-}3 = {}^{+}4$

10a. Possible answer: 15 red chips and 4 black chips; 12 red chips and 1 black chip

10b. See below left.

10c. $^{-}15 + {}^{+}4 = {}^{-}11$; $^{-}12 + {}^{+}1 = {}^{-}11$

11a. Possible answer: 10 black chips and 3 red chips; 8 black chips and 1 red chip

11b. See below left.

11c. $^{+}10 + {}^{-}3 = {}^{+}7$; $^{+}8 + {}^{-}1 = {}^{+}7$

10b.

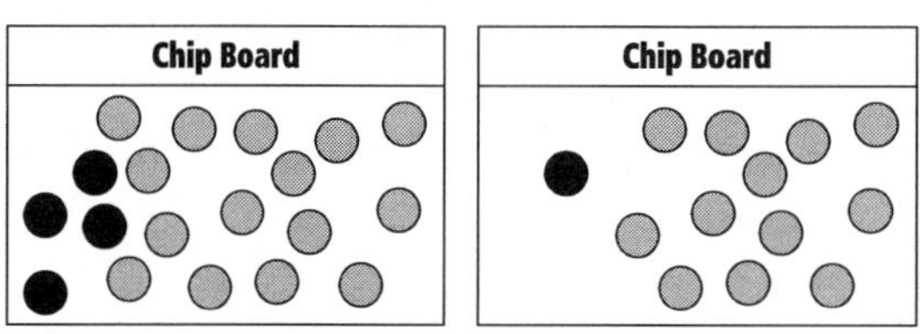

11b.

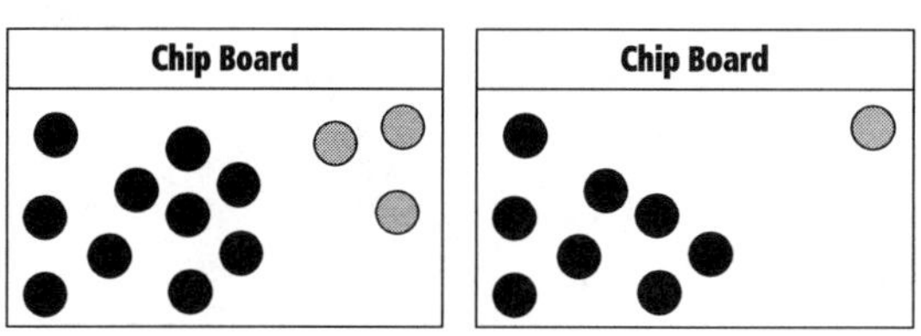

12. This board has 8 red chips and 11 black chips, so 3 black chips would remain, which represents $^{+}3$.

13a. $^{+}3 + {}^{+}4 = {}^{+}7$

13b. $^{+}7 + {}^{-}10 = {}^{-}3$

13c. $^{-}3 + {}^{+}6 = {}^{+}3$

13d. $^{+}3 + {}^{+}8 = {}^{+}11$

13e. $^{+}11 + {}^{-}8 = {}^{+}3$

14. See page 33k.

15. See page 33k.

16. See page 33l.

17. See page 33l.

18. $^{-}40$

19. 900

20. $^{-}146$

21. 10

22. $^{-}400$

23. $^{-}345$

24. $^{-}180$

25. $^{-}90$

26. 0

In 12 and 13, use the chip board shown below.

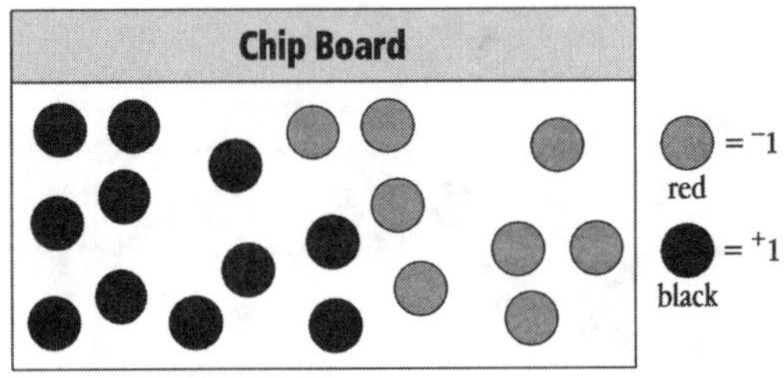

12. After you simplify the board by removing zeros (black-red pairs), what chips would remain? What integer do these chips represent?

13. Starting with the board as shown above, the following series of actions takes place. Write an addition sentence to describe each action. (A correct addition sentence will show the previous value represented by the board, the value of the chips that are added, and the new value represented by the board.)

a. Four black chips are added.

b. Ten red chips are added.

c. Six black chips are added.

d. Eight more black chips are added.

e. Eight red chips are added.

In 14–17, illustrate the addition problem on a number line or a series of chip boards, and give the answer.

14. $^{+}12 + {}^{-}4$

15. $^{-}5 + {}^{+}5$

16. $^{+}5 + {}^{-}9$

17. $^{-}3 + {}^{-}6$

In 18–26, find the sum.

18. $^{-}105 + {}^{+}65$

19. $^{+}1050 + {}^{-}150$

20. $^{-}99 + {}^{-}47$

21. $^{+}37 + {}^{-}12 + {}^{-}15$

22. $0 + {}^{-}400$

23. $^{-}120 + {}^{-}225$

24. $^{-}90 + {}^{-}90$

25. $^{-}90 + 0$

26. $^{+}35 + {}^{-}35$

In 27 and 28, decide whether the statement is always true, sometimes true, or always false. Give examples to illustrate your answer.

27. The sum of two negative integers is a negative integer.

28. The sum of a negative integer and a positive integer is a positive integer.

Connections

29. In Duluth, Minnesota, the temperature at 6:00 A.M. on January 1 was ⁻30°F. During the next 8 hours, the temperature rose 38°. Then, during the next 12 hours, the temperature dropped 12°. Finally, in the next 4 hours, it rose 15°. What was the temperature at 6:00 A.M. on January 2?

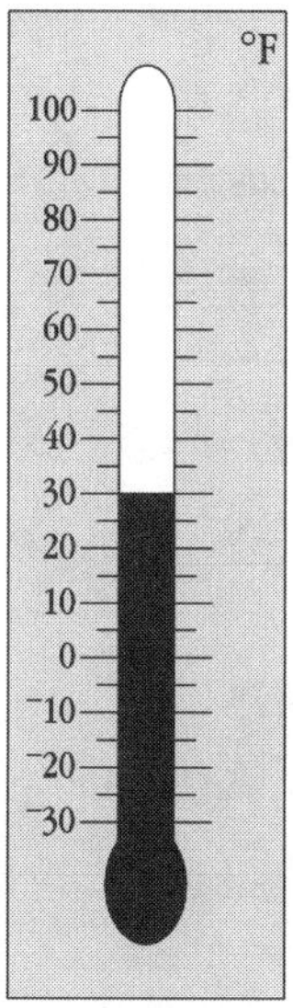

27. This is always true. Examples will vary. (One way to think of this is using a number line: start with a negative integer, and add a negative integer. You will always go to the left, so the answer will always be negative.)

28. This is sometimes true. Examples will vary. (This is true if the absolute value of the positive integer is greater than the absolute value of the negative integer. Students might express this as follows: If the positive integer is larger, the answer will be positive; if the negative integer is larger, the answer will be negative. This might be a good time to introduce the term *absolute value;* however, use your judgment about your students' readiness and the time you wish to devote here. It is not essential that you discuss this here, since students will encounter the concept in Investigation 3.)

Connections

29. ⁻30° + 38° + ⁻12° + 15° = 11°F

30a. $0 + {}^{-}1800 = {}^{-}\$1800$

30b. ${}^{-}1800 + {}^{-}2150 = {}^{-}\$3950$

30c. ${}^{-}3950 + {}^{-}675 = {}^{-}\$4625$

30d. ${}^{-}4625 + {}^{-}2300 = {}^{-}\$6925$

30e. ${}^{-}6925 + {}^{+}665 = {}^{-}\$6260$

30f. ${}^{-}6260 + {}^{+}95 = {}^{-}\$6165$

30g. ${}^{-}6165 + {}^{-}250 = {}^{-}\$6415$

30h. ${}^{-}6415 + {}^{+}1150 = {}^{-}\$5265$

30i. ${}^{-}5265 + {}^{-}225 = {}^{-}\$5490$

30j. ${}^{-}5490 + {}^{+}750 = {}^{-}\$4740$

30k. ${}^{-}4740 + {}^{+}530 = {}^{-}\$4210$ (Note: This is a refund from *return* of five bicycles *to manufacturer.* This is a profit to the bike shop.)

30. Most businesses try hard to make a profit. However, new businesses usually have start-up costs that put them "in the hole" at first. Suppose your family decides to open a bike shop. To get started, you'll have to make a down payment on the rent for your shop, buy bicycles and other supplies to stock the shop, and invest in business equipment and paper to keep track of income and expenses.

Below is a series of business transactions for the bike shop. For each transaction, write an addition sentence that shows how the new balance is calculated from the old balance.

a. Down payment of two months' shop rent: $1800

b. Payment for 20 new bicycles: $2150

c. Down payment of rent on office equipment: $675

d. Business insurance for 6 months: $2300

e. Sale of three bicycles: $665

f. Sale of two helmets and one baby seat: $95

g. Advertising in the yellow pages: $250

h. Sale of six bicycles: $1150

i. Refund for unhappy customer: $225

j. Sale of two bicycles, two helmets, and two air pumps: $750

k. Refund from return of five bicycles to manufacturer: $530

Extensions

31. **a.** Which integers, when added to $^-15$, give a sum greater than 0?

b. Which integers, when added to $^-15$, give a sum less than 0?

c. Which integers, when added to $^-15$, give a sum of 0?

32. A chip board starts out with five black chips. Chips are added to the board. After the board is simplified by removing zeros (black-red pairs), nine black chips remain.

a. What chips might have been added? Give two possibilities. (For example, adding five black chips and one red chip results in ten black chips and one red chip. After you remove zeros, nine black chips remain.)

b. Write an addition sentence for each of the possibilities you gave in part a. (For the example given in part a, the addition sentence would be $^+5 + {}^+5 + {}^-1 = {}^+9$).

33. A chip board starts out empty. Chips are added to the board. After the board is simplified by removing zeros (black-red pairs), one black chip remains.

a. What chips might have been added? Give two possibilities.

b. Write an addition sentence for each of the possibilities you gave in part a.

34. A chip board starts out with one black chip. Chips are added to the board. After the board is simplified by removing zeros (black-red pairs), five red chips remain.

a. What chips might have been added? Give two possibilities.

b. Write an addition sentence for each of the possibilities you gave in part a.

35. A chip board starts out with five red chips. Chips are added to the board. After the board is simplified by removing zeros (black-red pairs), eight red chips remain.

a. What chips might have been added? Give two possibilities.

b. Write an addition sentence for each of the possibilities you gave in part a.

Extensions

31a. Any integer greater than 15.

31b. Any integer less than 15.

31c. The only integer is 15.

32a. Possible answer: Add 6 black chips and 2 red chips, or add 12 black chips and 8 red chips.

32b. $^+5 + {}^+6 + {}^-2 = {}^+9$, $^+5 + {}^+12 + {}^-8 = {}^+9$

33a. Possible answer: Add 2 black chips and 1 red chip, or add 10 black chips and 9 red chips.

33b. $0 + {}^+2 + {}^-1 = {}^+1$, $0 + {}^+10 + {}^-9 = {}^+1$

34a. Possible answer: Add 1 black chip and 7 red chips, or add 9 black chips and 15 red chips.

34b. $^+1 + {}^+1 + {}^-7 = {}^-5$, $+1 + {}^+9 + {}^-15 = {}^-5$

35a. Possible answer: Add 1 black chip and 4 red chips, or add 5 black chips and 8 red chips.

35b. $^-5 + {}^+1 + {}^-4 = {}^-8$, $^-5 + {}^+5 + {}^-8 = {}^-8$

36a. Possible answer: Add 10 black chips and 12 red chips, or add 50 black chips and 52 red chips.

36b. $0 + {}^{+}10 + {}^{-}12 = {}^{-}2$, $0 + {}^{+}50 + {}^{-}52 = {}^{-}2$

37a. Possible answer: Add 9 black chips and 2 red chips, or add 15 black chips and 8 red chips.

37b. ${}^{-}2 + {}^{+}9 + {}^{-}2 = {}^{+}5$, ${}^{-}2 + {}^{+}15 + {}^{-}8 = {}^{+}5$

36. A chip board starts out empty. Chips are added to the board. After the board is simplified by removing zeros (black-red pairs), two red chips remain.

a. What chips might have been added? Give two possibilities.

b. Write an addition sentence for each of the possibilities you gave in part a.

37. A chip board starts out with two red chips. Chips are added to the board. After the board is simplified by removing zeros (black-red pairs), five black chips remain.

a. What chips might have been added? Give two possibilities.

b. Write an addition sentence for each of the possibilities you gave in part a.

Mathematical Reflections

In this investigation, you explored two ways to model the addition of integers—on a number line and with a chip board. These questions will help you summarize what you have learned:

1. When you add two integers, how can you decide whether their sum will be positive, negative, or zero?
2. Describe how to add any two integers.
3. Explain how you can find the opposite of a number. Use the following examples to illustrate your explanations.

   a. 7 **b.** 0 **c.** $^-12$

Think about your answers to these questions, discuss your ideas with other students and your teacher, and then write a summary of your findings in your journal.

Possible Answers

1. *Positive:* The sum of two positive integers will always be positive. The sum of a positive and a negative integer will be positive when the positive value is farther from 0 (for example, $^+10 + ^-7 = ^+3$). *Negative:* The sum of two negative integers will always be negative. The sum of a positive and a negative integer will be negative when the negative value is farther from 0 (for example, $^-10 + ^+7 = ^-3$). *Zero:* The sum of two opposites is 0.

2. When adding two positive or two negative integers, the numerical answer will be the sum of the two amounts, and the sign will be the same as the sign of the two integers. When adding a positive integer and a negative integer, the numerical answer is the difference between the two amounts, and the sign will be the same as the sign of the integer that represents the greater quantity without regard to sign. For example, in $^-10 + ^+7 = ^-3$, 3 is the difference between 10 and 7.

3. See page 33l.

Tips for the Linguistically Diverse Classroom

Original Rebus The Original Rebus technique is described in detail in *Getting to Know Connected Mathematics*. Students make a copy of the text before it is discussed. During the discussion, they generate their own rebuses for words they do not understand; the words are made comprehensible through pictures, objects, or demonstrations. Example: Question 1—key words for which students might make rebuses are *add* (+), *two* (2), *integers* (4, 3, $^-6$, $^-8$), *sum* (3 + 3 = ?), *positive* (+), *negative* (–), *zero* (0).

TEACHING THE INVESTIGATION

2.1 • Adding on a Number Line

The student edition describes a method for using a number line to add integers. The launch below is suggested to supplement that discussion, because many students will need more exposure than what is offered in the text. The discussion in the student edition will serve as a good reference for students (and their families) when they are at home working on the ACE questions and want to review the model.

Launch

While your students can add whole numbers, they may not be able to articulate their understanding of the operation of addition. One way to introduce this investigation is to have a conversation about addition.

> You have been adding numbers since you started school, and you all know how to find the sum of two or more whole numbers. My question is this: What is addition really about? What does it mean when you add two numbers?

Take a few ideas from the class. They should recognize that addition is about combining things and finding a total.

> If you have 7 cans of cola and 8 cans of cola and add them together, you would have a sum of 15 cans of cola. We combine two amounts—we *add*—to find the total number of something.
>
> We could also use addition to think about temperature, as we did in Investigation 1. If a thermometer reading is 7°F and the temperature rises 8°F, the temperature would be 15°F. This is the sum of the first temperature reading and the temperature increase.
>
> How might you show adding 7 and 8 and getting a sum of 15 on a number line?

You may want to distribute copies of the number lines to speed up this discussion. Have students work in pairs to search for a way to represent addition using a number line. Then, let them share their drawings. Look for several different representations.

After each representation is presented, ask the class whether the drawing makes sense and whether they think they could use that strategy to add any two integers on a number line. (At this point, negative integers will likely not be part of the conversation. The goal here is to have students find a way to use the number line to represent sums they already know and understand, then build on these representations once they feel comfortable with the model.)

Once several strategies have been presented and have been tried with other addition problems (such as 6 + 10 or 3 + 4 + 5), ask the class to find similarities and differences among the various representations. If no one presents the strategy used in the student edition, present it yourself for consideration.

For the Teacher: Number-line Addition

One way to use the number line to add integers is to start at 0. Represent the first integer by drawing an arrow above the number line the length of the first number in "number line" units—to the left if the integer is negative, to the right if it is positive. Represent the addition of the second number by drawing a second arrow above the first arrow, starting at the point where the first arrow ended and going to the left or right depending on whether the second integer is negative or positive. Here are two examples.

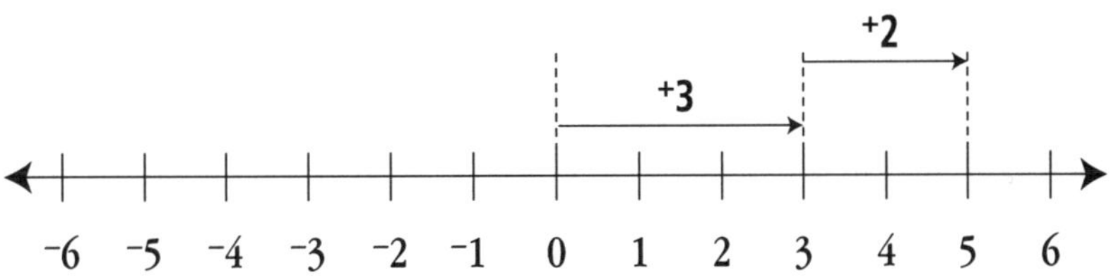

$^{+}3 + {}^{+}2 = 5$

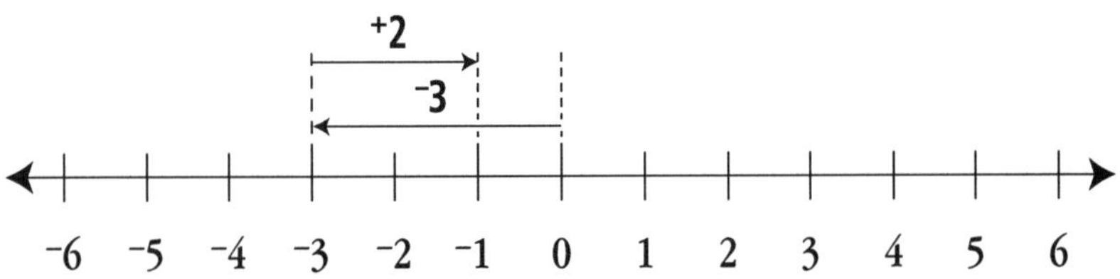

$^{-}3 + {}^{+}2 = {}^{-}1$

Continue the conversation by inquiring about negative numbers.

Now that we have some strategies for adding numbers like 7 and 8, let's look at a different set of addition problems and think about how we can use the number line to help us with them.

Consider this problem: $^{-}5 + {}^{-}4$. With your partner, use a number line to show the addition of these two numbers.

Give pairs some time to explore this question.

What did you get for the sum of these two numbers? *($^{-}9$)* Does it seem reasonable that the sum of $^{-}5$ and $^{-}4$ is $^{-}9$? *(Yes, because negative numbers can be thought of as losing, and if you lose 5 points and then lose 4 more, you will have lost a total of 9 points.)*

Ask for a volunteer to come to the board and show how he or she drew a representation of this addition problem on a number line.

Does everyone agree with this representation? Did anyone draw their representation differently?

If there are other representations, let students share them, and then ask the class to review their merits. If no one presents a drawing like the one below, draw it yourself and discuss why you drew what you did.

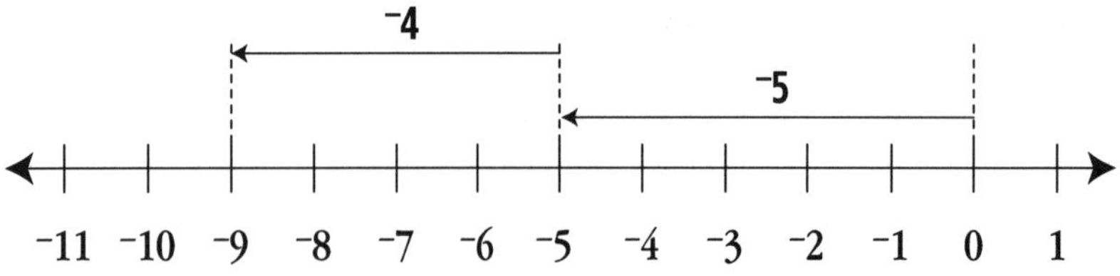

Now, I'd like you to show the addition of +5 and −4 on one number line and the addition of −5 and +4 on a second number line. Before you start, what do you think the two sums will be? Why?

After students have completed their drawings, ask for the sums and discuss why their answers seem reasonable. Have students share their drawings. When you feel that they have an idea of how to use a number line to show the addition of integers, have them work in pairs on the problem.

Explore

As you circulate, be aware that some students may not understand what a number sentence is and write only expressions for part A (for example, they may write the expression $^-3 - {}^-4$ instead of writing the sentence $^-3 - {}^-4 = {}^+1$). You will want to address this during the summary if you find that it is an issue in your class.

Summarize

Have students share their addition sentences for part A. Use this as an opportunity to help all students understand how to write number sentences properly and to check how well they understand and can use the number line model to find integer sums.

Question 3 of part B asks students to represent the sum of three integers on a number line. This is a nice problem for having a couple of groups share their representation. Discuss the representations and whether the answers make sense.

You will want to spend some time making sure students understand part C.

Why are these sums the same? Think what would happen if you switched the order of whole numbers when doing other operations, such as subtraction, multiplication, or division. Would the answers remain the same? Does order make a difference with any or all of these operations?

Students can test their ideas with whole numbers and quickly discover that order matters in subtraction and division but not in multiplication.

After discussing the problem, have students individually write out the number sentences for the follow-up and answer the questions. Some may write subtraction sentences rather than addition with negatives. If so, ask them to think about how to rewrite their answers as addition sentences using positive and negative values. You might have someone model how to do this. You could also ask why some related addition sentences and subtraction sentences give the same answer.

> Why is the sum of $^+200$ and $^-150$ ($^+200 + {}^-150$) the same as the difference of $^+200$ and $^+150$ ($^+200 - {}^+150$)?

This question will be addressed in Investigation 3 when subtraction of integers is discussed, so just raise the issue for the time being.

2.2 • Inventing a New Model

This problem introduces another tool that can be used to represent the addition of integers. The tool is connected to the language of business, with the idea of profits being a positive situation (often referred to as being "in the black") and losses being a negative situation (referred to as being "in the red").

Launch

Talk with students about how they used the number line to model the addition of integers. After using the model and finding sums, they have probably noticed some patterns they can use to predict sums of positive and negative integers.

> Some of you have started to notice patterns when adding certain integers. For example, when you add two positive integers, what do you know about the sum? *(The sum is simply the total of the two numbers and is positive.)* Give an example that demonstrates what you have said.
>
> What do you know about the sum of any two negative integers? *(The sum is the total of the two numbers, and it is negative.)* Give an example that demonstrates what you have said.
>
> What do you know about the sum of a positive and a negative integer?

Some students may say that sometimes the sum is positive and sometimes it is negative. If so, ask for examples of pairs of integers with a positive sum and examples of pairs of integers with a negative sum. Students may still be struggling with adding positive and negative integers and may not have noticed any patterns. If this is the case in your class, accept their explanations at this point.

> What is the sum of $^-5$ and $^+5$? *(0)* What is the sum of $^+1$ and $^-1$? *(0)* Why? *(Because they are opposites. Since you always start every problem at 0 on the number line, you just move back and forth the same amount and end up where you began.)*
>
> We are going to explore a different way to model the addition of integers. As you use this model, continue to think about what happens when you add positive and negative integers. Keep looking for patterns

that will allow you to predict sums of integers and to understand why the sum will be positive or negative.

Rather than have the students invent a method for showing addition of integers using chips (as they did with the number line), you may want to describe how to use this tool.

For the Teacher: Using the Chip Board

The chip board model uses one color of chips (black) to represent positive integers and another color (red) to represent negative integers. To use the model, begin with an empty board. Chips are placed on the board to represent each addend. If the integer is positive, that number of black chips is placed on the board. If the integer is negative, that number of red chips is placed on the board. If the two integers being added have the same sign, the sum is the total number of chips on the board. For example, to add $^-4 + {}^-3$, place 4 red chips and then another 3 red chips on the board, for a total of 7 red chips (representing a sum of $^-7$).

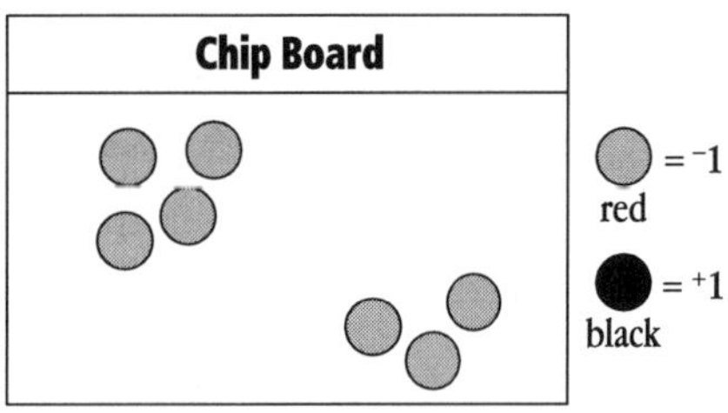

$^-4 + {}^-3 = {}^-7$

If the integers being added have different signs, the two values are represented by placing the appropriate number of red and black chips on the board. The board is then simplified by removing red-black pairs of chips. Red-black pairs represent opposites ($^-1$ and $^+1$), which add to 0. The chips that remain unmatched represent the sum of the two integers. For example:

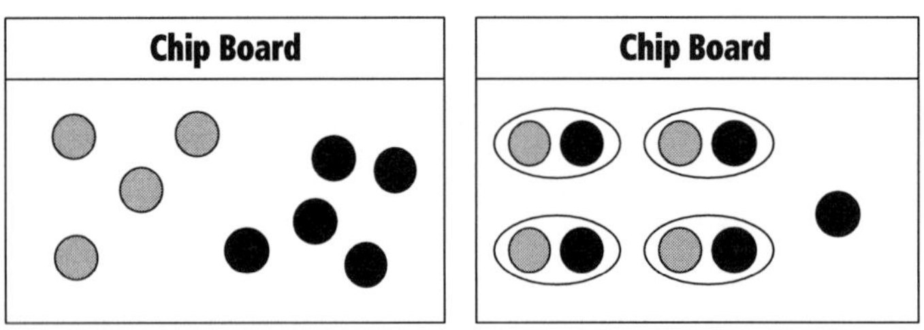

$^-4 + {}^+5$ $\quad$ $^-4 + {}^+5 = {}^+1$

Read the story in the student edition, or tell a similar story in your own words. Explain to the class that the idea and language of the chip board model is connected to the business world and to the ideas of making and losing money.

Distribute two different colors of chips or tiles (and, optionally, copies of the chip board) to each pair of students and have them work through a few addition problems until they understand how to use the chip board. Ask them why the pairing of a black chip ($^{+}1$) and a red chip ($^{-}1$) results in a sum of 0.

Save the follow-up questions for the summary discussion.

Explore

If students are stuck, suggest that they first work out one of the problems using a number line model and then see whether they can use their answer to help them make sense of the chip board model.

Summarize

Have students come to the board and share their chip board representations of the expressions in part A. Since all four sums involve the same numerical values, you might want to put all four drawings on the board or overhead projector at once and discuss their similarities and differences. Ask whether anyone has made a different drawing from that on the board for any of the problems. If so, let them share their drawings. Ask the class whether they agree with the representations presented. For drawings that are incorrect, have someone explain why the representation is wrong and how to fix it.

If students are using the chip board effectively and do not need to actually see the model to successfully do the problem, skip part B and review part C. Otherwise, do parts B and C together (students could show their chip boards and write their sentences beside them). Have several students share their sentences for each target integer, organizing them on the board in two groups:

- Addition sentences in which the integers being added have the same sign
- Addition sentences in which the integers being added have different signs

Collect several responses for each target integer. Ask the students to examine the lists for any addition sentences they disagree with.

At this point, you want students to notice patterns so that they can eventually add integers without relying on a model. Direct students' attention to the sentences that have integers with the same sign.

> Does anyone notice any patterns that would help us to predict the sum for two integers with the same sign?

Students should recognize that the sum will have the same sign as the sign of the addends and will be the sum of the numerical values.

> Does anyone notice any patterns that would help us to predict the sum when adding integers with different signs?

Students should mention that the sign for the sum will always be the same as the integer that is farther from 0 on the number line or that has the most chips on a chip board. Students should also notice that the sum will be the difference between the two numerical values.

For the Teacher: Absolute Value

Mathematically, we are looking at the *absolute value* of the integers being added. At this point, accept students' discussion of the distance from 0 or the relative "largeness" of the integers.

Ask questions to help students generalize their findings.

> When is the sum of two integers positive? When is it negative? When is it 0?

For follow-up question 1, ask the class how they might find the missing integer. Have a couple of students share their ideas, and ask the class to evaluate whether each idea is reasonable. For questions 2 and 3, ask questions until students can generalize each situation. If they only give examples, ask them to examine their examples to see what they have in common.

Have students share their solutions for question 4. They are to try to do these sums in their heads with the idea of using the following strategy:

- $^{+}9 + ^{-}7 = ^{+}2 + ^{+}7 + ^{-}7 = ^{+}2 + 0 = ^{+}2$
- $^{-}80 + ^{+}50 = ^{-}30 + ^{-}50 + ^{+}50 = ^{-}30 + 0 = ^{-}30$
- $^{+}35 + ^{-}27 = ^{+}8 + ^{+}27 + ^{-}27 = ^{+}8 + 0 = ^{+}8$
- Since $^{-}8 + ^{-}5$ do not involve integers of different signs, Conrado's method is not necessary.

Additional Answers

Answers to Problem 2.1

B. 1. $^{-}5 + ^{+}8 = ^{+}3$

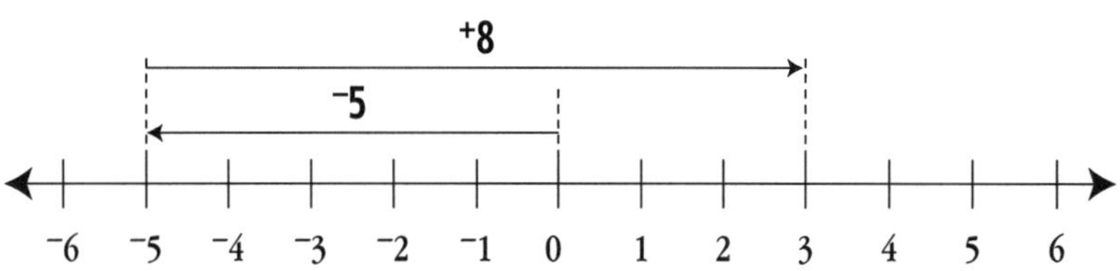

2. $^{-}4 + ^{-}3 = ^{-}7$

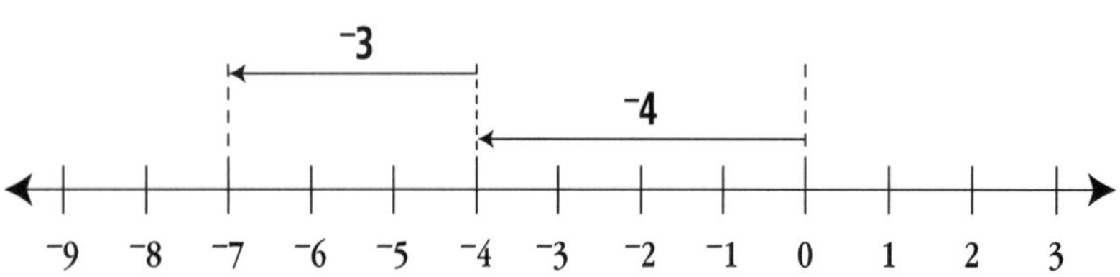

3. $^{-}2 + ^{-}3 + ^{+}10 = ^{+}5$

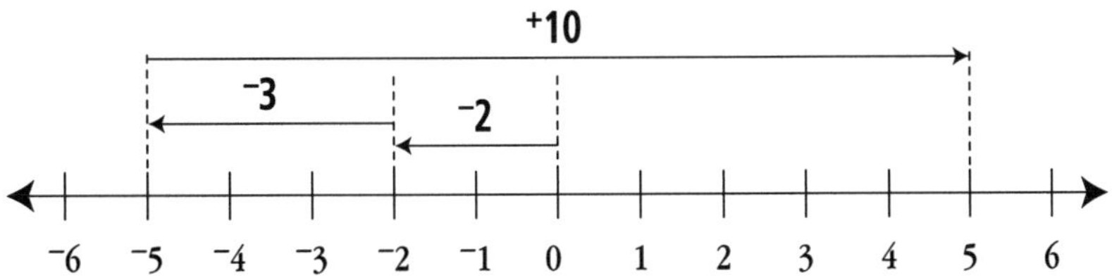

C. 1. The order of the integers does not matter; the answer is the same.

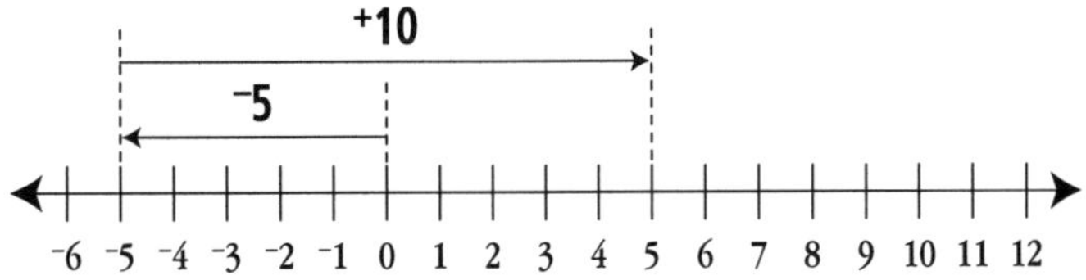

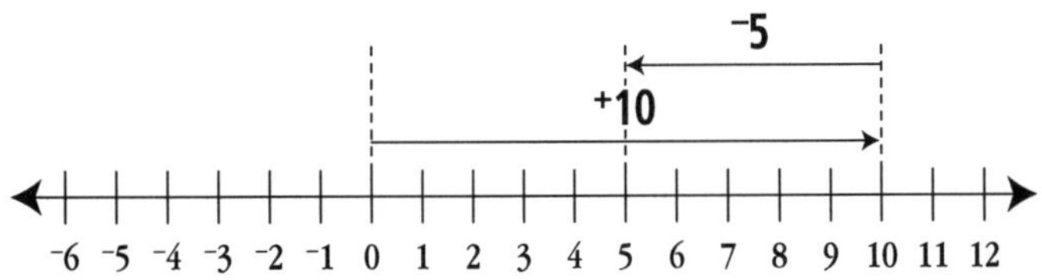

2.

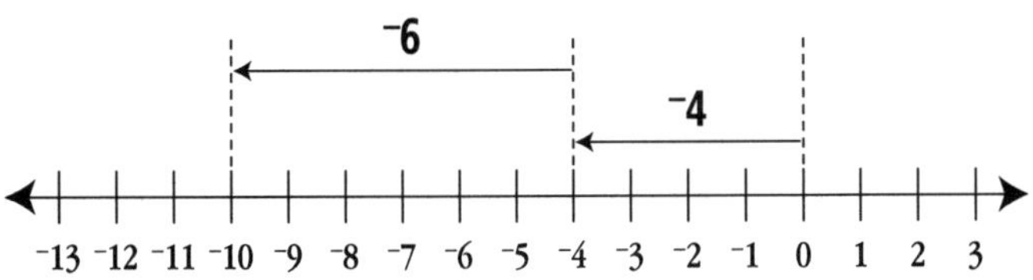

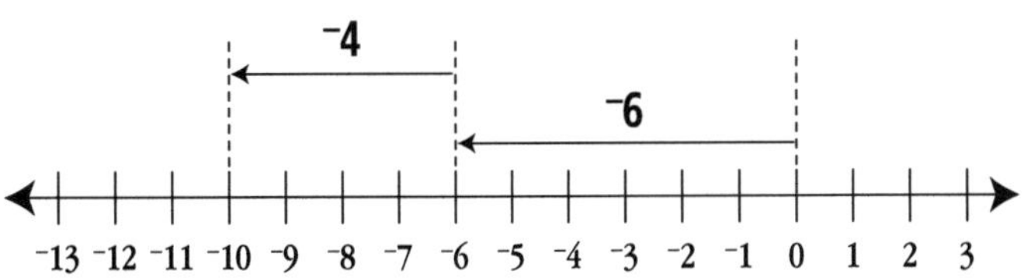

3.

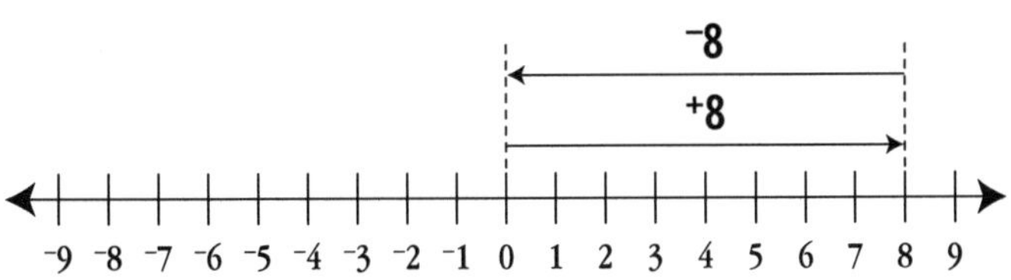

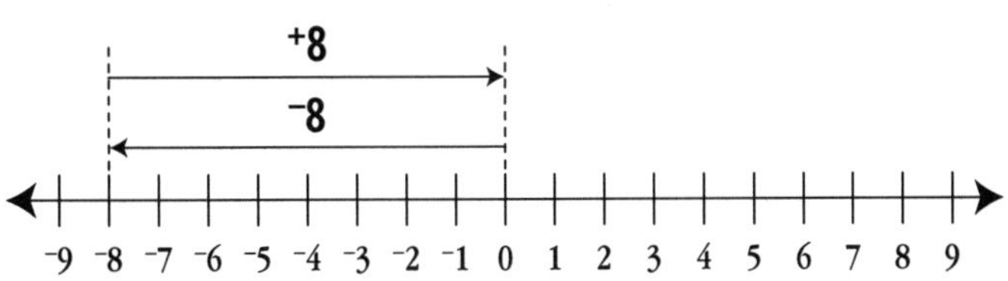

4.

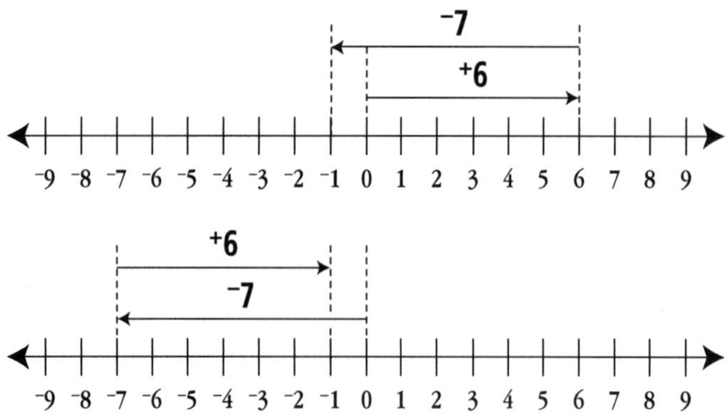

Answers to Problem 2.1 Follow-Up

2. a. $^{-}2 + {}^{+}2 = 0$

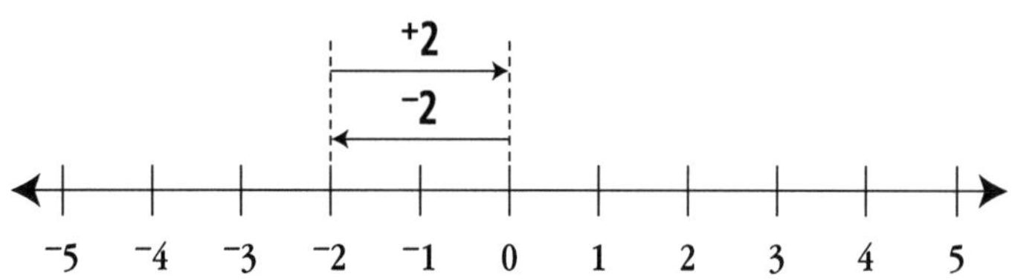

b. $^{+}8 + {}^{-}8 = 0$

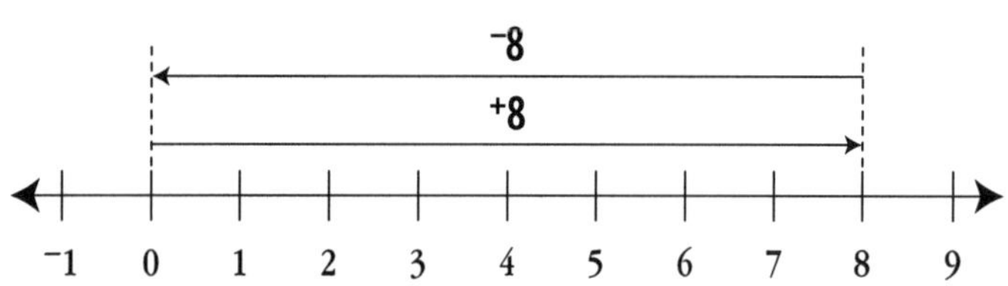

c. $^{-}1 + {}^{+}1 = 0$

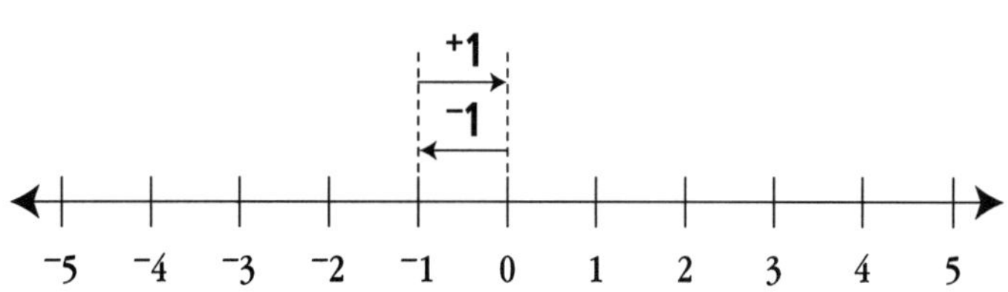

Answers to Problem 2.2

A. 1. $^{-}8 + {}^{-}7 = {}^{-}15$

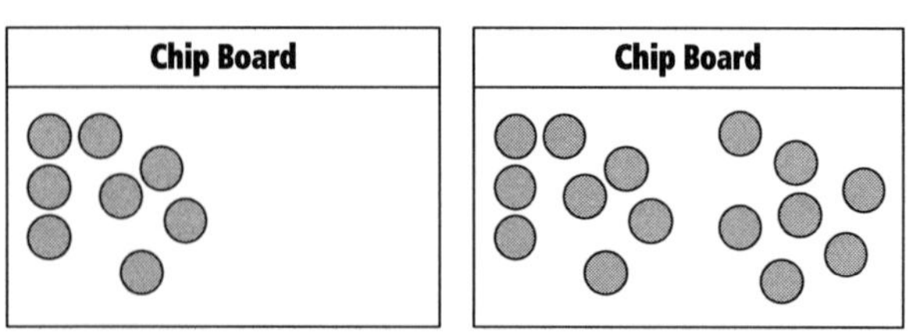

2. $^{-}8 + {}^{+}7 = {}^{-}1$

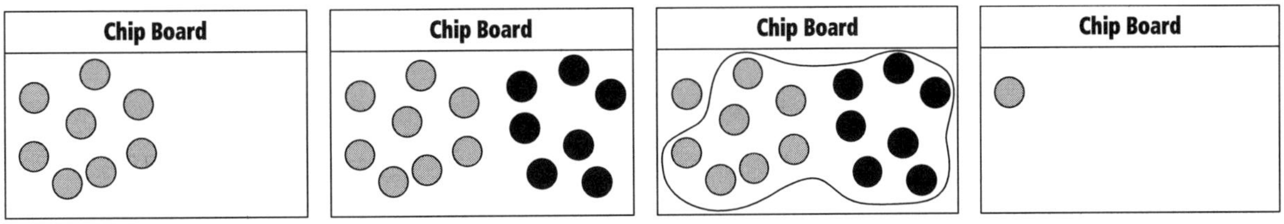

3. $^{+}8 + {}^{-}7 = {}^{+}1$

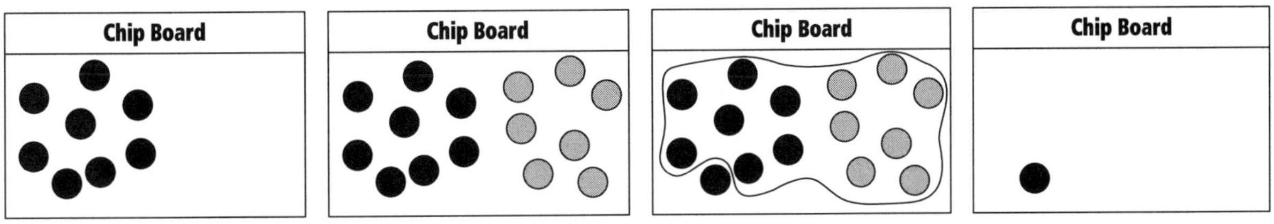

4. $^{+}8 + {}^{+}7 = {}^{+}15$

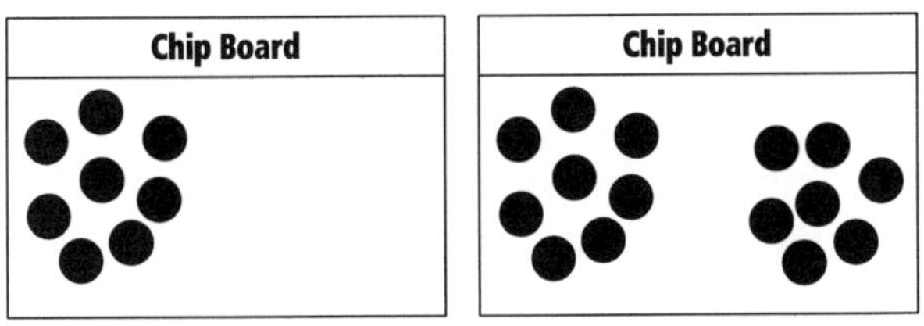

B. 1. Possible answer:

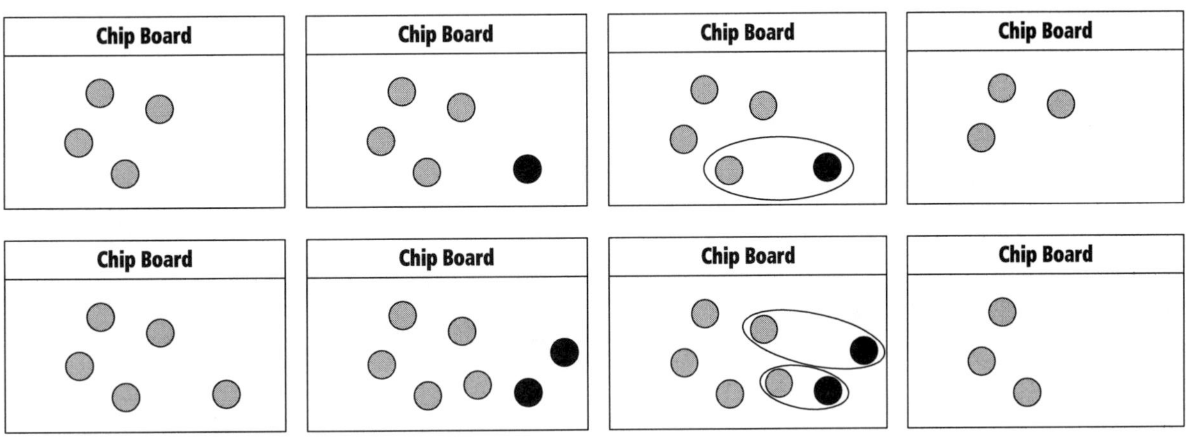

2. Possible answer:

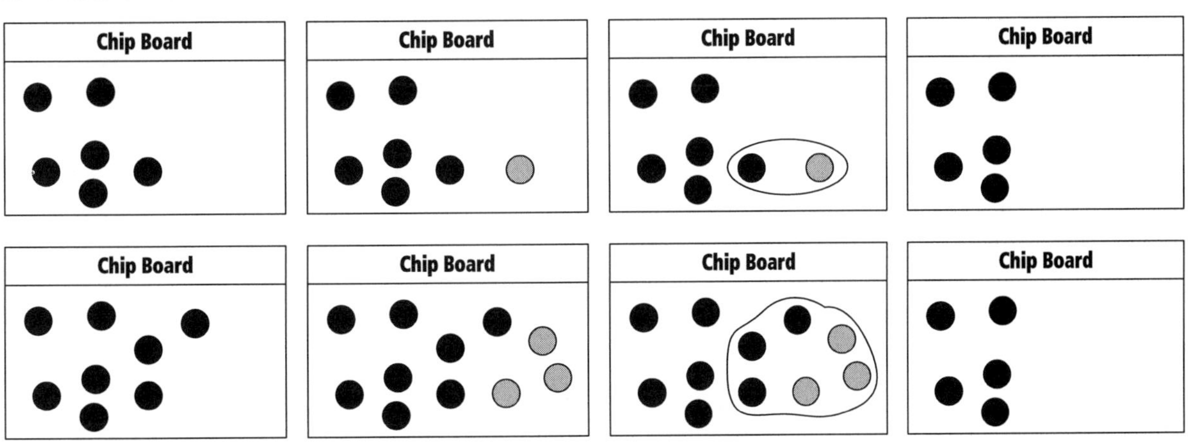

C. 1. Possible answer: ${}^-4 + {}^+1 = {}^-3$, ${}^-5 + {}^+2 = {}^-3$

2. Possible answer: ${}^+6 + {}^-1 = {}^+5$, ${}^+8 + {}^-3 = {}^+5$

ACE Answers

Applications

3. ${}^+8 + {}^-11 + {}^-9 = {}^-12$

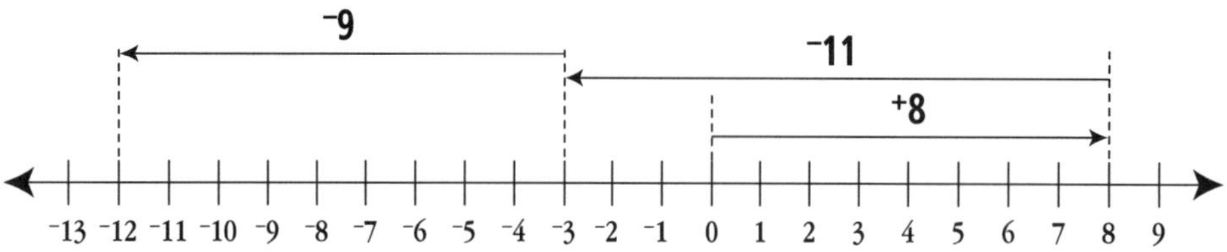

14. ${}^+12 + {}^-4 = {}^+8$

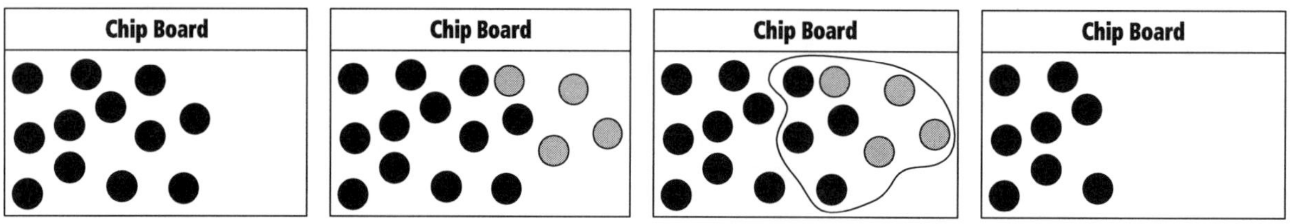

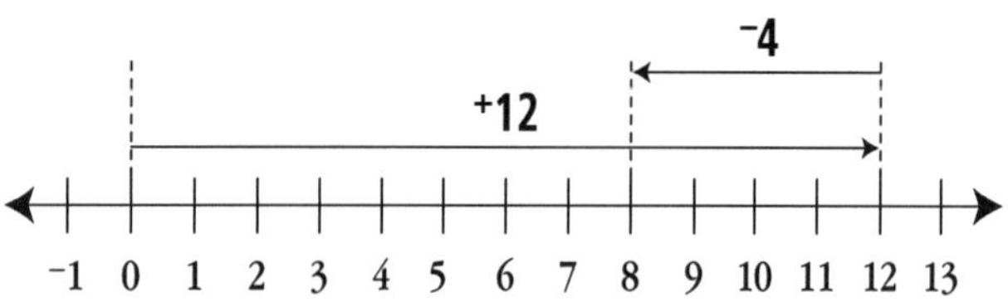

15. ${}^-5 + {}^+5 = 0$

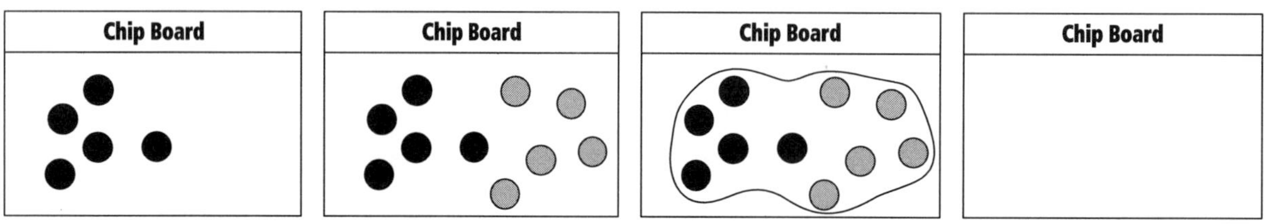

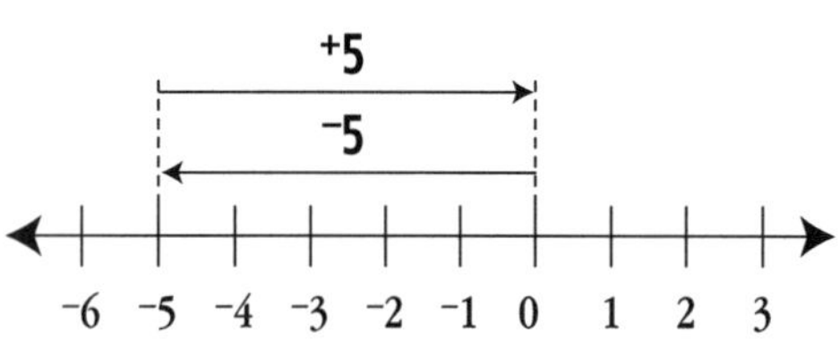

16. $^{+}5 + {}^{-}9 = {}^{-}4$

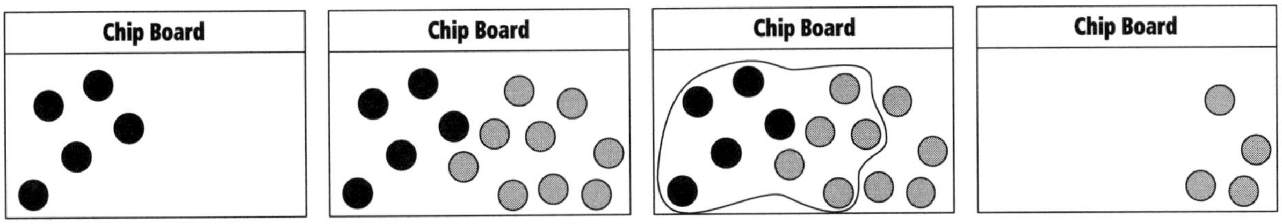

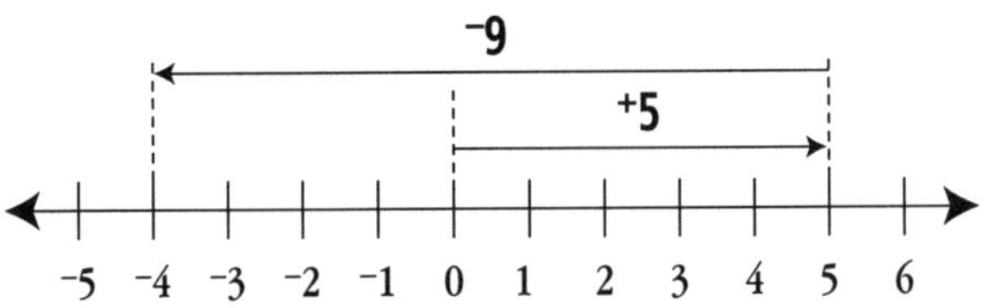

17. $^{-}3 + {}^{-}6 = {}^{-}9$

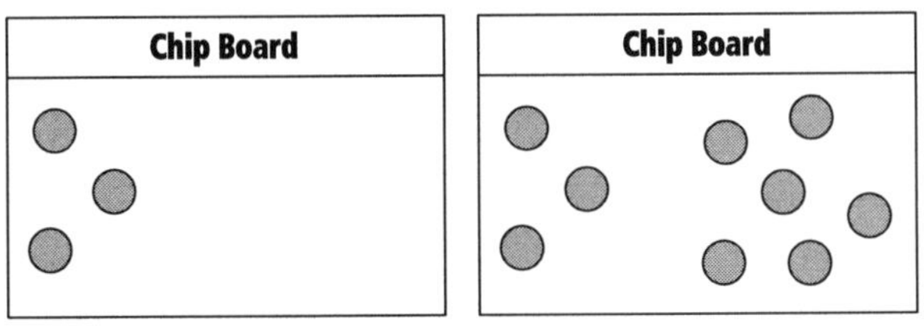

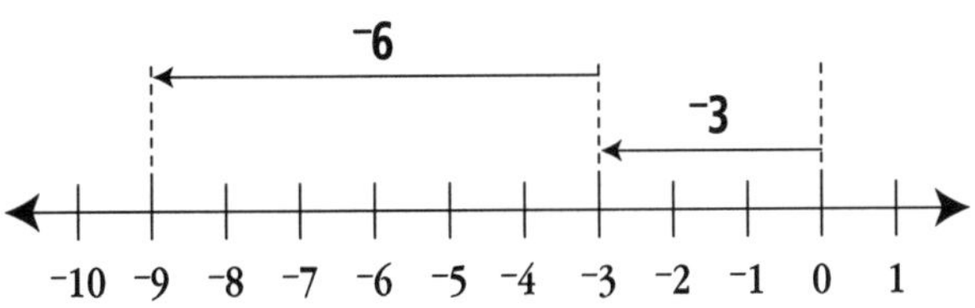

Mathematical Reflections

3. The opposite of a number is the number that is the same distance from 0 on a number line, only in the opposite direction. It is the number that, when added to the given number, gives a sum of 0.

3a. The opposite of 7 is $^{-}7$. It is 7 units from 0 in the opposite direction, and $7 + {}^{-}7 = 0$.

3b. The opposite of 0 is 0. It is the only number that is 0 units from 0, and $0 + 0 = 0$.

3c. The opposite of $^{-}12$ is 12. It is 12 units from 0 in the opposite direction, and $^{-}12 + 12 = 0$.

INVESTIGATION 3

Subtracting Integers

In this investigation, students develop strategies for subtracting integers. Subtraction with positive and negative integers is typically much more difficult for students to make sense of than addition.

In Problem 3.1, Subtracting on a Chip Board, students use chips to model subtraction of integers. In Problem 3.2, Subtracting on a Number Line, they use a number line model for subtraction. Subtraction is interpreted as the opposite of addition, which is modeled on a chip board as "taking away" and on a number line as reversing the direction of the second integer. In Problem 3.3, Exploring Patterns, students look for patterns in the subtraction of integers and further develop their rules for subtracting positive and negative integers. In Problem 3.4, "Undoing" with Addition and Subtraction, students continue to develop rules by looking more closely at the relationship between addition and subtraction.

Mathematical and Problem-Solving Goals

- *To explore subtraction of integers using two models (a number line and a chip board)*
- *To develop strategies for subtracting integers*
- *To recognize and use the relationship of addition and subtraction as inverse operations*
- *To recognize and solve problems involving subtraction of integers*

Materials

Problem	For students	For the teacher
All	Graphing calculators	Transparencies 3.1A to 3.4 (optional)
3.1	Chip boards (optional; provided as blackline masters, or students can simply label sheets of paper), chips or tiles in two colors (about 15–25 of each color per pair of students; student edition refers to red and black)	Transparency of chip boards (optional), transparent chips or tiles in two colors
3.2	Number lines (provided as a blackline master)	Transparency of number lines (optional)
3.3	Chip boards, number lines (optional)	Transparencies of chip boards and number lines (optional)
3.4	Chip boards (optional), chips or tiles in two colors	Transparency of chip boards (optional), transparent chips or tiles in two colors
ACE	Chip boards and number lines (optional)	

Student Pages 34–52 Teaching the Investigation 52a–52o

INVESTIGATION 3

Subtracting Integers

In the last investigation, you used number lines and chip boards to help you learn about the addition of integers. These tools are also helpful for modeling subtraction of integers. In this investigation, you will start by using a chip board to explore subtraction. Next, you will use the relationship between addition and subtraction to subtract numbers on the number line. Finally, you will study patterns involving subtraction of integers and use these patterns to make predictions.

Think about this!

You can use positive and negative numbers to describe elevations. If you think of sea level as 0 feet, you can express elevations above sea level with positive numbers and elevations below sea level with negative numbers.

The highest point in the United States is Mount McKinley (also known as Denali), Alaska, with an elevation of 20,320 feet above sea level. You can express this elevation as $^{+}20,320$ feet. The lowest point in the United States is Death Valley, California, with an elevation of 282 feet below sea level. You can express this elevation as $^{-}282$ feet.

Death Valley, California

How many feet higher is the highest point in the United States than the lowest point?

Tips for the Linguistically Diverse Classroom

Visual Enhancement The Visual Enhancement technique is described in detail in *Getting to Know Connected Mathematics*. It involves using real objects or pictures to make information more comprehensible. Example: While discussing positive and negative numbers used to describe elevations, show pictures of Mount McKinley and other places notably above or below sea level.

3.1 Subtracting on a Chip Board

Amber's friends Jing-mei and Drew liked Amber's chip board model for adding integers. They decided to use a chip board to explore subtracting integers.

To model 9 – 5, Jing-mei started with an empty chip board and then put nine black chips on the board to represent $^+9$.

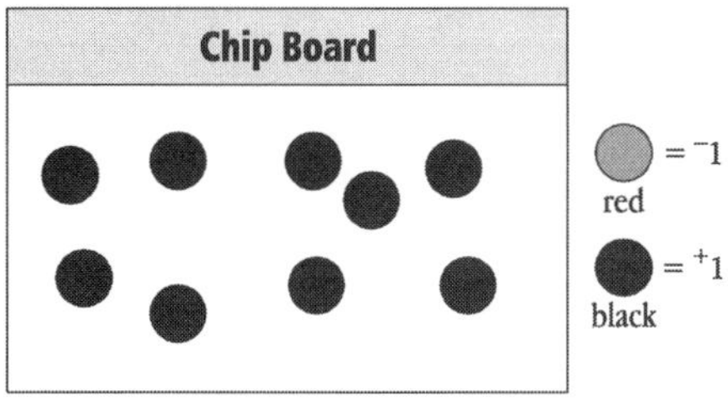

Jing-mei thinks about subtracting as "taking away." Therefore, to represent subtracting 5, she *removed* five black chips from the board.

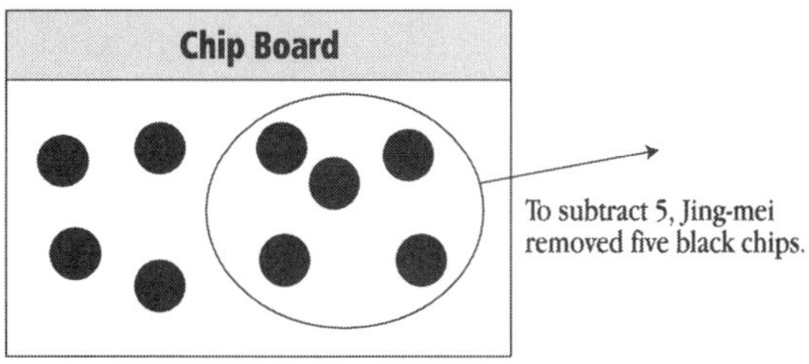

After removing the five black chips, four black chips remained.

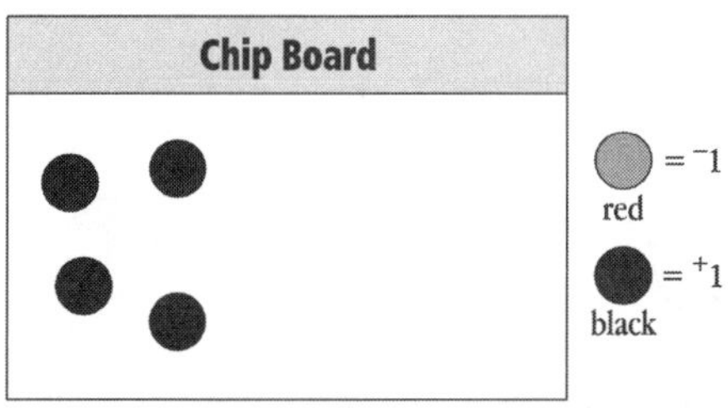

Jing-mei wrote the number sentence 9 – 5 = 4 to represent her work on the chip board.

3.1 Subtracting on a Chip Board

At a Glance

Grouping:* *pairs

Launch

- Talk with the class about the meaning of subtraction.
- Ask the class for ways to model subtraction on a chip board.
- Discuss the model shown in the student edition.

Explore

- As pairs work on the problem, if any are having trouble re-representing amounts on the board, suggest that they ask another pair for help.

Summarize

- Carefully review each part of the problem, analyzing the various representations students used.
- Once students understand how to model subtraction on a board, let them work on the follow-up.

Assignment Choices

ACE questions 11–14, 34, and unassigned choices from earlier problems

Drew tried Jing-mei's method to find $^{-}11 - ^{-}5$. He started with an empty board and then put on 11 red chips to represent $^{-}11$.

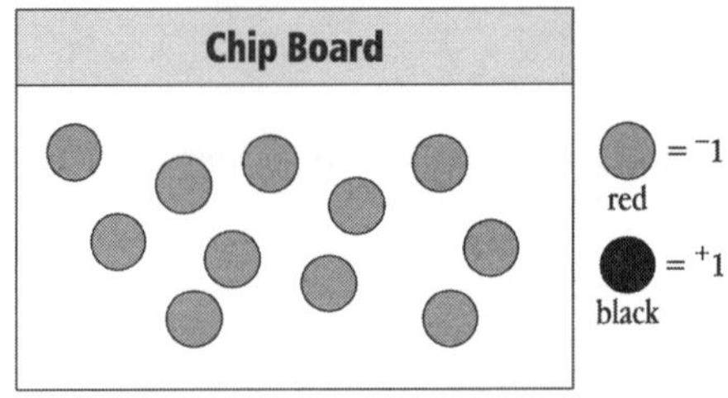

Like Jing-mei, Drew thought of subtracting as "taking away." To represent subtracting $^{-}5$, he removed five red chips from the board.

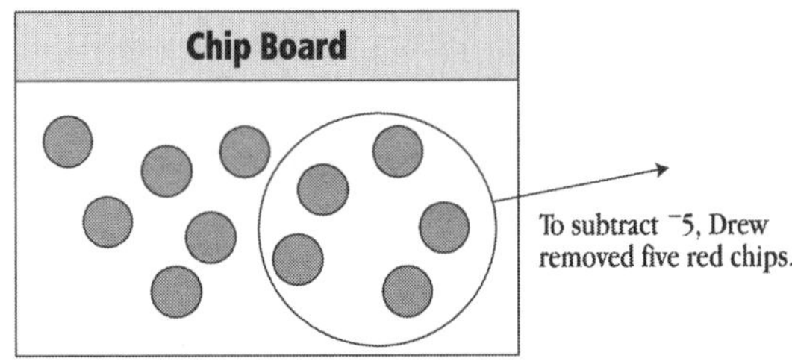

Six red chips remained on the board.

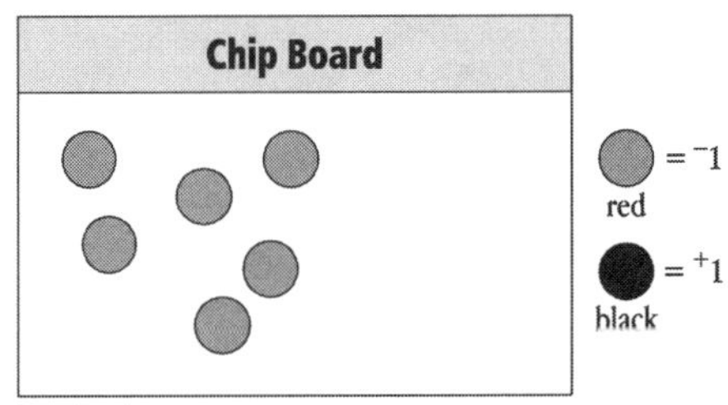

Drew wrote the number sentence $^{-}11 - ^{-}5 = ^{-}6$ to represent his work on the chip board.

Think about this!

Why does it makes sense that the difference between 9 and 5 is 4 (that is, $9 - 5 = 4$) and the difference between $^{-}11$ and $^{-}5$ is $^{-}6$ (that is, $^{-}11 - ^{-}5 = ^{-}6$)?

Answers to Problem 3.1

A. 1. $^{-}1$ 2. $^{+}1$ 3. $^{-}4$ 4. $^{+}4$

B. Possible answer:

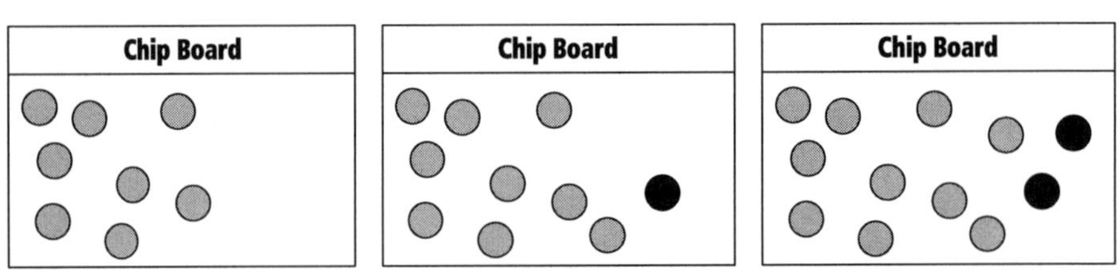

C. See page 52l.

Problem 3.1

A. Use a chip board and black and red chips to find each sum or difference.

1. $^{-}8 - {}^{-}7$ **2.** $^{+}8 + {}^{-}7$

3. $^{-}6 - {}^{-}2$ **4.** $^{+}6 + {}^{-}2$

B. In Problem 2.2, you simplified chip boards to find the number represented. For example, each chip board below represents $^{+}3$.

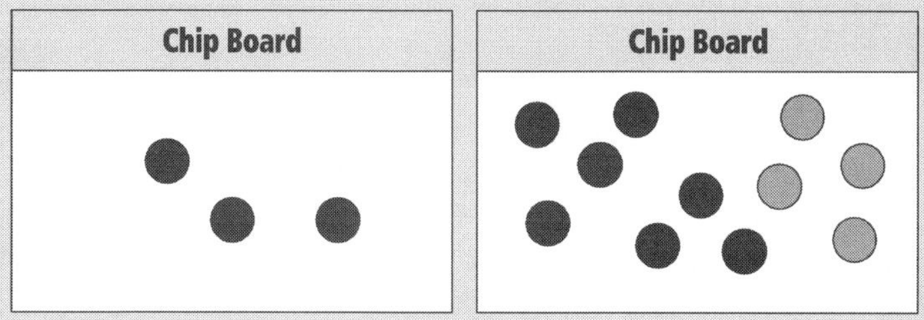

Find three ways to represent $^{-}8$ on a chip board.

C. Jing-mei wants to find $^{-}8 - {}^{-}10$ by using a chip board. She puts eight red chips on the board to represent $^{-}8$ but then gets stuck because she cannot remove ten red chips to represent subtracting $^{-}10$.

How can Jing-mei show $^{-}8$ on a chip board so that she can remove ten red chips? What is $^{-}8 - {}^{-}10$? Explain how you determined your answer.

D. Drew wants to find $^{+}5 - {}^{+}7$ by using a chip board. How can he show $^{+}5$ on a chip board so that he can remove seven black chips to represent subtracting $^{+}7$? What is $^{+}5 - {}^{+}7$? Explain how you determined your answer.

E. Use a chip board and black and red chips to find each difference. For each difference, tell how many chips of each color you used to represent the first integer so that you could take away chips to represent subtracting the second integer.

1. $10 - 12$ **2.** $7 - {}^{-}2$

3. $^{-}5 - 6$ **4.** $^{-}3 - {}^{-}7$

D. Drew can start by representing $^{+}5$ using 5 black chips. This is not enough to take away 7 black chips, so he needs to add two red-black pairs. He will be representing $^{+}5$ as 7 black chips and 2 red chips and taking away 7 black chips (leaving 2 red chips), so $^{+}5 - {}^{+}7 = {}^{-}2$.

E. 1. $^{-}2$; Represent 10 as 12 black chips and 2 red chips.

2. 9; Represent 7 as 9 black chips and 2 red chips.

3. $^{-}11$; Represent $^{-}5$ as 11 red chips and 6 black chips.

4. 4; Represent $^{-}3$ as 7 red chips and 4 black chips.

Problem 3.1 Follow-Up

To find $^{+}5 - {}^{+}7$, Drew started by showing $^{+}5$ as five black chips.

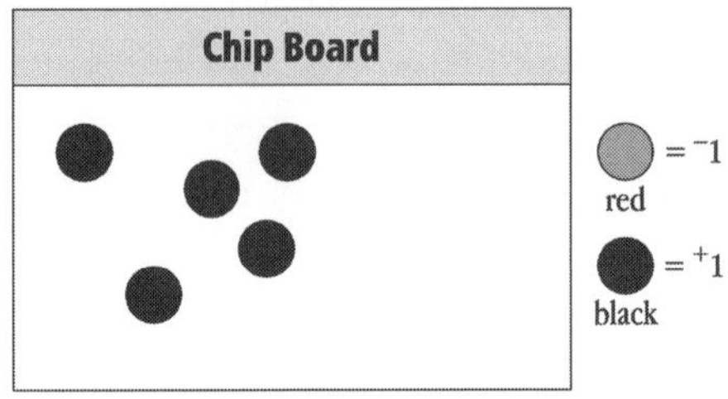

He could not represent subtracting $^{+}7$ because there were not seven black chips to remove from the board.
He recalled that adding or removing a black-red pair does not change the value of the board because such a pair represents 0 ($^{+}1$ and $^{-}1$ are opposites, so they combine to 0).
He added a black-red pair to the board.

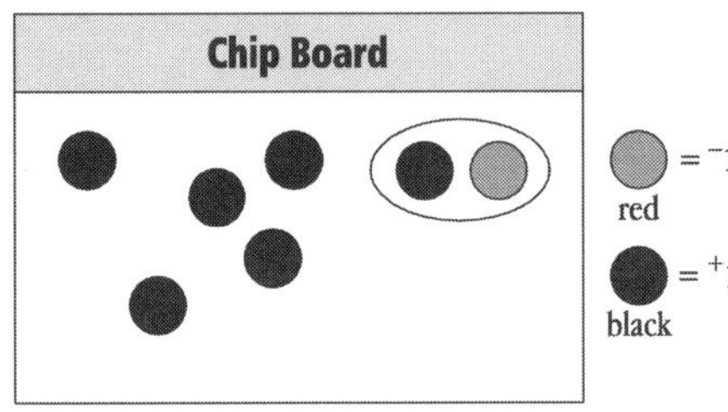

The board now had six black chips and one red chip. To subtract $^{+}7$, Drew needed to remove seven black chips, so he added one more black-red pair.

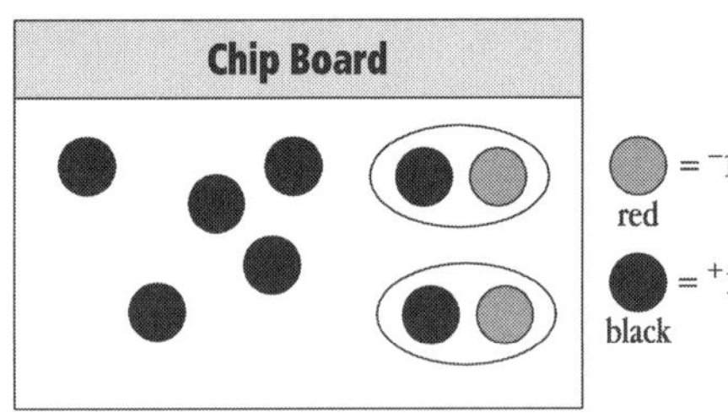

Answers to Problem 3.1 Follow-Up

1. Possible answer:

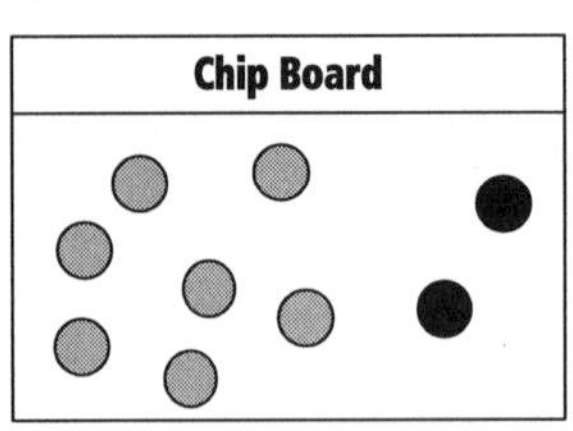

$^{-}5 - {}^{-}7$ or $^{-}5 - 2$

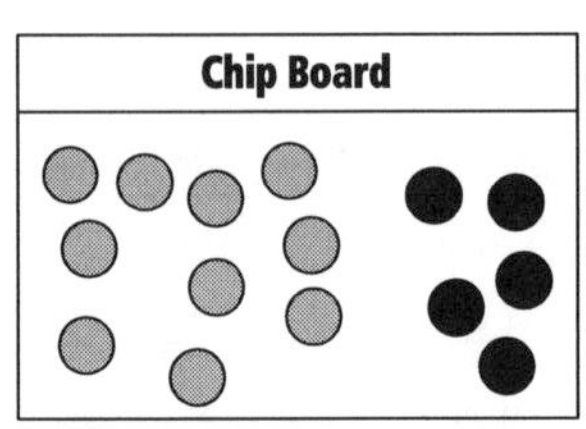

$^{-}5 - {}^{-}10$ or $^{-}5 - {}^{+}5$

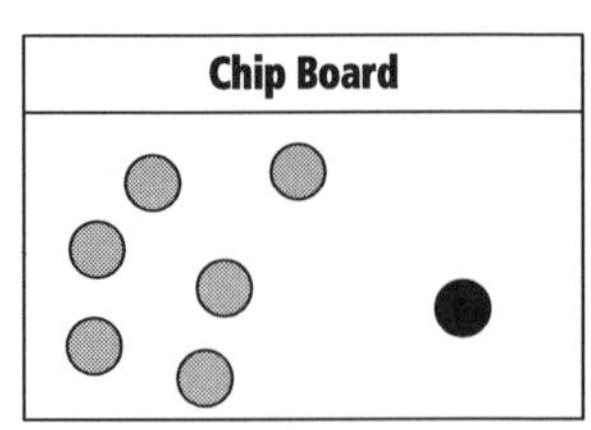

$^{-}5 - {}^{-}6$ or $^{-}5 - {}^{+}1$

Then Drew was able to represent the subtraction. He removed seven black chips from the board. Two red chips remained.

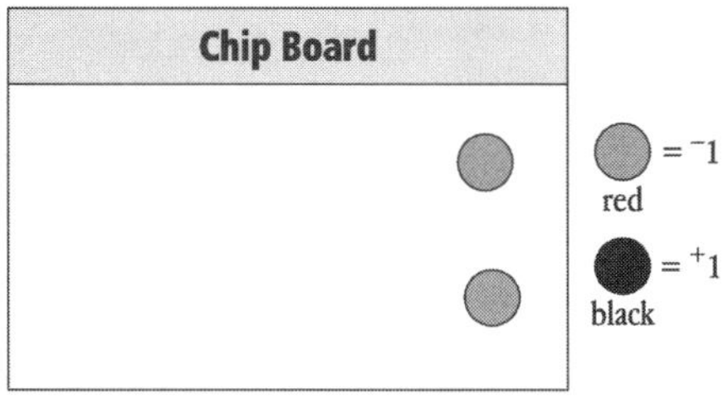

Drew wrote the number sentence ${}^{+}5 - {}^{+}7 = {}^{-}2$ to represent his work on the chip board.

1. Find three ways to show ${}^{-}5$ on the chip board. For each representation, write a subtraction problem that would be easy to solve if you started with that representation.

You have seen that there are lots of ways to represent a given integer on a chip board. For example, you could represent ${}^{+}5$ with eight black chips and three red chips or with six black chips and one red chip. However, there is only one way to represent a given integer with only one color. For example, the only way to represent ${}^{+}5$ with one color is by using five black chips, and the only way to represent ${}^{-}5$ with one color is by using five red chips.

The number of chips needed to represent an integer *with only one color* is the **absolute value** of the integer. Thus, the absolute value of 5 is 5, and the absolute value of ${}^{-}5$ is 5. We represent the absolute value of a number by writing a straight, vertical line segment on each side of the number. The equation $|{}^{-}5| = 5$ is read, "The absolute value of negative five equals five."

2. Find each absolute value.
a. $|{}^{-}7|$ **b.** $|18|$ **c.** $|{}^{-}42|$ **d.** $|0|$

3. Tell which numbers have the given number as their absolute value.
a. 12 **b.** 3 **c.** 31 **d.** 100

2. a. 7
   b. 18
   c. 42
   d. 0
3. a. ${}^{-}12$ and ${}^{+}12$
   b. ${}^{-}3$ and ${}^{+}3$
   c. ${}^{-}31$ and ${}^{+}31$
   d. ${}^{-}100$ and ${}^{+}100$

3.2

Subtracting on a Number Line

At a Glance

Grouping:* *pairs

Launch

- Review subtraction and how to model it with a chip board.
- Offer several problems for students to try to solve using a number line.
- Help the class interpret their results.

Explore

- Ask pairs who finish Problem 3.2 early to solve the same problems on a chip board.
- If pairs are struggling, suggest that they solve the problem on a chip board first, then try to model their results on a number line.

Summarize

- Review each part of the problem, helping students to summarize their learning.
- Talk about absolute value.
- Have pairs work on the follow-up.

Assignment Choices

ACE questions 1–10, 15–20, and unassigned choices from earlier problems

3.2 Subtracting on a Number Line

When you add integers by using a chip board, you add chips to the board. When you subtract integers, you remove chips from the board. Just as you can think of adding and removing chips as opposite "moves," you can think of adding and subtracting integers as opposite, or *inverse,* operations. This idea can help you understand how subtraction is modeled on a number line.

opposites attract

To model the *addition* sentence $^{+}7 + {}^{+}5 = {}^{+}12$ on a number line, you start at 0 and move 7 units to the right to represent $^{+}7$.

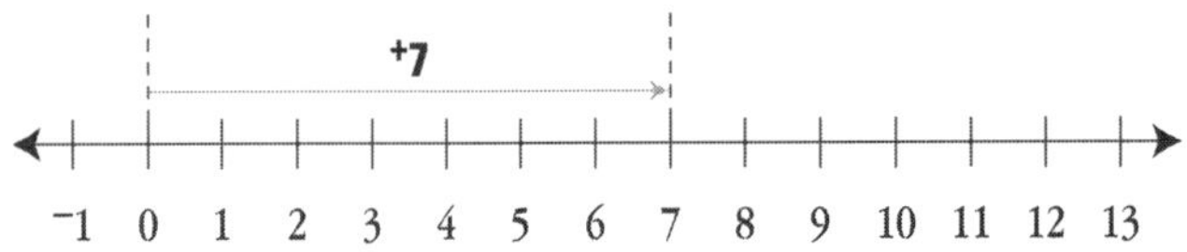

To *add* $^{+}5$, you move 5 more units to the *right.*

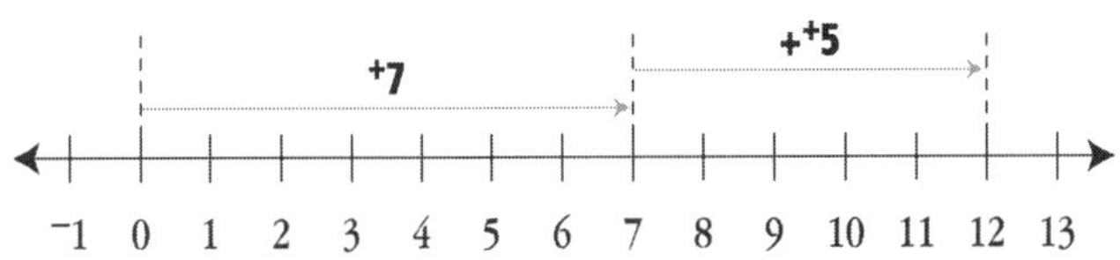

To model the *subtraction* sentence $^{+}7 - {}^{+}5 = {}^{+}2$, you can use the idea of opposite operations. Start at 0, and then move 7 units to the right to represent $^{+}7$.

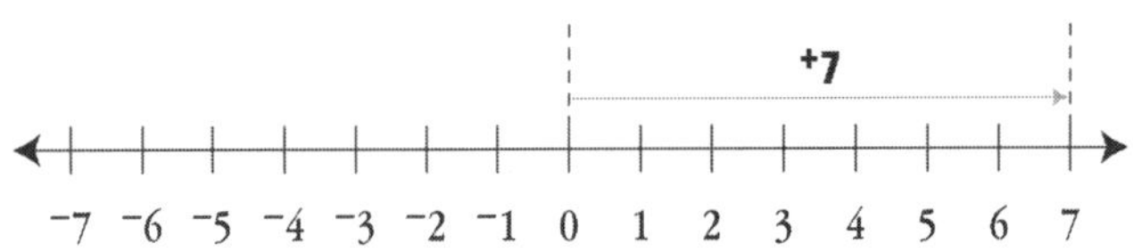

To *subtract* $^{+}5$, move to the *left*—opposite the direction you moved to add $^{+}5$.

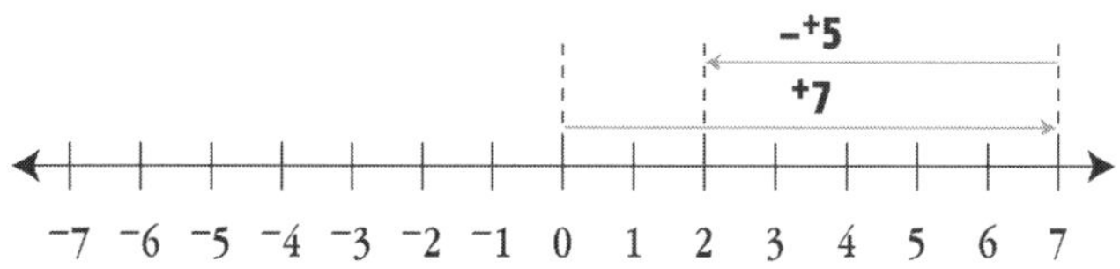

In other words, since subtraction is the opposite of addition, you subtract a number on the number line by moving in the opposite direction you would to add the number.

Let's use this idea to find $^{-}11 - {}^{-}5$. First, start at 0, and move 11 units to the left to represent $^{-}11$.

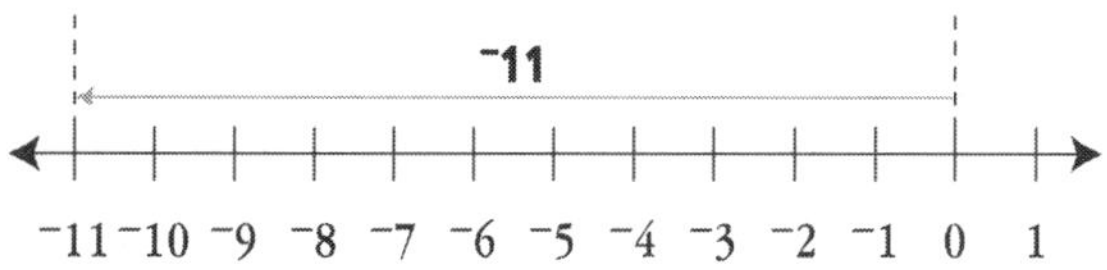

Next, you must subtract $^{-}5$. To add $^{-}5$, you would move 5 units to the left, so to subtract $^{-}5$, you must move 5 units to the right. You end at $^{-}6$.

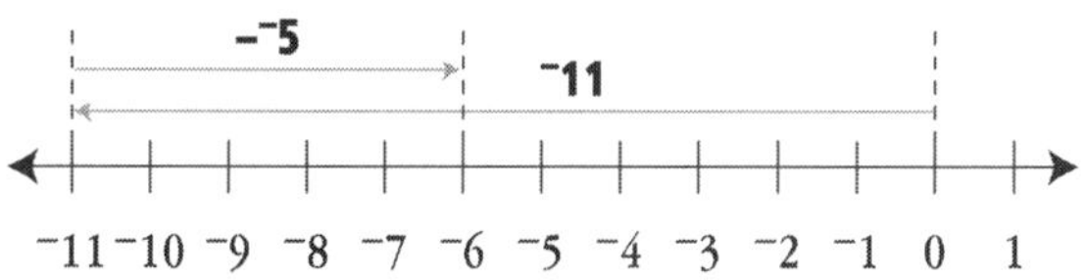

You can write the number sentence $^{-}11 - {}^{-}5 = {}^{-}6$ to represent your work on the number line.

Notice in the example above that *subtracting* $^{-}5$ is the same as *adding* $^{+}5$.

Problem 3.2

A. Use a number line to find each difference. Use a chip board to check your work.

1. $^+7 - ^+9$ **2.** $^-7 - ^+9$ **3.** $^+7 - ^-9$ **4.** $^-7 - ^-9$

B. Use a number line to find each sum or difference.

1. $^+12 - ^+3$ **2.** $^+12 + ^-3$ **3.** $^-10 - ^-7$ **4.** $^-10 + ^+7$

C. Find the distance between each pair of numbers on a number line. In each case, tell how the distance is related to the difference between the two numbers.

1. 1 and 5 **2.** $^-1$ and 5 **3.** $^-5$ and $^-9$ **4.** $^-3$ and 3

D. Write two number sentences illustrated by this figure.

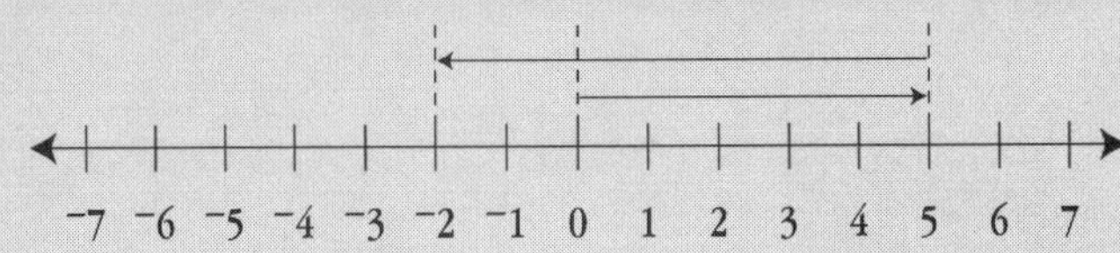

Problem 3.2 Follow-Up

1. When you add two positive integers, you get a positive sum. When you subtract two positive integers, do you always get a positive difference? Explain.

2. When you use the number line model, you can think of the ***absolute value*** of a number as its distance from 0. For example, 3 and $^-3$ are each 3 units from 0, so the absolute value of each number is 3.

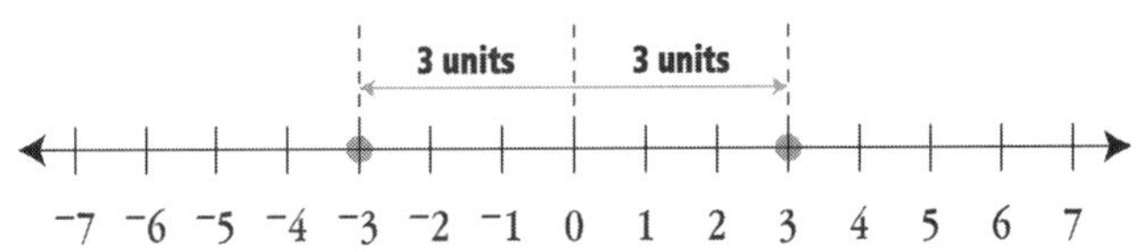

Use a number line to help you find a pair of numbers with the given absolute value.

a. 10 **b.** 5 **c.** 1 **d.** 7

Answers to Problem 3.2

A, B. See page 52m.

C. 1. 4; The distance between each set of points is the absolute value of the difference between the points.

2. 6 3. 4 4. 6

D. $5 + ^-7 = ^-2$ and $5 - 7 = ^-2$

Answers to Problem 3.2 Follow-Up

1. no; When you subtract two positive integers, if the integer being subtracted has a greater absolute value than the integer you are subtracting from, the difference will be negative.

2. a. $^+10$ and $^-10$ b. $^+5$ and $^-5$ c. $^+1$ and $^-1$ d. $^+7$ and $^-7$

3.3 Exploring Patterns

Studying and describing patterns are an important part of mathematics. Study the patterns in the equations below, and then work on the problem.

$15 - 5 = 10$
$15 - 4 = 11$
$15 - 3 = 12$
$15 - 2 = 13$
$15 - 1 = 14$
$15 - 0 = 15$

Problem 3.3

A. Describe any patterns you observe in the way the differences change as the integers subtracted from 15 get smaller.

B. Use the patterns you observed to predict the answer to $15 - {}^-1$. Check your prediction by using a chip board or number line.

C. Predict the answer to $15 - {}^-4$. Explain your reasoning.

Problem 3.3 Follow-Up

1. Study the equations below.

$^-10 - 5 = {}^-15$
$^-10 - 4 = {}^-14$
$^-10 - 3 = {}^-13$
$^-10 - 2 = {}^-12$
$^-10 - 1 = {}^-11$
$^-10 - 0 = {}^-10$

a. Describe any patterns you observe in the way the differences change as the integers subtracted from $^-10$ get smaller.

b. Use the patterns you observed to predict the answer to $^-10 - {}^-1$. Check your answer by using a chip board or number line.

c. Predict the answer to $^-10 - {}^-6$. Explain your reasoning.

2. When you add two negative integers, you get a negative sum. When you subtract two negative integers, do you always get a negative difference? Explain.

3.3 Exploring Patterns

At a Glance

Grouping: pairs

Launch

- Read the introduction and the problem with the class.
- Have pairs work on the problem.

Explore

- As pairs work, listen for the patterns they are finding.
- If students understand the problem, have them go on to the follow-up; if not, hold a class summary before they work on the follow-up.

Summarize

- Have students share the patterns they found in the problem and follow-up.
- Ask students what the patterns they have found tell them about subtracting *any* two integers.

Answers to Problem 3.3

A. As the integer being subtracted gets smaller, the difference becomes greater.

B. $15 - {}^-1 = 16$

C. $15 - {}^-4 = 19$; Possible explanation: $^-4$ is 3 units farther from 15 than $^-1$ is, so the difference between the integers is 3 units greater than the difference between 15 and $^-1$.

Answers to Problem 3.3 Follow-Up

See page 52n.

Assignment Choices

ACE questions 25–32, 35–38, and unassigned choices from earlier problems

3.4

"Undoing" with Addition and Subtraction

At a Glance

Grouping:* *pairs

Launch

- Read through the introduction to the problem.
- Make sure students understand the concept of "undoing."
- Let pairs work on the problem and follow-up.

Explore

- Offer additional examples to pairs who are struggling with the idea of "undoing."

Summarize

- Have pairs share their solutions and reasoning for the problem.
- Talk with the class about whether subtraction is commutative.

3.4 "Undoing" with Addition and Subtraction

You can use the chip boards below to think about the addition sentence $11 + 3 = 14$. The chip board on the left shows 11 black chips. On the chip board on the right, 3 more black chips have been added for a total of 14 black chips.

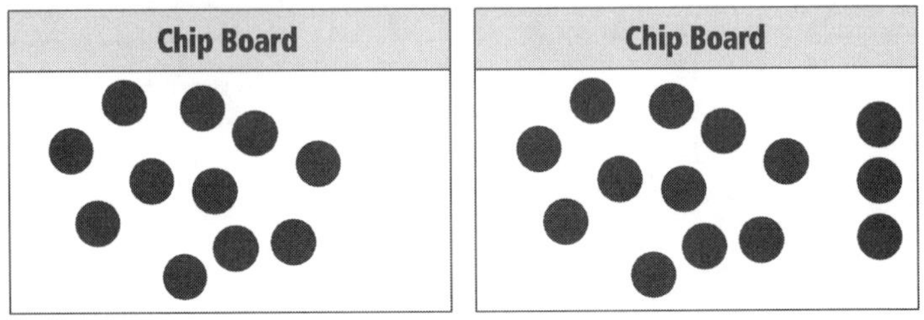

If you removed 3 black chips from the 14 black chips on the second board, you would end up with 11 chips, as you had on the starting board. In other words, removing chips from the board "undoes" placing chips on the board. You can represent this "undoing" with the subtraction sentence $11 = 14 - 3$. So, just as you can think of removing 3 chips from the board as "undoing" placing 3 chips on the board, you can think of the subtraction sentence $11 = 14 - 3$ as "undoing" the addition sentence $11 + 3 = 14$.

You can use this idea of undoing addition to find a subtraction sentence for a given addition sentence.

Problem 3.4

A. **1.** Complete the addition sentence $^-17 + 13 = ?$.

2. Write a subtraction sentence that "undoes" the addition sentence you found in part 1.

B. **1.** Complete the addition sentence $^-4 + {}^-18 = ?$.

2. Write a subtraction sentence that "undoes" the addition sentence you found in part 1.

C. Write a subtraction sentence that solves each problem.

1. $? + {}^-18 = 6$ **2.** $? + {}^-13 = {}^-41$

3. $? + 6.1 = {}^-3.2$ **4.** $? + {}^-\frac{1}{3} = \frac{1}{3}$

D. Write an addition sentence that solves each problem.

1. $? - {}^-6 = {}^-6$ **2.** $? - {}^-2 = 3$

3. $? - 5.3 = {}^-7.1$ **4.** $? - {}^-\frac{1}{4} = {}^-\frac{3}{4}$

Assignment Choices

ACE questions 21–24, 33, 39, 40, and unassigned choices from earlier problems

Assessment

It is appropriate to use Check-Up 2 after this problem.

Answers to Problem 3.4

A. 1. $^-17 + 13 = {}^-4$ 2. $^-17 = {}^-4 - 13$

B. 1. $^-4 + {}^-18 = {}^-22$ 2. $^-4 = {}^-22 - {}^-18$

C. 1. $6 - {}^-18 = 24$ 2. $^-41 - {}^-13 = {}^-28$

3. $^-3.2 - 6.1 = {}^-9.3$ 4. $\frac{1}{3} - {}^-\frac{1}{3} = \frac{2}{3}$

D. 1. $^-6 + {}^-6 = {}^-12$ 2. $3 + {}^-2 = 1$

3. $^-7.1 + 5.3 = {}^-1.8$ 4. $^-\frac{3}{4} + {}^-\frac{1}{4} = {}^-1$

Problem 3.4 Follow-Up

1. In the introduction to this problem, we wrote the number sentence $11 = 14 - 3$ from the sentence $11 + 3 = 14$. We could also write $3 + 11 = 14$. Can you write a different subtraction sentence to go with this addition sentence?

2. a. Complete the addition sentence $3.8 + {}^{-}2.6 = ?$.

b. Write all the subtraction sentences you can that are related to the addition sentence you found in part a.

3. a. Complete the subtraction sentence ${}^{-}11 - 6 = ?$.

b. Write all the addition sentences you can that are related to the subtraction sentence you found in part a.

4. When you add positive and negative integers, sometimes you get a positive sum and sometimes you get a negative sum. Is the same true when you subtract positive and negative integers? Explain.

Answers to Problem 3.4 Follow-Up

1. $3 = 14 - 11$

2. a. $3.8 + {}^{-}2.6 = 1.2$ b. $3.8 = 1.2 - {}^{-}2.6$ and ${}^{-}2.6 = 1.2 - 3.8$

3. a. ${}^{-}11 - 6 = {}^{-}17$

   b. ${}^{-}11 = {}^{-}17 + 6$ (Note: You cannot write a second addition sentence—except the same sum with addends commuted, or ${}^{-}11 = 6 + {}^{-}17$—because subtraction is not commutative.)

4. yes; If you subtract a smaller integer from a greater integer, you get a positive result. If you subtract a greater integer from a smaller integer, you get a negative result. For example, ${}^{-}5 - 4 = {}^{-}9$ makes sense because 4 is greater than ${}^{-}5$, so the answer is negative. However, in ${}^{-}5 - {}^{-}9 = {}^{+}4$, we are subtracting the smaller integer, ${}^{-}9$, from the greater, ${}^{-}5$, and we get a positive result.

ACE

Answers

Applications

1a. $50.25 + $44.00 = $94.25

1b. $94.25 – $8.00 = $86.25

1c. $86.25 + $25.00 = $111.25

1d. $111.25 – $50.00 = $61.25

1e. $61.25 + $50.00 = $111.25

Applications • Connections • Extensions

As you work on these ACE questions, use your calculator whenever you need it.

Applications

1. When the finance committee for the Westover School Dance met on October 22, they had a balance of $50.25 in their checking account. Since then, the following transactions have taken place. Find the balance in the checking account after each transaction.

a. The committee deposited $44 they received from ticket sales.

b. Two students asked for refunds for their tickets. These tickets were worth a total of $8. The committee treasurer wrote these students checks for their refunds.

c. The finance committee got a $25 refund from the bakery because the refreshments committee decided to bake their own cookies and cakes. They deposited the refund into the checking account.

d. The committee gave the school principal $50 to pay the custodian who would open, clean, and close the school on the night of the party.

e. The DJ called to say she couldn't work at the party because her sound system was broken. She returned the committee's $50 deposit, which they deposited into the checking account.

In 2–10, find the sum or difference. Be prepared to explain how you got your answer.

2. $^{+}12 + {}^{+}4$ **3.** $^{+}5 - {}^{+}9$ **4.** $^{+}5 + {}^{-}9$

5. $^{-}3 - {}^{+}6$ **6.** $^{-}3 + {}^{-}6$ **7.** $^{+}7 - {}^{-}5$

8. $^{+}7 - {}^{+}5$ **9.** $^{-}7 - {}^{-}5$ **10.** $^{+}3.8 - {}^{-}4.2$

11. Write an addition sentence to describe this chip board.

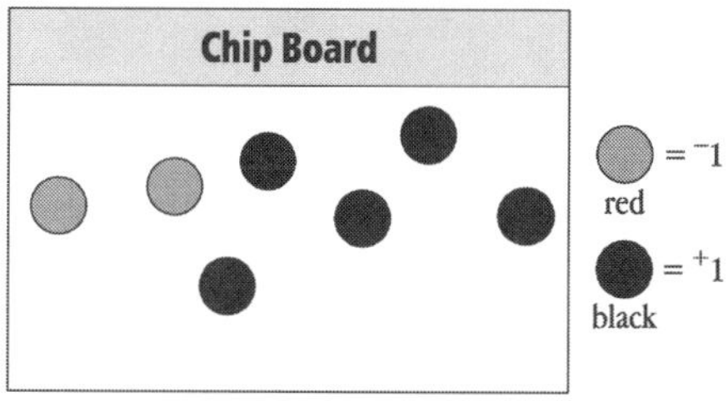

In 12–14, draw chip boards to help you find the difference.

12. $3 - 5$ **13.** $5 - 3$ **14.** $3 - {}^{-}2$

In 15 and 16, write an addition sentence and a subtraction sentence to represent what is shown on the number line.

15.

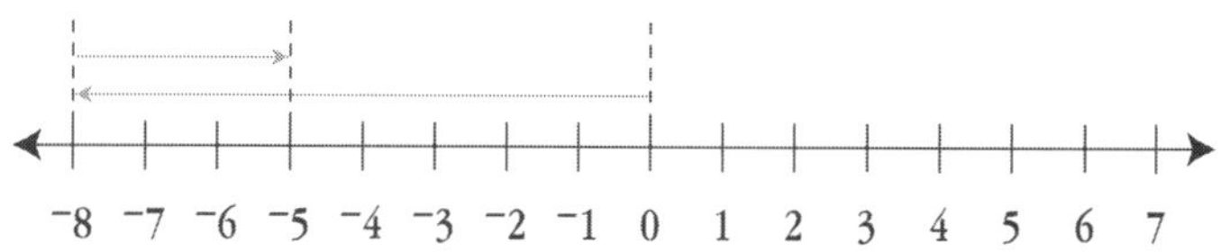

16.

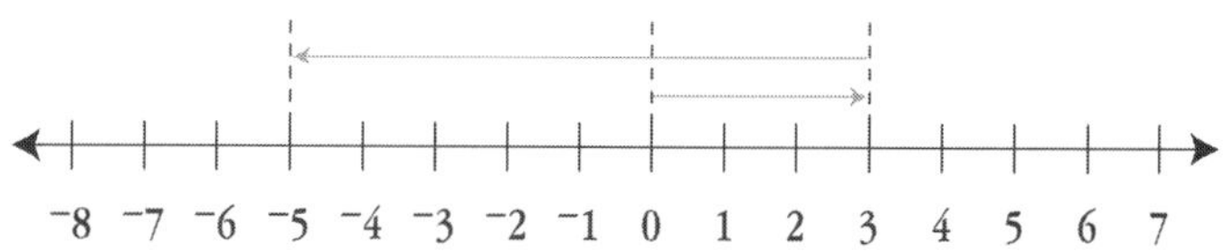

In 17–20, find the distance between the two numbers on the number line.

17. 9 and 4 **18.** $^{-}9$ and 4 **19.** $^{-}9$ and $^{-}4$ **20.** 0 and $^{-}7$

2. $^{+}16$

3. $^{-}4$

4. $^{-}4$

5. $^{-}9$

6. $^{-}9$

7. $^{+}12$

8. $^{+}2$

9. $^{-}2$

10. 8.0

11. Possible answers: $^{-}2 + {}^{+}5 = {}^{+}3$, $5 + {}^{-}2 = 3$

12. See below left.

13. See below left.

14. See page 52n.

15. $^{-}8 + {}^{+}3 = {}^{-}5$, $^{-}8 - {}^{-}3 = {}^{-}5$

16. $^{+}3 + {}^{-}8 = {}^{-}5$, $^{+}3 - {}^{+}8 = {}^{-}5$

17. 5 units

18. 13 units

19. 5 units

20. 7 units

12. $3 - 5 = {}^{-}2$

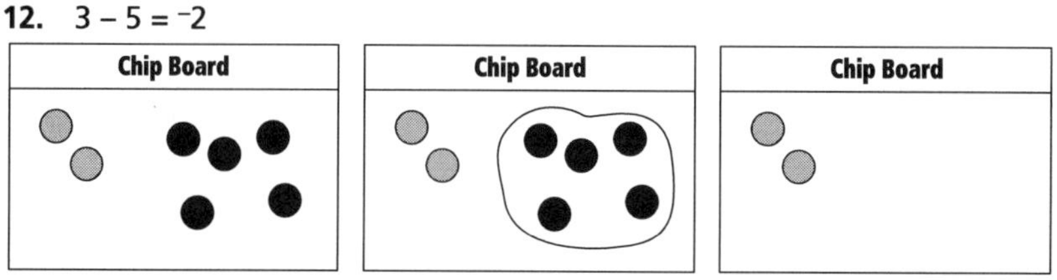

13. $5 - 3 = 2$

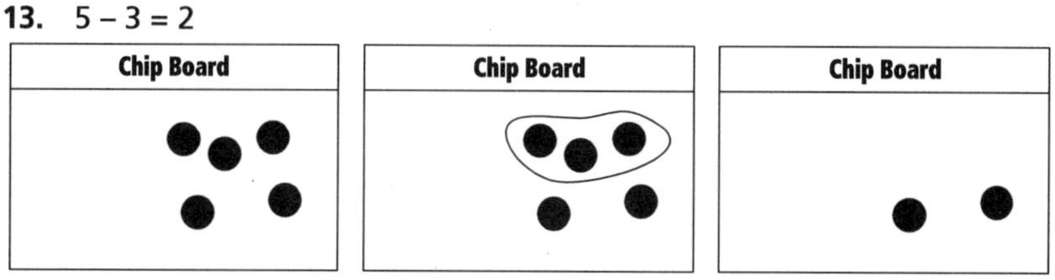

21. Three red chips remain, which represents ⁻3.

22a. ⁻3 + ⁺9 = ⁺6 (The balance of 6 black chips is represented by this number sentence.)

22b. ⁺6 – ⁺7 = ⁻1 (The actions are cumulative; students must use their previous answer to obtain the amount remaining after the next action. The balance of 1 red chip is represented by this number sentence.)

22c. ⁻1 – ⁻4 = ⁺3 (Students can add three black-red pairs to obtain this number sentence.)

22d. ⁺3 – ⁺3 = 0 (This represents a clear board.)

23. The board has 8 red chips and 13 black chips, an excess of 5 black chips, or $5.

In 21 and 22, refer to the chip board below.

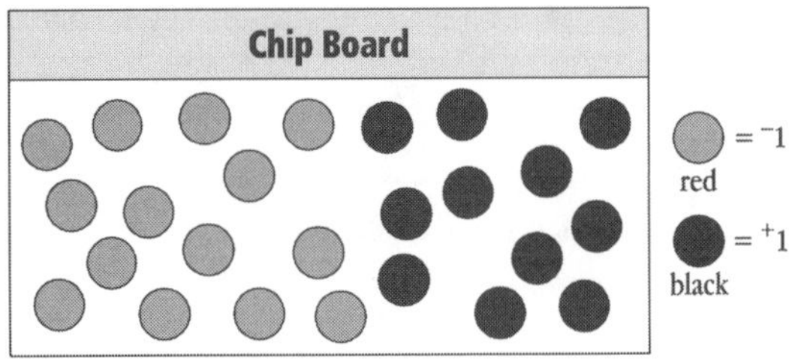

21. After you simplify the board by removing zeros (black-red pairs), what chips would remain? What integer do these chips represent?

22. Starting with the board as shown above, the following series of actions takes place. Write a number sentence to describe each action.

a. Nine black chips are added.

b. Seven black chips are removed.

c. Four red chips are removed.

d. Three black chips are removed.

In 23 and 24, refer to the chip board below. Each black chip represents $1, and each red chip represents ⁻$1.

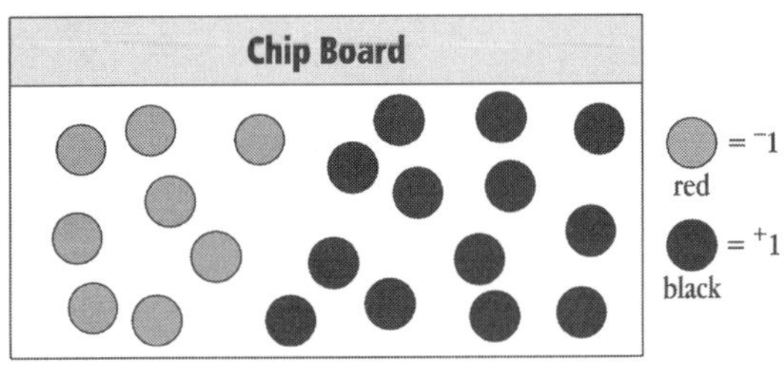

23. What "balance" is shown on this board?

24. Starting with the board as shown on the previous page, the following series of "transactions" takes place. Find the new balance after each transaction.

- **a.** Four black chips are added.
- **b.** Ten red chips are added.
- **c.** Six black chips are added.
- **d.** Eight black chips are removed.
- **e.** Five red chips are removed.

In 25 and 26, decide whether the statement is always true, sometimes true, or always false. Give examples to illustrate your thinking.

25. If a negative integer is subtracted from a positive integer, the difference is a negative integer.

26. If a negative integer is subtracted from a negative integer, the difference is a negative integer.

In 27–32, find the sum or difference.

27. $^-756 + 398$ **28.** $^-756 + {}^-398$

29. $3138 + {}^-2149$ **30.** $3138 - {}^-2149$

31. $3138 - 5149$ **32.** $^-3138 - 5149$

33. **a.** Name all integers that have an absolute value of 12.

- **b.** Name all integers that are 12 units from 0 on the number line.
- **c.** Name all integers that are 12 units from $^-8$ on the number line.
- **d.** Write two subtraction problems that relate to your answer in part c.

ACE

24a. $^+5 + {}^+4 = {}^+9$ or \$9

24b. $^+9 + {}^-10 = {}^-1$ or $^-$\$1

24c. $^-1 + {}^+6 = {}^+5$ or \$5

24d. $^+5 - {}^+8 = {}^-3$ or $^-$\$3

24e. $^-3 - {}^-5 = {}^+2$ or \$2

25. This is always false. Possible explanation: One way to think about this is using the chip board. In order to remove red chips (to subtract a negative), you have to add black chips to keep the board balanced. If you start with a positive balance, the result will always be positive, because the final change will be adding black chips. On a number line, subtraction is shown as reversing the direction of the arrow in an addition, so you would be moving in a positive direction from a positive integer.

26. This is sometimes true. It will be true if the absolute value of the integer being subtracted is less than the absolute value of the other integer. For example, $^-3 - {}^-5 = {}^+2$ and $^-5 - {}^-3 = {}^-2$.

27. $^-358$

28. $^-1154$

29. 989

30. 5287

31. $^-2011$

32. $^-8287$

33a. $^+12$ and $^-12$

33b. $^+12$ and $^-12$

33c. $^+4$ and $^-20$

33d. $^-8 - {}^+4 = {}^-12$ and $^-8 - {}^-20 = 12$

ACE

Connections

34. 12 – 9 + 14 – 21 + 5 – 14 + 11 – 10 = $^-12$ patients (or $^+12 + ^-9 + 14 + ^-21 + 5 + ^-14 + 11 + ^-10 = ^-12$ patients). There were 12 fewer patients at the end of the four-day period then at the start of the four-day period.

35. Possible answer: $^-3 + ^-4 = ^-7$, $2 + ^-9 = ^-7$, $^-8 + ^+1 = ^-7$

36. Possible answer: $5 + 7 = 12$, $14 + ^-2 = 12$, $^-6 + 18 = 12$

37. Possible answer: $-3 - ^+4 = ^-7$, $2 - 9 = ^-7$, $0 - 7 = ^-7$

38. Possible answer: $20 - 8 = 12$, $^-2 - ^-14 = 12$, $0 - ^-12 = 12$

Connections

34. Records at Jefferson Hospital showed the following information about the number of patients received and discharged:

Day 1: received 12 patients and discharged 9 patients
Day 2: received 14 patients and discharged 21 patients
Day 3: received 5 patients and discharged 14 patients
Day 4: received 11 patients and discharged 10 patients

How did the number of patients in the hospital at the end of the four-day period compare with the number of patients at the start of the four-day period?

35. Write three addition problems that have $^-7$ as a sum.

36. Write three addition problems that have 12 as a sum.

37. Write three subtraction problems that have $^-7$ as a difference.

38. Write three subtraction problems that have 12 as a difference.

Extensions

39. Juan said that he had discovered a new method for subtracting integers. He gave this example to illustrate his method:

$^+7 - {}^+9 = {}^+7 - ({}^+7 + {}^+2) = ({}^+7 - {}^+7) - {}^+2 = 0 - {}^+2 = {}^-2$

a. Is Juan's method correct? Draw chip boards to explain your answer.

b. Explain Juan's method in words.

40. On many scientific calculators, you use the [+/–] or [(–)] key to enter a negative number. This means that evaluating problems with lots of negative numbers like the ones below requires many keystrokes. For each problem below, find an equivalent problem that you could enter into a calculator to avoid using the [+/–] or [(–)] key as much as possible.

a. $^-12 - {}^-7 - {}^-9 - {}^-10 - {}^-4$

b. $^-12 - 7 - {}^-9 + 10 - {}^-4 + 13 + {}^-20$

Extensions

39a. Juan's method works. Possible explanation: Start with 9 black chips and 2 red chips to represent $^+7$. Separate the 9 black chips into two groups, 7 chips and 2 chips. Now we can remove 7 black chips and 2 black chips, leaving 2 red chips, or $^-2$.

39b. Possible answer: First, represent the number to be subtracted as two parts, and separate the number so you have an opposite to pair up with the starting number. These two together equal 0, and the leftover portion is the answer.

40a. Possible answer: Change all the subtractions to adding opposites: $^-12 + 7 + 9 + 10 + 4$.

40b. Possible answer: Change all the subtracting negatives to adding opposites and the adding negatives to subtraction: $^-12 - 7 + 9 + 10 + 4 + 13 - 20$.

Possible Answers

1. See page 52n.

2. If the two integers are both positive, the sum will be positive. For example, 5 + 6 = 11. If the two integers have different signs, the sum will be positive if the integer farthest from 0 (on a number line) is positive. If the two integers are both negative, the sum will be negative (for example, $^-5 + ^-6 = ^-11$). If the integers have different signs, the sum will be negative if the integer farthest from 0 is negative. In other words, the sign of the answer when adding two integers with different signs will have the sign of the integer with the greater absolute value (for example, $5 + ^-6 = ^-1$). If you are adding opposites, the sum will be 0.

3. The difference will be positive if the integer being subtracted is smaller than the integer it is subtracted from (for example, 8 – 2 = 6 and $^-6 - ^-9 = 3$). The difference will be negative if the integer being subtracted is greater than the integer it is subtracted from (for example, $8 - 10 = ^-2$ and $^-6 - ^-4 = ^-2$). If you are subtracting an integer from itself, the difference will be 0.

4. Addition and subtraction are opposite operations. In addition, you combine things; in subtraction, you take things apart.

5. See page 52o.

Mathematical Reflections

In this investigation, you explored situations that involve subtraction of integers. You explored subtraction by using chip boards and number lines and by looking at patterns. These questions will help you summarize what you have learned:

1. Write a strategy for finding the difference of two integers. Be sure to consider all possible combinations of positive integers, negative integers, and 0. Verify your strategy by finding the following differences.

   a. $5 - 9$ **b.** $^-5 - ^+3$ **c.** $^-5 - ^-3$ **d.** $5 - ^-9$

2. Without actually calculating the sum, how can you decide if the sum of two integers is positive? Negative? Zero?

3. Without actually calculating the difference, how can you decide if the difference of two integers is positive? Negative? Zero?

4. Describe how addition and subtraction of integers are related.

5. Describe how to find the absolute value of any number.

Think about your answers to these questions, discuss your ideas with other students and your teacher, and then write a summary of your findings in your journal.

Tips for the Linguistically Diverse Classroom

Diagram Code The Diagram Code technique is described in detail in *Getting to Know Connected Mathematics*. Students use a minimal number of words and drawings, diagrams, or symbols to respond to questions that require writing. Example: Question 5—A student might answer this question by drawing a number line from $^-3$ to 3 and underlining the number 0. Below the line, the student might write *+1* between the intervals of 0 and $^-1$, $^-1$ and $^-2$, and $^-2$ and $^-3$; above the line, the student might write *absolute value of 3 and $^-3$ is 3.*

3.1 • Subtracting on a Chip Board

This problem introduces students to subtracting integers on a chip board. The problem involves helping students understand the operation of subtraction and how they might model it on a chip board. While your students can subtract whole numbers, they may not be able to articulate their understanding of the operation of subtraction.

Launch

To introduce this investigation have a conversation about subtraction.

> You all know how to find the difference between two whole numbers. But, what is subtraction really about? How can we interpret what is happening when you subtract one number from another? How is subtraction different from addition?

Take a few ideas from students. The class should recognize that subtraction is about taking something away and that it is the opposite of addition.

> If you have 10 basketball tickets and you give 3 to a friend, you would have 7 left. We use subtraction to find out how many of an item remain. We could say we *subtracted* to find the *difference* between the amounts.
>
> You could use a chip board to model this procedure. If you had 10 black chips (to represent the tickets) and you want to subtract 3 black chips (tickets), how could you model that on the chip board?

Have someone model this problem using the chip board. Ask if what was modeled seems a reasonable way to represent subtraction and whether anyone sees a different way to model the subtraction on a chip board. You want students to model and discuss subtraction as "taking away," whereas addition was combining or "putting together."

> When you subtracted, what did you do differently from what you would do to add 10 black chips and 3 black chips? *(Instead of adding the amount of the second integer to the board, you take that amount off the board. You do the opposite of what you do when you add, because the operations are the opposite of each other.)*

If students simply say that "you do the opposite of addition," question them further to be sure they understand what this means. The first integer is represented on the board the same way the first integer is represented in an addition problem. It is the second integer that tells how much of a change to make, and the operation sign tells whether we are adding or taking away the second number from the first.

We could write $10 - 3 = 7$, a number sentence, to represent what we just modeled on the chip board. How could you model $^{-}10 - {}^{-}3$ using the chip board?

Students should put 10 red chips on the board and then remove 3 of them, leaving 7 red chips.

What did you get for the difference between these two integers? *($^{-}7$)*

Why does it seem reasonable that the difference between $^{-}10$ and $^{-}3$ is $^{-}7$? *(If you started with 3 red chips, you would need 7 more red chips to get to 10 red chips, and red chips represent a negative amount.)*

Can you think of a real-life situation that would show that this is a reasonable answer for $^{-}10 - {}^{-}3$?

Possible example: "I owe my father \$10, and he let me work off \$3 of debt by washing the car. So I got to subtract \$3 of debt. I still owe my father \$7, which is the same as $^{-}7$."

If the subtraction model offered by students is different from the one presented in the student edition, show that model to your class as another way to model subtraction.

For the Teacher: Chip Board Subtraction

To model subtraction of integers on a chip board, black is again used to represent positive integers and red to represent negative integers. Begin with an empty board. If the first integer in the subtraction sentence is positive, place that number of black chips on the board. If it is negative, place that number of red chips on the board. If the second integer has the same sign as the first (and is therefore represented by the same color), check to see whether there are enough chips on the board to "take away" the number of chips that represent the second integer. In each example below, the two integers in the expression have like signs and there are enough chips representing the first integer to allow the chips representing the second integer to be removed.

To do $^{+}9 - {}^{+}5$, put 9 black chips on a chip board. Then, since subtraction is the opposite of addition, rather than adding 5 black chips ($^{+}5$), remove 5 black chips. Four black chips remain, so $^{+}9 - {}^{+}5 = 4$.

To do $^{-}11 - {}^{-}5$, place 11 red chips on a board to represent $^{-}11$. Remove 5 red chips to represent subtracting $^{-}5$. The 6 red chips that remain represent $^{-}6$, so $^{-}11 - {}^{-}5 = {}^{-}6$.

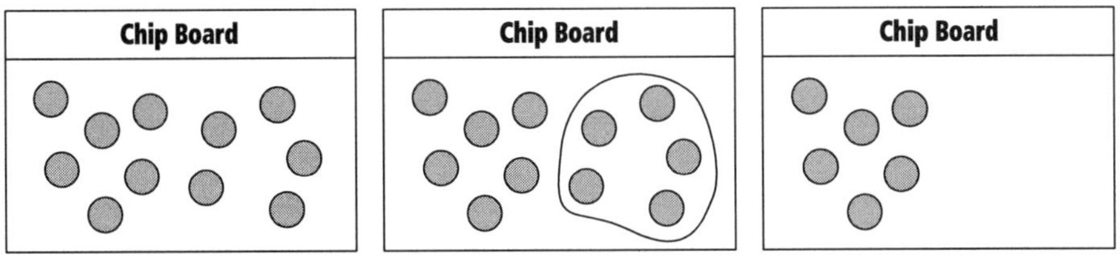

If the integers being subtracted have different signs, or if there are not enough chips on the board to allow chips for the second integer to be removed, the first integer must be re-represented. This is done by adding pairs of red and black chips to the board, which has no effect on the board's value. (A red-black pair represents 0, since $^+1$ and $^-1$ are opposites.)

To do $^+5 - {}^+7$, place 5 black chips on a board to represent $^+5$. Since the board does not have 7 black chips to remove, add red-black pairs until a total of 7 black chips are on the board. So, $^+5$ is re-represented as 7 black chips and 2 red chips. Now 7 black chips can be taken away (subtracted). The 2 red chips that remain represent $^-2$, so $^+5 - {}^+7 = {}^-2$.

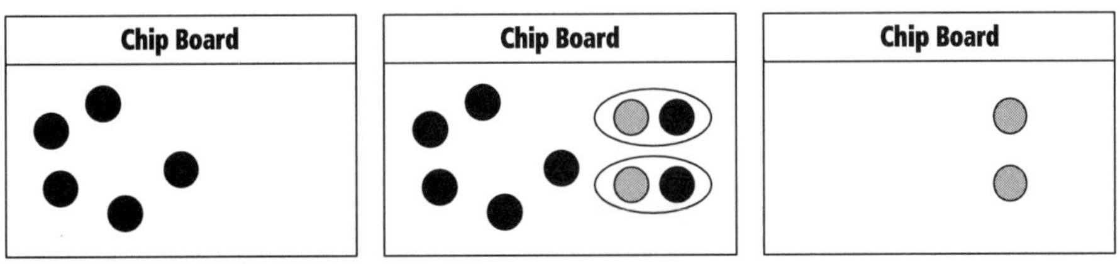

If students seem comfortable working through the subtraction situations suggested above, have pairs work on the problem. If some are still struggling with the model, present a few additional problems until they can subtract integers with like signs using the model.

Explore

Part A asks students to find differences similar to those found in the Launch. In the remaining questions, pairs will investigate situations in which they will need to re-represent their original amount in order to model the subtraction.

Allow the class time to experiment with different representations. If a pair is stuck, suggest they ask another pair to explain the procedure. The pair that is sharing should have developed a strategy for subtracting numbers such as $8 - 12$ and $8 - {}^-7$, problems that require students to re-represent the amount they started with originally.

Summarize

Have students share their solutions for part A. If they are having difficulty with any of these, have someone demonstrate how they used their chip board to find a solution.

Does the given answer seems reasonable? Why it is reasonable?

For part B, have some pairs draw their models on the board. Ask the class whether they agree that each model presented represents $^{-}8$. For any that are incorrect, have someone explain why they are incorrect and how to fix them.

Talk about how the models are alike and how they are different. Each representation, for example, should have 8 red chips plus as many additional red chips as there are black chips.

Spend some time having students model how they did part C. One way is to first represent $^{-}8$ as 10 red chips and 2 black chips. Remove the 10 red chips (to represent subtracting $^{-}10$), and you are left with 2 black chips, which represent a value of $^{+}2$.

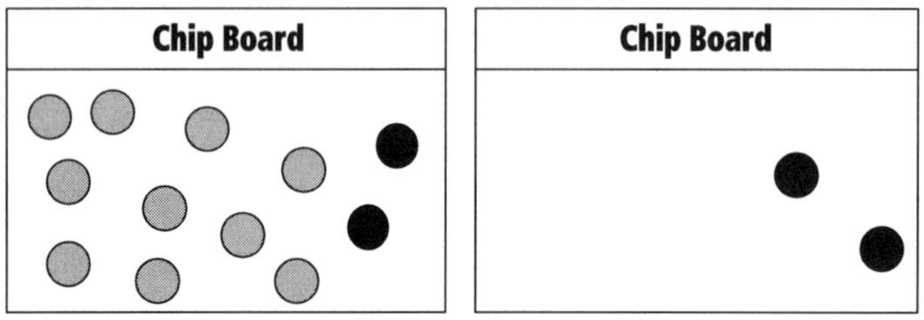

If students have used more chips, such as 15 red chips and 7 black chips, they still need to take away 10 red chips to model subtracting $^{-}10$. They will then need to simplify their board to show what remains.

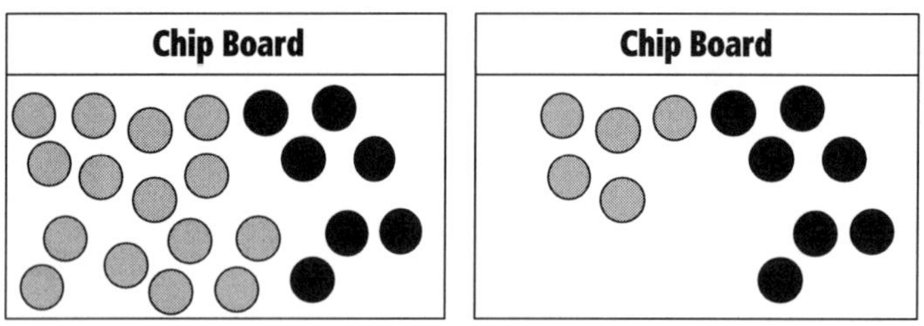

They can do this by pairing opposites—one red and one black chip—and removing them. Two black chips will remain on the board.

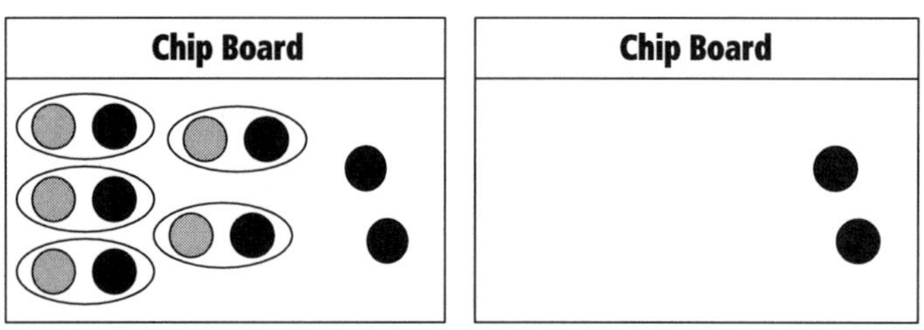

Again, pose the question of why it makes sense that $^{-}8 - {}^{-}10$ is $^{+}2$. This fact is much harder to explain and make sense of than were the problems in part A. You might use a debt example to explain this.

> Suppose you owe your mother \$8. She agrees to let you work off the debt by doing yard work, for which you can subtract \$10 of debt. This is subtracting a negative number, or $^{-}8 - {}^{-}10$. The result is that your mother now owes you \$2; you are \$2 ahead rather than \$2 in debt.

If students are struggling with their explanations, move on, but remind them that they need to be thinking about the answers they find and why they are reasonable.

Have someone model their answer to part D on a chip board, and ask the class whether they agree with the representation. If they do and the student has given a complete explanation, ask if anyone did part D a different way. As students share any other representations, ask the class whether each is correct and reasonable. Students' representations should involve re-representing $^+5$ by placing red-black pairs on the board until they have enough black chips to subtract (take away) the value of the second integer in the equation ($^+7$). A typical student description is the following: "I represented the first integer, $^+5$, on my board using 5 black chips. I couldn't subtract $^+7$, because there weren't 7 black chips on the board, so I added pairs of red and black chips until I had 7 black chips on the board. I needed to add two pairs of red and black chips. Then I took away 7 black chips, and there were 2 red chips left. This means that the difference between these two numbers is $^-2$."

Ask students to demonstrate and explain their solutions for part E. Offer a few more problems if they are still having difficulty, and again have several students demonstrate and explain their solutions.

If students struggled with parts D and E, go through Drew's method, which is at the beginning of the follow-up. Then, as a class, use his method to rework parts D and E.

Pairs can move on to the follow-up once they are able to find differences when working with both positive and negative numbers. Take time to discuss these questions. (Note: Question 2 introduces the term ***absolute value*** to the students. This idea is revisited in the follow-up for Problem 3.2.)

3.2 • Subtracting on a Number Line

This problem uses the number line to represent the subtraction of integers. The number line model focuses on the idea that subtraction is the opposite, or inverse, of addition. Subtracting "undoes" addition. If we add one number to another, we can find the original number by subtracting the amount added from the sum, in effect undoing the addition by subtraction. Students have used this familiar checking strategy in the elementary grades. They will need time, however, to make sense of this model.

Launch

Begin by reviewing what subtraction means (taking away, or the opposite of addition). Then review how to model subtraction using a chip board. Have a student model a problem, and discuss any patterns the class has noticed when subtracting integers (such as if the integers you are subtracting have the same sign and the first has a greater numerical value, you just take away the amount of chips indicated by the second integer).

Distribute copies of the number lines, and explain to the class that they will be revisiting the number line model. Begin by having a student demonstrate how to use a number line to model an addition problem, such as 8 + 2.

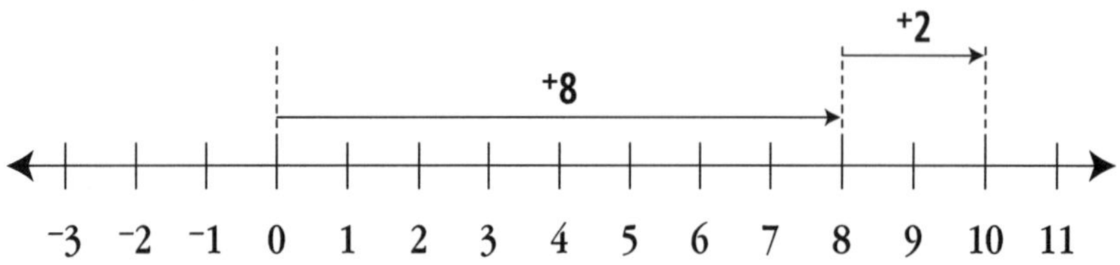

Next, ask the class how they would use a number line to represent the problem 8 – 2.

> **We all know that the answer to this subtraction problem is 6, but how could you represent this with a number line and arrows?**

Most students will draw the first arrow 8 units in length, starting at 0 and ending 8 units to the right. From there they will draw an arrow 2 units in length, starting at 8, going to the left, and ending at 6.

> **I understand why you drew your first arrow 8 units long and pointing to the right: the arrow represents what you are starting with, a value of positive 8. Why did you draw your next arrow 2 units in length and pointing to the left, when the second integer is also positive and the positive direction is to the right?**

You are trying to engage students in a conversation that involves opposites and that leads them to an understanding of subtraction as the opposite of addition. To represent subtraction, we move in the opposite direction on the number line from the direction we would move if we were adding.

Write 8 – 10 on the board.

> **Let's try another problem. What is the answer to this problem? Before you use the number line to represent this problem, ask yourself this: What is a reasonable answer to the problem? What would make sense?**

Students should draw their first arrow 8 units long starting at 0 and ending at $^{+}8$. From there they should draw an arrow 10 units long, pointing to the left and ending at $^{-}2$.

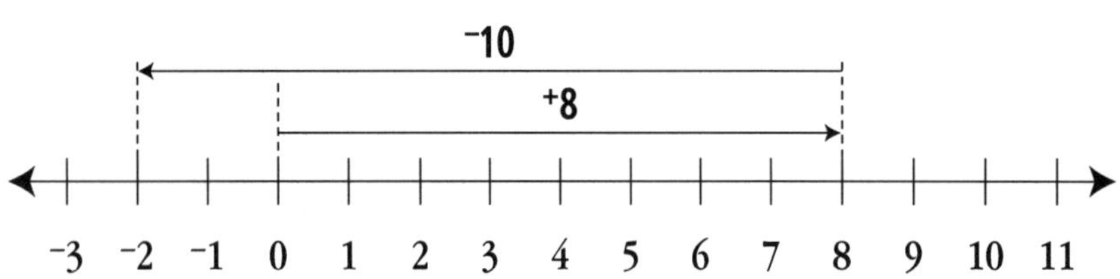

> **Explain your drawing and why you drew it as you did. What is represented on your number line?**

Students should explain that they first represented $^{+}8$ because that is how much they have at the start. The second arrow is drawn to the left because this is a subtraction problem and we are taking away a positive amount. In general, since subtraction is the opposite of addition, to subtract the second integer, the arrow is drawn in the opposite direction from the sign of the integer because that sign represents the direction the arrow would be drawn for addition.

Is it reasonable that 8 – 10 would be $^-2$?

This can be explained in different ways. You have 8, and you need to take away 10. Since you don't have 10 to take, you must go in the hole. That is what $^-2$ means: you are 2 in the hole. It is like buying something that costs $10 when you only have $8 and must borrow $2 from a friend. Now you are $2 in debt, which can be represented as $^-2$.

Offer students another problem, such as $^-6 - {}^-1$. They should draw their first arrow 6 units long and to the left, starting at 0 and ending at $^-6$. From there they should draw an arrow 1 unit long, to the right and ending at $^-5$.

Again ask for explanations of students' drawings. They should explain that they first draw an arrow to the left 6 units because the first integer is $^-6$ and negative numbers are to the left of 0. The second arrow is drawn to the right because we are subtracting a negative integer. To subtract, you must move in the direction opposite to the direction you would if you were adding We could think of this as being $6 in debt and working off or subtracting $1 of that debt. Now the debt is only $5.

For the Teacher: Number-line Subtraction

Modeling subtraction on a number line involves essentially the same kinds of moves as addition. Addition requires that the arrow for the second addend be drawn to the right or left depending on the sign of that addend; subtraction requires that the arrow representing the second number be drawn in the reverse direction from the addition direction because we are doing the opposite of adding; we are subtracting. Subtracting a positive integer requires that the arrow be drawn to the left; subtracting a negative integer requires that the arrow be drawn to the right.

To represent 7 + 5 = 12, draw an arrow 7 units long that starts at 0 and goes to the right. Draw a second arrow, 5 units in length, starting at 7 (where the last arrow ended) and going to the right (because 5 is positive). It will end at 12.

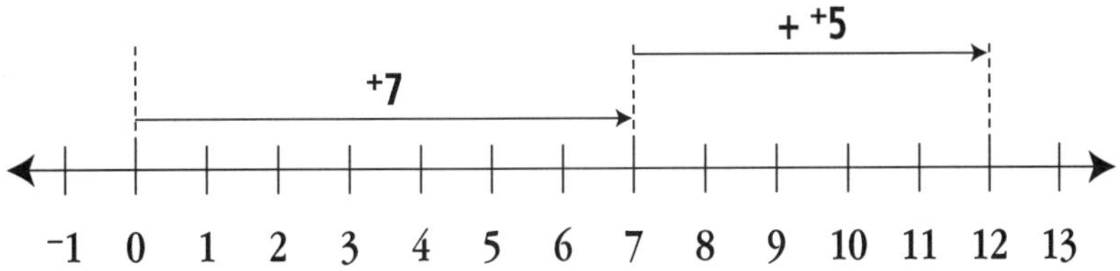

To show 7 – 5 = 2, draw an arrow 7 units long that starts at 0 and goes to the right. Draw a second arrow going to the left, 5 units in length. Though 5 is a positive amount, it is being subtracted, and subtraction is the opposite of addition. This is represented on the number line by reversing the direction of the arrow used to represent the second integer.

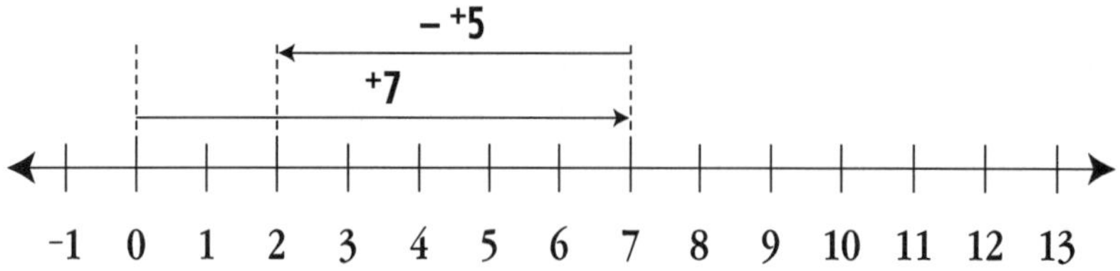

Once students have modeled several of these equations on a number line, some will observe that the number line model for subtraction represents both $7 - 5$ and $7 + {}^{-}5$. This may lead them to the conclusion that subtracting an integer is the same as adding the opposite of the integer.

Subtracting a positive integer using a number line makes sense to students. The difficult part of the model is subtracting a negative integer, such as ${}^{+}7 - {}^{-}5$ or ${}^{-}7 - {}^{-}5$. This requires students to reason that we move to the left to draw an arrow representing a negative integer, but we must change the direction of the arrow to subtract. So pointing the arrow left for the integer and then changing its direction for the operation of subtraction means that it will now be pointing to the right.

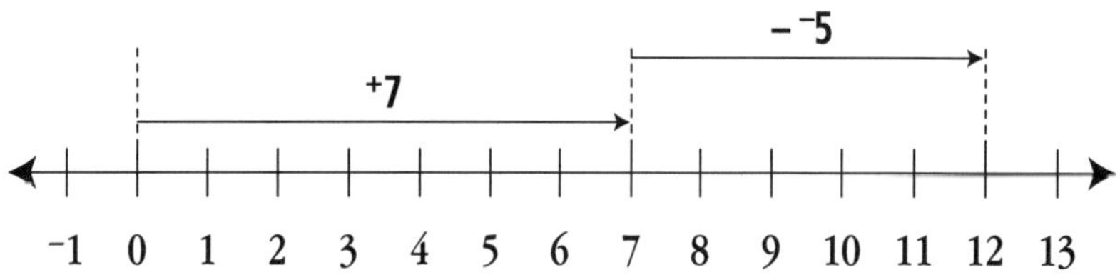

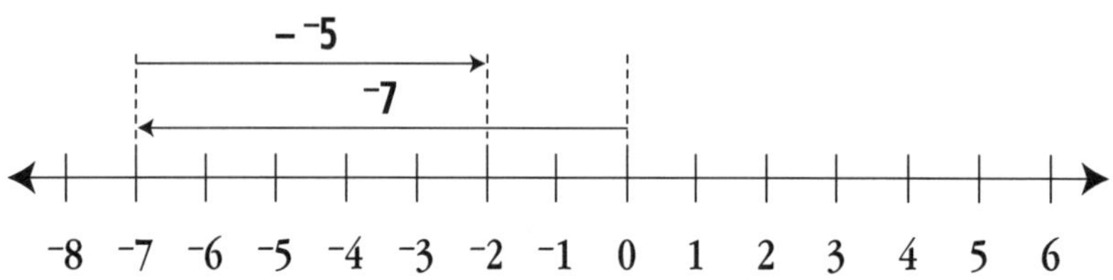

If students are still struggling with the model and the ideas, have them do a few more problems (such as those in the introduction to Problem 3.2 in the student edition). When they are comfortable with the model, have them work on Problem 3.2 in pairs.

Explore

Have additional copies of the number lines available. If students finish the problems quickly, ask them to check their solutions using chip boards. If some students are struggling, suggest that they work out the problems using a chip board first and, once they have the solution, find a way to represent that solution on a number line.

Summarize

An important goal of this problem is to demonstrate the idea that subtraction and addition are inverse operations and that all subtraction statements can be written as equivalent addition statements. For example, $8 - 10$ is the same problem as $8 + {}^{-}10$. This idea should be part of the summary discussion.

Have students share their solutions and drawings for part A. Take turns having them explain their drawings and justify their solutions. Once the class has agreed that the drawings and solutions are correct, discuss the following ideas about what conclusions they can draw from their work.

> Look at your answers to questions 1 and 4 and to questions 2 and 3. Is there a relationship between the answers in each pair? *(The integers in each pair are the opposites of each other, as are the answers.)*
>
> If you locate each of the integers in one of the pairs of answers on a number line, where would they lie relative to 0? *(The two integers that are opposites are the same distance from 0, but in opposite directions.)*
>
> Earlier in the unit, we described the *absolute value* of a number as the number of same-color chips it would take to represent the number. Which numbers have an absolute value of 10? *($^{+}10$ and $^{-}10$, because they would each require 10 chips.)*
>
> Where are the numbers with an absolute value of 12 located on a number line? *(They are 12 units from 0 and on opposite sides of 0. They are $^{+}12$ and $^{-}12$.)*
>
> Summarize what we can say about the pairs of answers to questions 1 and 4 and to questions 2 and 3. *(The answers are opposites of each other. They have the same absolute value; they are located the same distance from 0 on opposite sides of 0.)*
>
> How far apart are $^{+}7$ and $^{+}9$ on a number line? *(2 units)* How far apart are $^{-}7$ and $^{-}9$ on a number line? *(2 units)*
>
> How does the distance between two integers compare to the answer to the subtraction problem, and why? *(The answer to the subtraction problem without the sign—the absolute value—tells how far apart the two numbers are.)*
>
> When you subtract any two integers, will the difference always tell you how far apart they are on a number line?

Test students' ideas with another set of integers. Write these two expressions on the board: $10 - 1$ and $^{-}10 - {}^{-}1$.

> What are the solutions to these? *(9 and $^{-}9$)* Do the solutions tell how far apart the integers are? *(yes)*
>
> Do you think it will work if we choose another set of integers in which the signs are different?

Write $7 - {}^{-}5$ on the board.

> What is the answer to this problem? *(12)* Is this the distance between the two integers? *(Yes. They are 12 units apart on the number line. If you start at $^{-}5$, you must move 12 units to the right to get to $^{+}7$.)*

Can someone write a subtraction problem to pair with $7 - {}^{-}5$ that has ${}^{-}12$ as its difference? *(${}^{-}7 - 5$)*

Where are these two pairs of integers on a number line? *(The integers 7 and ${}^{-}5$ are 12 units apart on a number line, and ${}^{-}5$ is to the left of 7. The integers ${}^{-}7$ and 5 are also 12 units apart, but 5 is to the right of ${}^{-}7$.)*

Have students share their solutions and drawings for part B. Again, take turns having them explain their drawings and justify their solutions. Once the class has agreed that the drawings and solutions are correct, help them to draw conclusions.

Notice that questions 1 and 2 have the same solution and drawing and that questions 3 and 4 have the same solution and drawing. How do the expressions for questions 1 and 2 compare?

Help students to see that both expressions start with ${}^{+}12$, but in one the operation is subtraction and in the other it is addition. Also, the integers being added or subtracted have opposite signs (${}^{-}3$ and ${}^{+}3$). The two expressions have opposite operations, that are being applied to integers that are the opposite of each other.

Is that true for expressions 3 and 4? Do they also have the same beginning integer but opposite operations and opposite second integers? *(yes)*

Do you think that if we took another pair of integers and changed the operation sign to its opposite and changed the sign of the second integer to its opposite, the solution for those two expressions would be the same?

Offer a couple of pairs of problems, such as $7 - 9$ and $7 + {}^{-}9$ or ${}^{-}6 - {}^{-}3$ and ${}^{-}6 + 3$. Have students work these out on their own and then share their results. Do a few more problems with the class to help build students' confidence that this is always true.

For part C, ask students to give the distance between each pair of points. Make sure they understand that they could find these distances by counting. Discuss how the distance between points relates to the solution they would get if they subtracted the numbers.

For part D, make sure both possibilities ($5 + {}^{-}7 = {}^{-}2$ and $5 - 7 = {}^{-}2$) are presented during the discussion. Talk about why both are possible.

After discussing the problem, have pairs work on the follow-up. Walk around the room, and listen for what sense students are making of these questions and how they are incorporating the ideas from the summary. These conversations should help you decide what else to discuss when you bring them back together to share their responses to the follow-up. If students are having a hard time understanding the concepts, you may want to work through a few more problems during the class session.

3.3 • Exploring Patterns

In this problem, students continue to look at subtracting integers but are not asked to use a particular model (although many students may still be using one of the models).

Launch

Read the introduction and problem with your students. By now, they should be able to find the difference between two integers. Have students work in pairs on the problem.

Explore

As pairs work, listen for what patterns they are noticing. If they seem to be making sense of the problem, have them continue their work with the follow-up. If they are having trouble finding patterns, discuss the problem as a class, then have pairs do the follow-up.

Summarize

Have pairs share the patterns they found. Students should see that as the integer being subtracted from 15 gets smaller, the difference increases. Have students give solutions for parts B and C. You may want to ask about a couple of additional expressions (for example, $15 - {}^{-}5$ and $15 - {}^{-}10$) to make sure they understand the pattern.

For the follow-up, have a similar discussion. Again, students should see that as the integer being subtracted from $^{-}10$ gets smaller, the difference increases. This is a bit more difficult than the first set of equations, as students may still be struggling with the idea that $^{-}14$ is less than $^{-}13$. You will want to discuss question 2 in detail. This question is suggesting that students look for patterns so as to be able to predict the difference between two numbers without using a model.

Continue the discussion and questioning until students are able to generalize rules.

> How do you subtract integers if you don't use one of the models? What patterns have you noticed that will allow you to find the difference between any two integers?

Here are some subtraction rules students have given.

- Letty: "Since subtraction is the opposite of addition, you just rewrite the subtraction as adding the opposite of the second number and use the rules for addition."
- Hani: "If the two integers in the subtraction problem have the same sign and the integer being subtracted is a smaller amount [meaning a smaller absolute value], just subtract the integers. The answer will be the difference between the two numbers, and it will have the same sign as they have."
- Daniela: "If the integers have the same sign but the number being subtracted is larger [meaning a greater absolute value], you still subtract the two integers, but the answer will be the difference between them and will have an opposite sign to the sign they have."
- Curt: "If the two integers have different signs, you add them, just ignoring the signs, and the sign of the answer will match the sign of the first integer."

Students will return to these ideas in the Mathematical Reflections for this investigation. At that time, they are expected to be able to give complete rules for subtracting positive and negative integers.

3.4 • "Undoing" with Addition and Subtraction

The idea of "undoing" is familiar from students' earliest contacts with subtraction. Seeing it in the context of negative numbers will help them look more deeply at the relationship between addition and subtraction and further refine their ideas about subtracting positive and negative integers.

Launch

Read through the introduction to the problem with the class. To help students understand the idea of "undoing," work through a few more problems, such as ${}^-8 + 4 = {}^-4$ and ${}^-1 + {}^-6 = {}^-7$, modeling them on a chip board and writing the original sentence and the sentence that "undoes" the work (${}^-8 = {}^-4 - 4$ and ${}^-1 = {}^-7 - {}^-6$).

When students understand the concept of undoing, have them work on the problem and follow-up in pairs.

Explore

If pairs do not catch on relatively quickly, offer them some additional examples. Select simple problems so they can focus on the relationship between addition and subtraction.

Summarize

Have pairs share their results for each part of the problem, explaining how they got their solutions and why their solutions are reasonable.

The follow-up asks students to think about the fact that addition is commutative. Discuss with your students whether the same is true for subtraction. For example, $7 + {}^-3$ and ${}^-3 + 7$ have the same sum. Does $7 - {}^-3$ have the same answer as ${}^-3 - 7$?

Additional Answers

Answers to Problem 3.1

C. Possible answer: The representation of ${}^-8$ as 10 red chips and 2 black chips allows you to take away ${}^-10$.

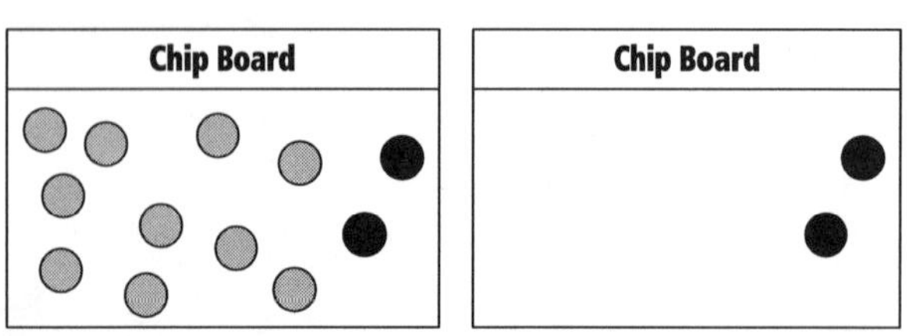

Answers to Problem 3.2

A. 1. $^{+}7 - {}^{+}9 = {}^{-}2$

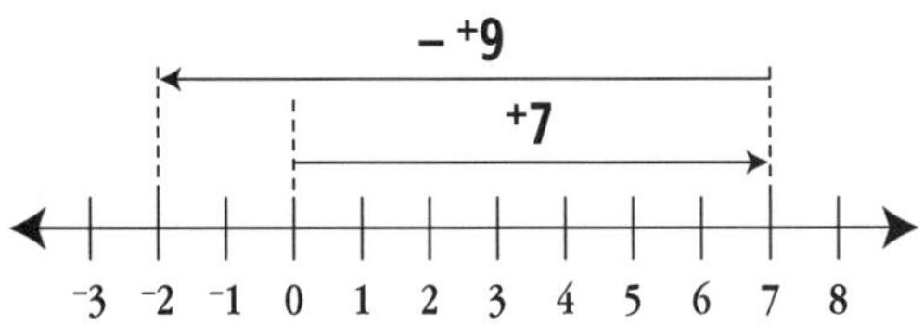

2. $^{-}7 - {}^{+}9 = {}^{-}16$

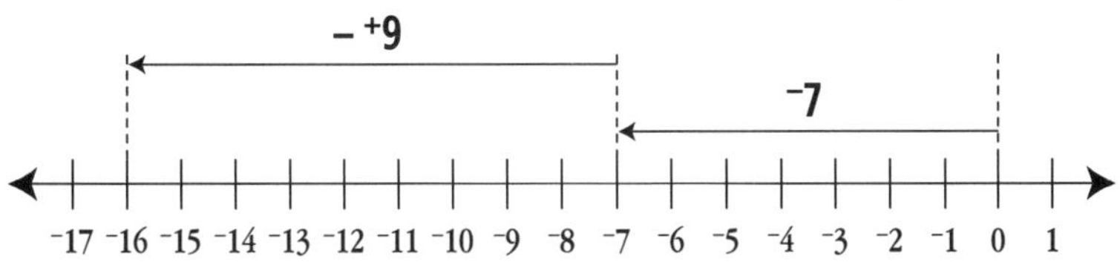

3. $^{+}7 - {}^{-}9 = 16$

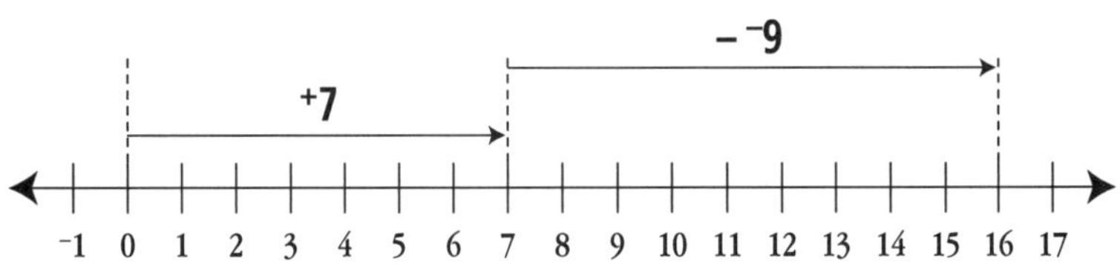

4. $^{-}7 - {}^{-}9 = 2$

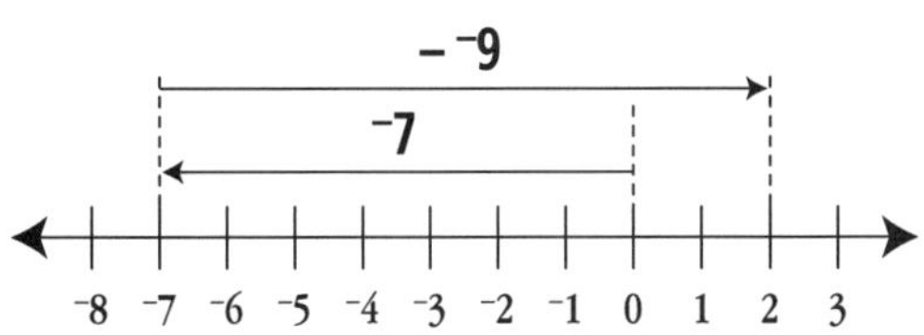

B. 1. $^{+}12 - {}^{+}3 = 9$

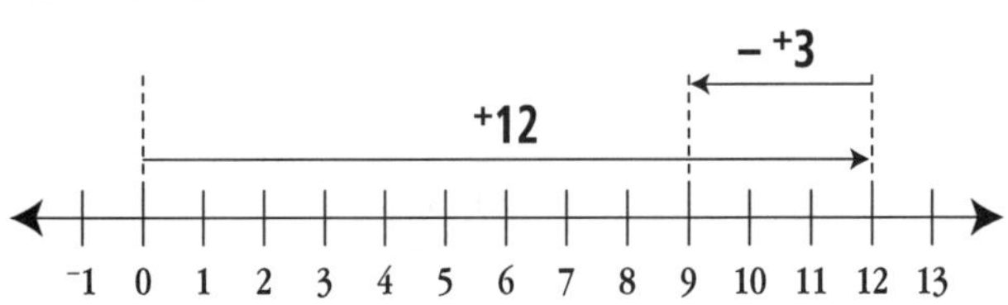

2. $^{+}12 + {}^{-}3 = 9$

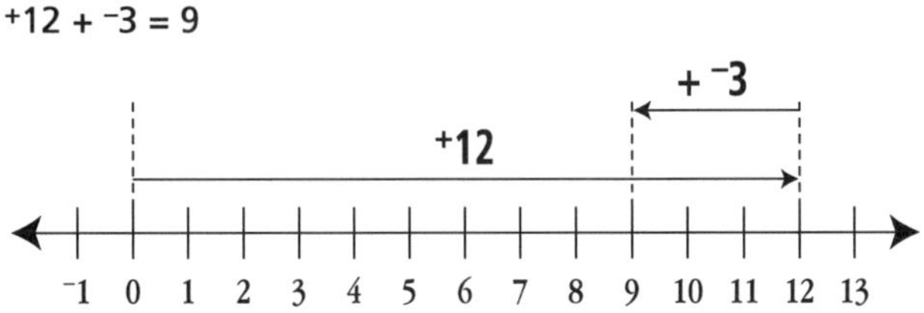

3. $^{-}10 - {}^{-}7 = {}^{-}3$

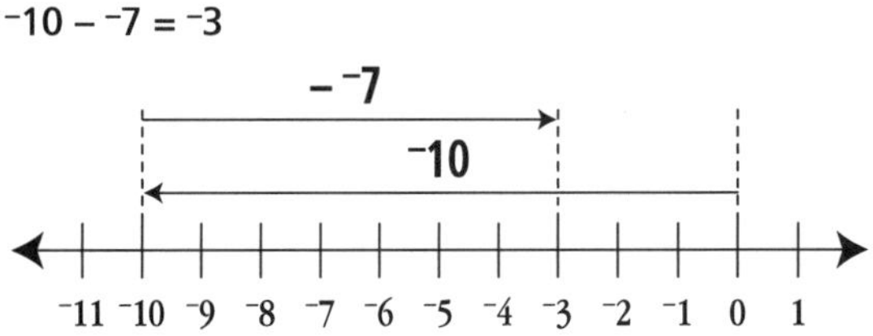

4. $^{-}10 + {}^{+}7 = {}^{-}3$

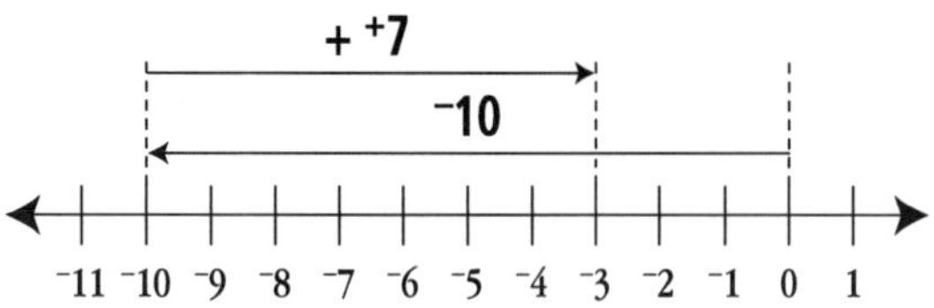

Answers to Problem 3.3 Follow-Up

1. a. As the integer being subtracted gets smaller, the difference becomes greater.

   b. $^{-}10 - {}^{-}1 = {}^{-}9$

   c. $^{-}10 - {}^{-}6 = {}^{-}4$; Possible explanation: $^{-}6$ is 5 units farther from $^{-}10$ than $^{-}1$ is, so the difference is 5 units greater than the difference between $^{-}10$ and $^{-}1$.

2. You do not always get a negative difference when you subtract two negative integers; when you subtract a smaller integer from a larger integer, you get a positive difference. For example, in $^{-}10 - {}^{-}12 = 2$, because $^{-}12$ is smaller than $^{-}10$, you get a positive difference.

ACE Answers

Applications

14. $3 - {}^{-}2 = 5$

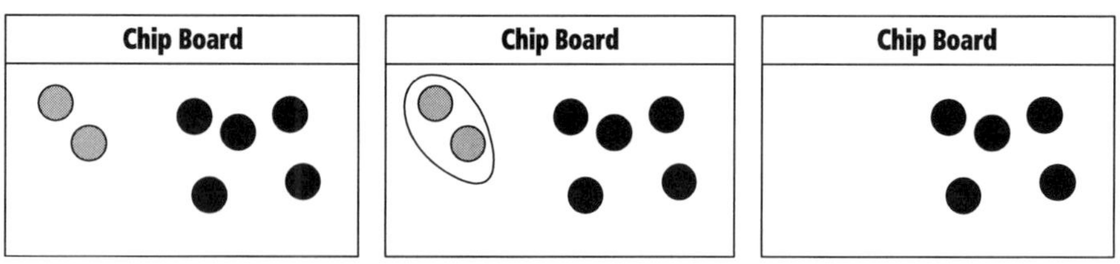

Mathematical Reflections

1. Since subtraction is the opposite of addition, rewrite the subtraction problem as adding the opposite of the second integer, and then add. If the two integers have the same sign and the integer being subtracted has a smaller absolute value, just subtract them, and the answer will be that difference and have the same sign as the integers. If the integers have the same sign but the integer being subtracted has a greater absolute value, just do the subtraction, and the answer will have the opposite sign of the two integers. If the two integers have different signs, add them, and the sign will be the same as the sign of the first integer in the expression.

1a. $5 - 9 = {}^{-}4$

1b. $^{-}5 - {}^{+}3 = {}^{-}8$

1c. $^{-}5 - {}^{-}3 = {}^{-}2$

1d. $5 - {}^{-}9 = 5 + 9 = 14$

(Note: Some students will describe how to find the difference by using one of the two models presented in the investigation. Encourage these students to look for patterns that will help them to predict the difference so that they can find the solution without having to use the model. By no means are we implying that using a model is wrong. The first goal is always that students have some means of finding solutions. However, learning general rules will be more useful in the long run.)

5. The absolute value of a number is the distance that number is from 0 on a number line. Absolute value is the number of units and does not involve direction (on a number line) or color (on a chip board).

INVESTIGATION 4

Multiplying and Dividing Integers

In this investigation, students develop rules for multiplying and dividing integers.

In Problem 4.1, Rising and Falling Temperatures, students investigate a thermometer (which can be thought of as a vertical number line) and repeated constant changes in temperature (which is essentially repeated addition) to show that, for example, $^-3 + ^-3 + ^-3 + ^-3 + ^-3$ is the same as $5 \times ^-3$. Problem 4.2, Studying Multiplication Patterns, asks students to look for patterns that will help them to predict the product of any two integers and to develop rules for finding products of integers. In Problem 4.3, Playing the Integer Product Game, students play a game involving negative and positive factors and products and try to make products using certain factors. The game helps them develop their skill at finding products of integers. In Problem 4.4, Dividing Integers, students look at the relationship between multiplication and division and derive rules for dividing integers based on what they already know about multiplying integers.

Mathematical and Problem-Solving Goals

- ***To develop strategies for multiplying and dividing integers***
- ***To recognize and use the relationship of multiplication and division as inverse operations***
- ***To recognize and solve problems involving multiplication and division of integers***

Materials		
Problem	**For students**	**For the teacher**
All	Graphing calculators	Transparencies 4.1A to 4.4 (optional)
4.3	Labsheet 4.3 (1 per pair); chips or tiles in two colors (about 12 of each color per pair of students) or colored pens, markers, or pencils; paper clips (2 per pair)	Transparency of Labsheet 4.3 and colored transparency markers (optional)

Student Pages 53–66 Teaching the Investigation 66a–66j

INVESTIGATION 4

Multiplying and Dividing Integers

In the previous investigations, you looked at various ways to think about and model addition and subtraction of integers. In this investigation, you will explore ways to think about multiplying and dividing integers.

4.1 Rising and Falling Temperatures

In Investigation 1, you used a thermometer to explore positive and negative numbers. In this problem, you will use a thermometer to help you think about multiplying integers.

In this investigation, we will use a positive symbol to represent a rise in temperature and a negative symbol to represent a drop in temperature. That means, for example, if the temperature rises 3°, we will say that it changes by $^{+}3°$, and if the temperature drops 3°, we will say that it changes by $^{-}3°$.

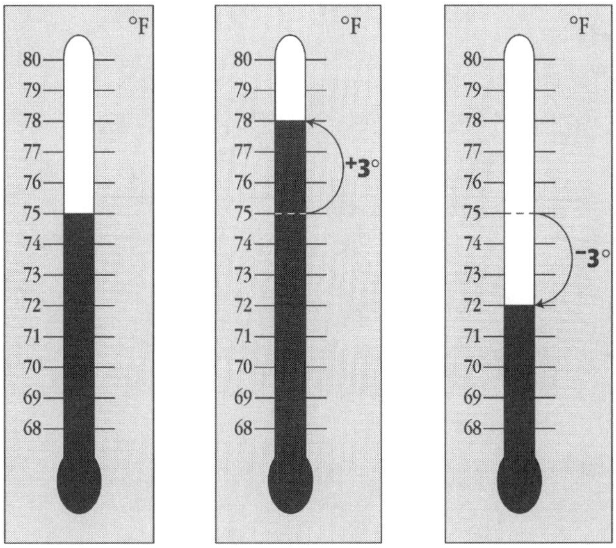

4.1

Rising and Falling Temperatures

At a Glance

Grouping: pairs

Launch

- Talk with the class about the introduction to the problem.
- Ask questions relating temperature changes to number sentences.

Explore

- As pairs work on the problem, remind them to write complete number sentences and to make sure they can explain their answers.

Summarize

- Discuss with the class the relation between multiplication and repeated addition and the order of the two integers in a multiplication sentence.
- Discuss the follow-up questions.

Assignment Choices

ACE questions 1–3 and unassigned choices from earlier problems

Problem 4.1

A. 1. Suppose the temperature changed by an average of $^+3°$ per hour for a 10-hour period. Copy and complete the table below, and use it to find the total temperature change for the first 5 hours.

Number of hours	1	2	3	4	5
Total temperature change	$^+3°$	$^+6°$			

2. Write a multiplication sentence that represents the total change in temperature for the first 5 hours. Write a multiplication sentence that represents the total change in temperature for the entire 10-hour period.

B. 1. Suppose the temperature changed by an average of $^-3°$ per hour for a 10-hour period. Copy and complete the table below, and use it to find the total temperature change for the first 5 hours.

Number of hours	1	2	3	4	5
Total temperature change	$^-3°$	$^-6°$			

2. Write a multiplication sentence that represents the total change in temperature for the first 5 hours. Write a multiplication sentence that represents the total change in temperature for the entire 10-hour period.

C. 1. Write the addition sentence illustrated by each diagram below.

2. Write the multiplication sentence illustrated by each diagram below.

a. 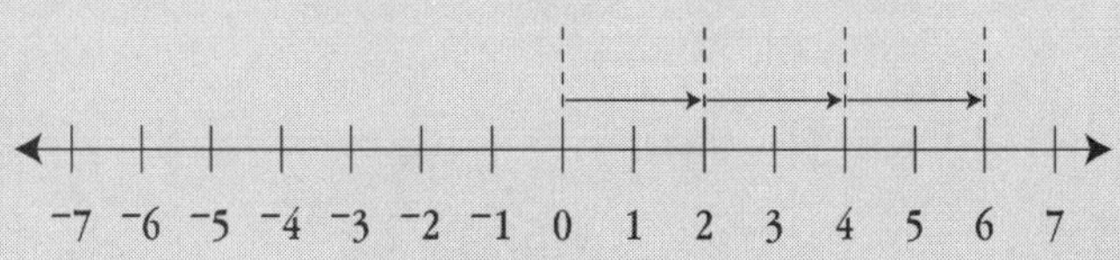

b. 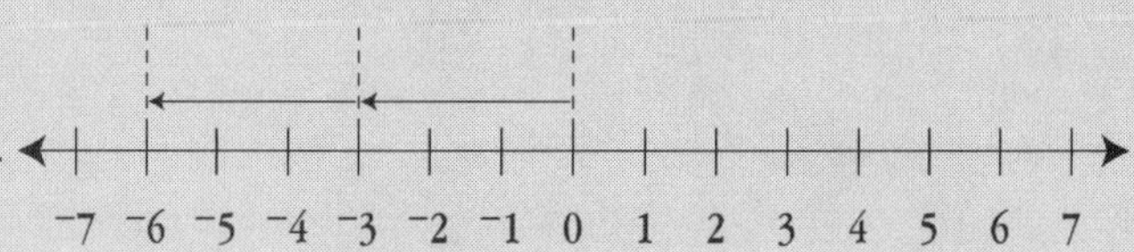

c. 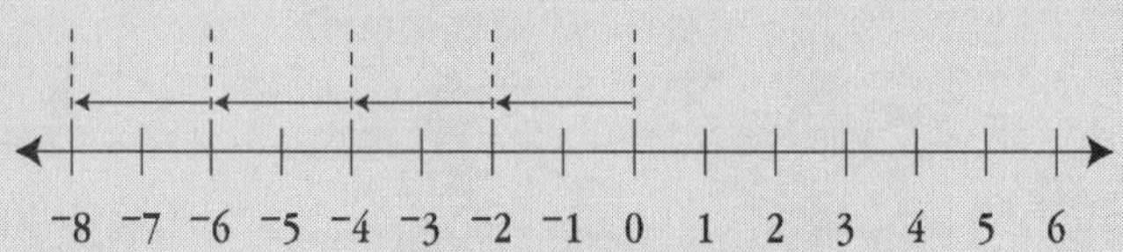

D. Make up a situation about temperatures that can be expressed as $4 \times {}^-10$.

E. Find each product.

1. $5 \times {}^-4$ **2.** $20 \times {}^-4$ **3.** $^-4 \times 20$ **4.** $^-5 \times 4$

Answers to Problem 4.1

A. 1.

Number of hours	1	2	3	4	5
Total temperature change	+3°	+6°	+9°	+12°	+15°

2. $5 \times 3° = 15°$; $10 \times 3° = 30°$

B. 1.

Number of hours	1	2	3	4	5
Total temperature change	$^-3°$	$^-6°$	$^-9°$	$^-12°$	$^-15°$

2. $5 \times {}^-3° = {}^-15°$; $10 \times {}^-3° = {}^-30°$

C. 1. a. $2 + 2 + 2 = 6$ b. $^-3 + {}^-3 = {}^-6$ c. $^-2 + {}^-2 + {}^-2 + {}^-2 = {}^-8$

2. a. $3 \times 2 = 6$ b. $2 \times {}^-3 = {}^-6$ c. $4 \times {}^-2 = {}^-8$

D. Possible answer: The temperature drops about 10° for each of the next 4 hours.

E. 1. $^-20$ 2. $^-80$ 3. $^-80$ 4. $^-20$

Problem 4.1 Follow-Up

1. Suppose the temperature changed by an average of $^{+}2°$ per hour from its low of $^{-}4°F$ at 3:00 A.M. What was the temperature at 1:00 P.M.?

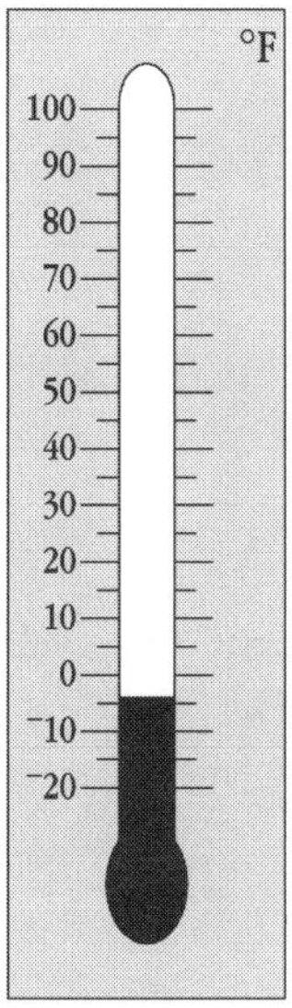

2. Suppose the temperature changed by an average of $^{-}1.5°$ per hour from its high of $^{+}25°F$ at noon. What was the temperature at 10:00 P.M.?

3. When you add a positive integer and a negative integer, you sometimes get a positive result and sometimes get a negative result. Is the same true when you multiply a positive integer and a negative integer? Explain.

Did you know?

The temperature at the center of the Sun is estimated to be about 15,000,000°C. The temperature at the center of a thermonuclear fusion bomb is about 400,000,000°C! Temperature does not appear to have an upper limit. However, there does seem to be a lower limit. Scientists believe that $^{-}273.15°C$, a temperature known as ***absolute zero,*** is the lowest temperature attainable. At this temperature the molecules and atoms of a substance have the least possible energy.

Answers to Problem 4.1 Follow-Up

1. Ten hours separate 3 A.M. and 1 P.M., so the temperature increased $10 \times 2° = 20°$ and at 1 P.M. was $^{-}4° + 20° = 16°$.
2. Ten hours separate noon and 10 P.M., so the temperature decreased $10 \times {}^{-}1.5° = {}^{-}15°$ and at 10 P.M. was $25° + {}^{-}15° = 10°$.
3. You always get a negative result. Possible answer: Multiplying a positive and a negative integer is like adding the same negative integer a certain number of times, which always gives a negative sum. For example, $4 \times {}^{-}7$ means you have 4 groups of negative 7, so you add four $^{-}7$s.

4.2

Studying Multiplication Patterns

At a Glance

***Grouping:* pairs**

Launch

- Read the introduction and problem with the class.

Explore

- As pairs work on the problem, listen for the patterns they are noticing.
- If pairs have trouble with parts E and F, suggest that they think about what seems reasonable.

Summarize

- Discuss students' answers and thinking strategies for the problem.
- Assist the class in looking for patterns that will help predict the product of any two integers.
- Discuss the follow-up questions.

4.2 Studying Multiplication Patterns

In Investigation 3, you studied patterns to help you understand subtraction of integers. Studying patterns can also help you think about multiplication of integers. Study the equations below, and then work on the problem.

$$5 \times 5 = 25$$
$$5 \times 4 = 20$$
$$5 \times 3 = 15$$
$$5 \times 2 = 10$$
$$5 \times 1 = 5$$
$$5 \times 0 = 0$$

Problem 4.2

A. Describe any patterns you observe in the way the products change as the integers multiplied by 5 get smaller.

B. **1.** Use the patterns you observed to predict $5 \times {}^-1$. Explain your reasoning.

2. Write the next four equations in the pattern.

C. Complete the equations below, and use them to help you answer parts D and E.

$$5 \times {}^-4 = ?$$
$$4 \times {}^-4 = ?$$
$$3 \times {}^-4 = ?$$
$$2 \times {}^-4 = ?$$
$$1 \times {}^-4 = ?$$
$$0 \times {}^-4 = ?$$

D. Describe any patterns you observe in the way the products change as the integers multiplied by $^-4$ get smaller.

E. **1.** Use the patterns you observed to predict $^-1 \times {}^-4$. Explain your reasoning.

2. Write the next four equations in the pattern.

F. Find the following products.

1. $^-3 \times 7$ **2.** $5 \times {}^-8$ **3.** $^-11 \times {}^-12$ **4.** $^-3.6 \times 2.7$

Assignment Choices

ACE questions 26, 29, 32, and unassigned choices from earlier problems

Answers to Problem 4.2

A. As the size of the groups decreases, the products decrease by 5 at each step.

B. 1. $5 \times {}^-1 = {}^-5$; Possible explanation: With each equation, there is one fewer group of 5, and 5 less than 0 is $^-5$.

2. $5 \times {}^-2 = {}^-10$, $5 \times {}^-3 = {}^-15$, $5 \times {}^-4 = {}^-20$, $5 \times {}^-5 = {}^-25$

C. $5 \times {}^-4 = {}^-20$, $4 \times {}^-4 = {}^-16$, $3 \times {}^-4 = {}^-12$, $2 \times {}^-4 = {}^-8$, $1 \times {}^-4 = {}^-4$, $0 \times {}^-4 = 0$

D. The product increases each time because you are accumulating fewer negatives (one less group of $^-4$).

E. 1. $^-1 \times {}^-4 = 4$; Possible explanation: With each equation, the product increases by 4, and 4 more than 0 is 4.

2. $^-2 \times {}^-4 = 8$, $^-3 \times {}^-4 = 12$, $^-4 \times {}^-4 = 16$, $^-5 \times {}^-4 = 20$

F. 1. $^-21$ 2. $^-40$ 3. 132 4. $^-9.72$

Problem 4.2 Follow-Up

1. a. Find $^-6 \times 7$ and $7 \times {}^-6$.
   b. When you multiply integers, does the order of the numbers matter?
2. a. Find $^-6 + 7$ and $7 + {}^-6$.
   b. When you add integers, does the order of the numbers matter?
3. a. Find $^-6 - 7$ and $7 - {}^-6$.
   b. When you subtract integers, does the order of the numbers matter?
4. When you add two negative integers, you get a negative result. Is the same true when you multiply two negative integers? Explain.

4.3 Playing the Integer Product Game

In this problem, you will practice multiplying integers by playing the Integer Product Game. The Integer Product Game board consists of a list of factors and a grid of products. Two players compete to get four squares in a row—up and down, across, or diagonally. To play the game, you will need Labsheet 4.3, two paper clips, and colored markers or game chips. The rules for the game and the game board are given on the next page.

Problem 4.3

Play the game with a partner. Look for interesting patterns and ideas that might help you devise a winning strategy. Make notes of your observations.

Problem 4.3 Follow-Up

1. Give every combination of two factors from the factor list that will give each of the following products.
   a. 5 b. $^-12$ c. 12 d. $^-25$
2. Your opponent starts the game by putting a paper clip on $^-4$. What products are possible on your turn?
3. At the end of your opponent's turn, the paper clips are on $^-5$ and $^-2$. What move would you make to get a product of $^-15$?
4. At the end of your opponent's turn, the paper clips are on $^-3$ and $^-2$. What move would you make to get a product of $^-6$?
5. Why doesn't $^-35$ appear on the board?

4.3 Playing the Integer Product Game

At a Glance

Grouping: pairs

Launch

- Review the rules of the Integer Product Game with the class.
- As a class, play a sample game.

Explore

- Have pairs or teams of two play the game several times.
- Remind students to make notes of any patterns or winning strategies they see.

Summarize

- Discuss any patterns and winning strategies students discovered.
- Go over the follow-up questions.

Answers to Problem 4.2 Follow-Up

1. a. Both products are $^-42$.
   b. The order of two integers does not affect their product.
2. a. Both sums are 1.
   b. The order of two integers does not affect their sum.
3. a. $^-6 - 7 = {}^-13$, $7 - {}^-6 = 13$
   b. The order of two integers does affect their difference.
4. no; When you multiply two negative integers, the product is always positive.

Answers to Problem 4.3 Follow-Up

See page 66j.

Assignment Choices

ACE questions 4–8, 17–21, 34, and unassigned choices from earlier problems

Integer Product Game Rules

1. Player A puts a paper clip on a number in the factor list. Player A does not cover a square on the product grid because only one factor has been marked; it takes two factors to make a product.

2. Player B puts the other paper clip on any number in the factor list (including the same number marked by Player A) and then shades or covers the product of the two factors on the product grid.

3. Player A moves *either one* of the paper clips to another number and then shades or covers the new product using a different color from Player B.

4. Each player, in turn, moves a paper clip and marks a product. If a product is already marked, the player does not get a mark for that turn. The winner is the first player to mark four squares in a row—up and down, across, or diagonally.

The Integer Product Game

1	−1	2	−2	3	−3
4	−4	5	−5	6	−6
8	−8	9	−9	10	−10
12	−12	15	−15	16	−16
18	−18	20	−20	24	−24
25	−25	30	−30	36	−36

Factors:
−6 −5 −4 −3 −2 −1 1 2 3 4 5 6

Answers to Problem 4.4

A. 1. $^-5 \times 6 = {}^-30$ 2. $^-5 = {}^-30 \div 6$, $6 = {}^-30 \div {}^-5$

B. 1. $^-8 \times {}^-4 = 32$ 2. $^-4 = 32 \div {}^-8$, $^-8 = 32 \div {}^-4$

C. 1. $^-132 \div 12 = {}^-11$ 2. $^-56 \div {}^-8 = 7$

3. $132 \div {}^-4 = {}^-33$ 4. $^-8.84 \div 5.2 = {}^-1.7$

D. 1. $^-8 \times {}^-3 = 24$ 2. $91 \div {}^-7 = {}^-13$

3. $^-17 \times 11 = {}^-187$ 4. $^-19.95 \div 9.5 = {}^-2.1$

4.4 Dividing Integers

In Investigation 3, you saw that subtraction is the opposite, or inverse, of addition. You observed that for any addition sentence, you can write a subtraction sentence that undoes the addition. Similarly, division is the opposite, or inverse, of multiplication, and for any multiplication sentence, you can write a division sentence that undoes the multiplication.

For example, given the multiplication sentence $5 \times 6 = 30$, you can write two division sentences:

$$5 = 30 \div 6 \text{ and } 6 = 30 \div 5$$

Problem 4.4

A. **1.** Complete the multiplication sentence $^-5 \times 6 = ?$.

2. Write two division sentences that are equivalent to the multiplication sentence you found in part 1.

B. **1.** Complete the multiplication sentence $^-8 \times {}^-4 = ?$.

2. Write two division sentences that are equivalent to the multiplication sentence you found in part 1.

C. Write a division sentence that solves each problem.

1. $? \times 12 = {}^-132$ **2.** $^-8 \times ? = {}^-56$

3. $? \times {}^-4 = 132$ **4.** $5.2 \times ? = {}^-8.84$

D. Write a division or a multiplication sentence that solves each problem.

1. $? \div {}^-3 = {}^-8$ **2.** $91 \div ? = {}^-7$

3. $? \div 11 = {}^-17$ **4.** $^-19.95 \div ? = 9.5$

Problem 4.4 Follow-Up

1. Find each quotient.

a. $^-121 \div 11$ **b.** $121 \div {}^-11$ **c.** $^-96 \div {}^-4$ **d.** $96 \div 4$

2. **a.** Find $18 \div 3$.

b. How does your answer from part a help you find $^-18 \div 3$, $18 \div {}^-3$, and $^-18 \div {}^-3$?

4.4 Dividing Integers

At a Glance

Grouping:* *pairs

Launch

- Talk with the class about the meaning of division.
- Discuss the relationship between multiplication and division.
- Work through examples of multiplication sentences and their two related division sentences.

Explore

- Have pairs work on the problem.
- If students have made sense of Problem 4.4, have them do the follow-up before the summary.

Summarize

- Have students share solutions and strategies.
- Help the class generalize rules for dividing positive and negative integers.

Answers to Problem 4.4 Follow-Up

1. a. $^-11$
   b. $^-11$
   c. 24
   d. 24
2. a. 6
   b. Because I know the quotient for part a is 6, the quotient for each of these problems must be 6 or $^-6$.

Assignment Choices

ACE questions 9–16, 22–25, 27, 28, 30, 31, 33, 35–38, and unassigned choices from earlier problems

ACE

Answers

Applications

1a. There are 4 hours between noon and 4:00 P.M. In 4 hours, the temperature changed $4 \times {}^-2° = {}^-8°$, so the temperature at 4:00 P.M. was $75° + {}^-8° = 67°$.

1b. There are 21 hours between noon and 9:00 A.M. In 21 hours, the temperature changed $21 \times {}^-2° = {}^-42°$, so the temperature at 9:00 A.M. was $75° + {}^-42° = 33°$.

2a. $^-2 + {}^-2 + {}^-2 = {}^-6$

2b. $^-2 \times 3 = {}^-6$ or $3 \times {}^-2 = {}^-6$

3a. $3 + 3 + 3 = 9$

3b. $3 \times 3 = 9$

4. 1 and 11, $^-1$ and $^-11$

5. 1 and $^-21$, $^-1$ and 21, 3 and $^-7$, $^-3$ and 7

6. $^-1$ and $^-12$, 1 and 12, $^-2$ and $^-6$, 2 and 6, $^-3$ and $^-4$, 3 and 4

7. 1 and $^-12$, $^-1$ and 12, 2 and $^-6$, $^-2$ and 6, 3 and $^-4$, $^-3$ and 4

Applications • Connections • Extensions

As you work on these ACE questions, use your calculator whenever you need it.

Applications

1. On Tuesday, a cold front passed through, causing the temperature to change $^-2$°F per hour from noon until 10:00 A.M. the next morning. The temperature at noon on Tuesday was 75°F.

a. What was the temperature at 4:00 P.M. Tuesday?

b. What was the temperature at 9:00 A.M. Wednesday?

2. a. Write the addition sentence illustrated by the number line below.

b. Write the multiplication sentence illustrated by the number line below.

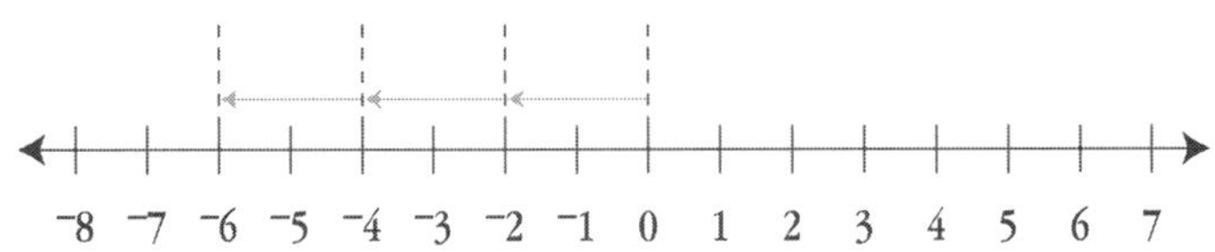

3. a. Write the addition sentence illustrated by the number line below.

b. Write the multiplication sentence illustrated by the number line below.

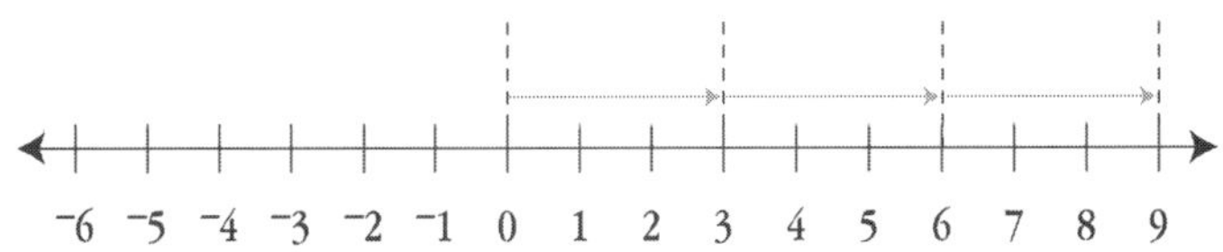

In 4–7, list all the integer factor pairs for the number.

4. 11 **5.** $^-21$ **6.** 12 **7.** $^-12$

8. Iseku and Kylie are making a version of the Integer Product Game in which players need three products in a row to win. What factors do they need for their game?

Iseku and Kylie's Product Game

4	$^-4$	6	$^-6$
9	$^-9$	10	$^-10$
15	$^-15$	25	$^-25$

In 9–16, find the sum, difference, product, or quotient.

9. 52×75 **10.** $52 \times {}^-75$ **11.** $2262 \div 58$ **12.** $10{,}680 \div {}^-120$

13. $137 + 899$ **14.** $5679 - 7890$ **15.** $^-4329 - {}^-1234$ **16.** $^-9908 \div {}^-89$

Connections

In 17–21, write a number sentence to represent the situation described. Then tell whether more than one number sentence is possible, and explain your reasoning.

17. The temperature at noon was $^-13$°C. For the next 6 hours, the temperature changed by an average of $^+1.8$° per hour. What was the temperature at 6:00 P.M.?

18. The temperature at noon was $^-13$°C. From 6:00 A.M. until noon, the temperature had changed by an average of $^+5$° per hour. What had the temperature been at 6:00 A.M.?

19. In a game of MathMania, the Extraterrestrials had a score of $^-300$, and then they answered four 50-point questions incorrectly. What was their score after missing the four questions?

20. After answering three 100-point questions correctly, the Supermutants had 200 points. What was their score before answering the three questions?

8. 2, $^-2$, 3, $^-3$, 5, $^-5$

9. 3900

10. $^-3900$

11. 39

12. $^-89$

13. 1036

14. $^-2211$

15. $^-3095$

16. 111.33

Connections

17. $^-13° + (6 \times 1.8°) = {}^-2.2°$

18. $^-13° - (5° \times 6) = {}^-43°$, $^-13° + ({}^-6 \times 5°) = {}^-43°$

19. $^-300 - (4 \times 50) = {}^-500$, $^-300 + (4 \times {}^-50) = {}^-500$

20. $200 - (3 \times 100) = {}^-100$, $200 + ({}^-3 \times 100) = {}^-100$

ACE

21. 25 – (3 × 4) = 13-yard line, 25 + (3 × ⁻4) = 13-yard line

22. ⁻34 × ⁺15 = ⁻510; ⁻510 ÷ ⁺15 = ⁻34 or ⁻510 ÷ ⁻34 = ⁺15

23. ⁻12 × ⁻23 = 276; 276 ÷ ⁻23 = ⁻12 or 276 ÷ ⁻12 = ⁻23

24. ⁺532 ÷ ⁻7 = ⁻76; ⁻76 × ⁻7 = ⁺532

25. ⁻777 ÷ ⁻37 = 21; 21 × ⁻37 = ⁻777

26a. $C = {}^{-}7H$

26b. $C = {}^{-}7(3) = {}^{-}21°$

26c. ⁻42 = ⁻7*H*, so ⁻42 ÷ ⁻7 = *H*, and *H* = 6 h

27. The sum of all the temperatures is ⁻41, giving a mean temperature of ⁻41 ÷ 12 = ⁻3.4°.

21. The Bigtown Bears were on their own 25-yard line. For the next three plays, they lost an average of 4 yards per play. Where did the Bears end up after the three plays?

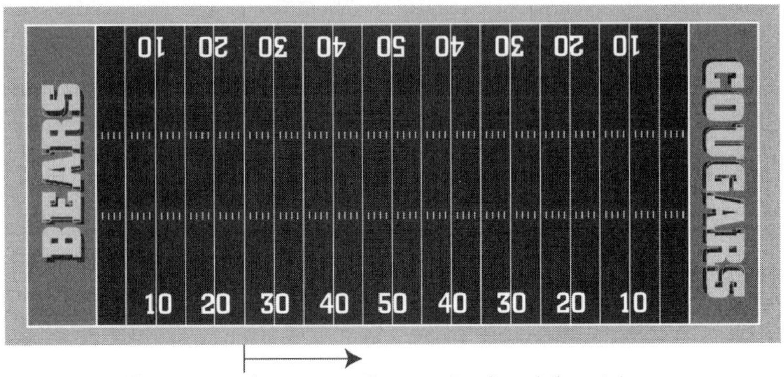

The Bears are here now and are moving from left to right—that is, they move right when they gain yards.

In 22–25, complete the number sentence, and then write an equivalent sentence using the inverse operation.

22. $^{-}34 \times {}^{+}15 = ?$ **23.** $^{-}12 \times {}^{-}23 = ?$

24. $^{+}532 \div {}^{-}7 = ?$ **25.** $^{-}777 \div {}^{-}37 = ?$

26. **a.** Suppose the temperature changes by an average of ⁻7° per hour. Write an equation you can use to determine the temperature change, *C*, after *H* hours.

b. Use your equation to find the temperature change after 3 hours.

c. How many hours will it take for the temperature to change by ⁻42°?

27. The list below gives average temperatures (in °C) for Fairbanks, Alaska, for each month of the year from January through December. What is the mean of these monthly temperatures?

⁻25, ⁻20, ⁻13, ⁻2, ⁺9, ⁺15, ⁺17, ⁺14, ⁺7, ⁻4, ⁻16, ⁻23

28. The R-80 Trucking Company carried freight along interstate 80 from New York City to San Francisco. The home base of R-80 Trucking was in Omaha, Nebraska, which is roughly midway between the ends of its line. R-80 truckers averaged about 50 miles per hour on this route, allowing time for rest stops.

R-80 Trucking Company Route Map

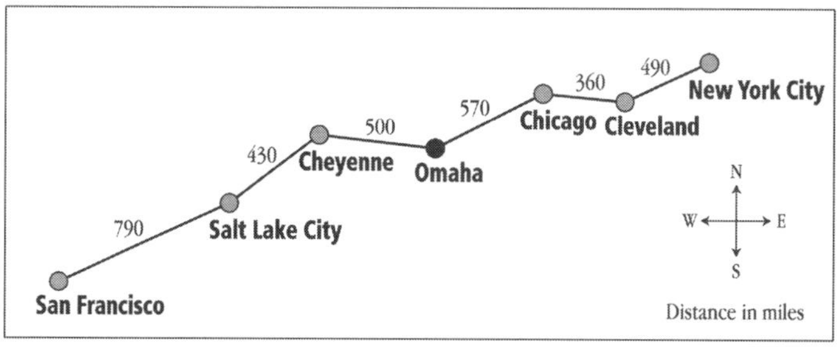

a. Make a number line to represent this truck route. Put Omaha at 0, and use positive numbers for cities east of Omaha and negative numbers for cities west of Omaha.

b. A truck left Omaha, heading east, and traveled for 7 hours. About how far did the truck go? Where on the number line did it stop? Show all your calculations.

c. A truck left Omaha, heading west, and traveled for 4.5 hours. About how far did the truck go? Where on the number line did it stop? Show all your calculations.

d. A truck heading east arrived in Omaha. About where on the number line was the truck 12 hours before it reached Omaha? Show all your calculations.

e. A truck heading west arrived in Omaha. About where on the number line was the truck 11 hours before it reached Omaha? Show all your calculations.

28a. See below left.

28b. The truck would be $50 \times 7 = 350$ miles east of Omaha, a coordinate of $^{+}350$ and more than halfway to Chicago.

28c. The truck would be $50 \times 4.5 = 225$ miles west of Omaha, a coordinate of $^{-}225$ and about halfway to Cheyenne.

28d. The truck would be $50 \times 12 = 600$ miles west of Omaha, a coordinate of $^{-}600$.

28e. The truck would be $50 \times 11 = 550$ miles east of Omaha, a coordinate of $^{+}550$.

28a. Note: Increments on number lines should be spaced equally.

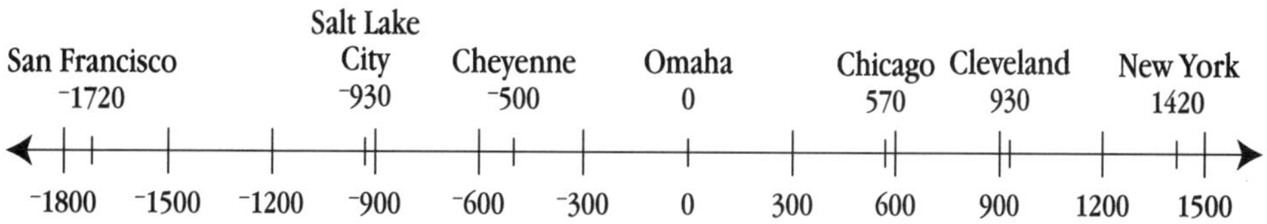

ACE

29. The sum of the gains and losses is 37, giving an average gain per play of $37 \div 10 = 3.7$ yards.

30. $7 \times {}^{-}3 = {}^{-}21$, ${}^{-}21 \div 7 = {}^{-}3$, ${}^{-}21 \div {}^{-}3 = 7$

31. ${}^{-}4 \times {}^{-}5 = 20$, $20 \div {}^{-}4 = {}^{-}5$, $20 \div {}^{-}5 = {}^{-}4$

32a. If the signs are the same, the product will be positive.

32b. If the signs are different, the product will be negative.

32c. If either or both of the factors are 0, the product is will be 0.

33a. If the divisor and the dividend have the same sign, the quotient will be positive.

33b. If the divisor and the dividend have opposite signs, the quotient will be negative.

33c. If the dividend is 0 and the divisor is a nonzero number, the quotient will be 0. (Division by 0 is not possible, so the divisor cannot be 0.)

Extensions

34. See possible Sum Game below right. Warning: This problem is not as easy as it appears.

29. The list below shows the yards gained and lost on each play by the Mathville Mudhens in the fourth quarter of their last football game. What was their average gain or loss per play?

${}^{-}8, 20, 3, 7, {}^{-}15, 4, {}^{-}12, 32, 5, 1$

In 30 and 31, write a set of number sentences that shows the related multiplication and division facts for the set of integers. For example, for the integers 27, 9, and 3, the sentences would be

$$9 \times 3 = 27 \qquad 3 = 27 \div 9 \qquad 9 = 27 \div 3$$

30. $7, {}^{-}3$, and ${}^{-}21$

31. ${}^{-}4, {}^{-}5$, and 20

32. Without actually multiplying, how can you decide whether the product of two integers is

a. positive

b. negative

c. 0

33. Without actually dividing, how can you decide whether the quotient of two integers is

a. positive

b. negative

c. 0

Extensions

34. Make a Sum Game with a 6-by-6 grid of sums. Each sum in the grid must be the sum of two integers (addends) listed below the grid.

34.

⁻24	⁻22	⁻20	⁻18	⁻16	⁻14
⁻12	⁻11	⁻10	⁻9	⁻8	⁻7
⁻6	⁻5	⁻4	⁻3	⁻2	⁻1
0	1	2	3	4	5
6	7	8	9	10	11
12	14	16	18	20	22

Addends:
⁻12 ⁻10 ⁻8 ⁻6 ⁻4 ⁻2 0 1 3 5 7 9 11

In 35–38, use the following information: Many towns and small cities have water towers to store water and help maintain water pressure. Water flows into and out of the towers all day long. Generally, flow out of the tower is greatest during the hours when most people are awake and active. The flow into the towers is greatest at night when most people are asleep.

35. If water flows into a tower at the rate of 5000 gallons per hour, how will the supply in the tower change over a 4-hour period? Assume no water flows out of the tower during this time. Show your calculations.

36. If water flows into a tower at the rate of 4000 gallons per hour for a 7-hour period, by how much will the supply at the end of the 7 hours differ from the supply at the beginning of the 7 hours? Assume no water flows out of the tower during this time. Show your calculations.

37. If water flows out of a tower at the rate of 7500 gallons per hour, how will the supply in the tower change over a 3-hour period? Assume no water flows into the tower during this time. Show your calculations.

38. If water flows out of a tower at the rate of 5000 gallons per hour for a 6.5-hour period, by how much will the supply at the end of the 6.5 hours differ from the supply at the beginning of the 6.5-hour period? Assume no water flows into the tower during this time. Show your calculations.

35. $5000 \times 4 = 20{,}000$ gal will be added.

36. The supply will be $4000 \times 7 = 28{,}000$ gal greater.

37. The change is $^-7500 \times 3 = {^-22{,}500}$ gal. So, the supply will decrease by 22,500 gal.

38. The change is $^-5000 \times 6.5 = {^-32{,}500}$. So, the supply will be 32,500 gal less at the end of the 6.5-hour period.

Possible Answers

1. The product will be positive if the two integers have the same sign and negative if the two integers have different signs. Once the sign of the product is determined, the "number part" of the product can be calculated by multiplying the "number parts" of the factors (disregarding the signs). The product will be 0 if one of the integers being multiplied is 0.

1a. $^-13 \times 7 = {}^-91$

1b. $11 \times {}^-20 = {}^-220$

1c. $^-12 \times 0 = 0$

1d. $^-18 \times {}^-22 = 396$

2. See page 66j.

Mathematical Reflections

In this investigation, you explored the multiplication and division of integers. These questions will help you summarize what you have learned:

1. Write a strategy for multiplying two integers. Be sure to consider all possible combinations of positive integers, negative integers, and 0. Verify your strategy by finding the following products.

   a. $^-13 \times 7$ **b.** $11 \times {}^-20$

   c. $^-12 \times 0$ **d.** $^-18 \times {}^-22$

2. Write a strategy for dividing two integers. Be sure to consider all possible combinations of positive integers, negative integers, and 0. Verify your strategy by finding the following quotients.

   a. $126 \div {}^-9$ **b.** $^-36 \div {}^-12$

   c. $^-2592 \div 32$ **d.** $0 \div 18$

Think about your answers to these questions, discuss your ideas with other students and your teacher, and then write a summary of your findings in your journal.

Tips for the Linguistically Diverse Classroom

Diagram Code The Diagram Code technique is described in detail in *Getting to Know Connected Mathematics*. Students use a minimal number of words and drawings, diagrams, or symbols to respond to questions that require writing. Example: Question 1—A student might answer this question by writing + × + *is* +; – × – *is* +; – × + *is* –; beneath this, *If same sign, then +. If not, then –.*

4.1 • Rising and Falling Temperatures

In this problem, students consider the multiplication of two positive integers and of a positive and a negative integer. (The multiplication of two negative integers is considered in Problem 4.2.)

Launch

Read the problem introduction with your class. Ask students questions about the relationship between changes on a thermometer to number sentences.

> What would the reading be on the middle thermometer if the temperature rose another 3°? *(81°)*
>
> What number sentence could we write to show the total change for two consecutive temperature changes of 3°? *(3° + 3° = 6° or 2 × 3° = 6°)*
>
> What would the reading be on the third thermometer if the temperature dropped another 3°? *(69°)*
>
> What number sentence could we write to show the total change for two consecutive temperature changes of $^-3$°? *($^-3$° + $^-3$° = $^-6$° or 2 × $^-3$° = $^-6$°)*

Have student work in pairs on the problem and follow-up.

Explore

As pairs work, make sure they are writing complete number sentences reflecting totals and not just expressions. For part E, remind them that they need to be able to explain why their solutions make sense and are reasonable.

For the follow-up, you might suggest to students who are struggling that they draw thermometers to help them answer questions 1 and 2.

Summarize

Review students' solutions to parts A and B. For part C, have pairs share their number sentences. Help them analyze how each pair of addition and multiplication sentences are related.

> What does the number sentence 3 × 2 = 6 mean? *(3 × 2 means that you have 3 groups of 2.)*
>
> What does the operation of multiplication mean?

For the Teacher: A Need for Consistency

The sentence 2×3 could also be read as 3 groups of 2. You and your class will need to decide how you will read and write multiplication sentences. Although it doesn't influence the solution, 3 groups of 2 and 2 groups of 3 are two different situations. At this point, it is important to be consistent when reading and writing multiplication sentences, because students are trying to make sense of multiplying with negative integers. We have written 3 groups of 2 as 3×2 because it matches the language and notational order used in the *Bits and Pieces II* unit, in which students multiplied fractions and decimals.

Most students think of multiplication as a shorthand for writing repeated addition. Write 8×4 on the board.

> What does this expression mean? *(the total amount in 8 groups of 4)*
> How much is 8 groups of 4? *(32)*

Write $8 \times {}^{-}4$ on the board.

> What does this expression mean? *(the total amount in 8 groups of ⁻4)*
> How much is 8 groups of ⁻4? *(⁻32)*

As pairs share their situations for part D, ask the class to verify that each could be expressed as $4 \times {}^{-}10$. If pairs have written addition or subtraction situations instead of multiplication situations, help them to see that their answers can also be written as multiplication sentences.

Question E involves the order of the numbers as well as their signs. Have students explain what each expression is saying and why their solutions make sense. Expressions 1 and 2 are similar to those already discussed in class. Expression 3 is the same as expression 2, except for the order of the factors.

> Does switching the order of the integers change the product?

The class could investigate products they already know and then see, for example, that 5×8 is the same as 8×5. Based on this reasoning, it seems that $20 \times {}^{-}4$ should be the same as ${}^{-}4 \times 20$. However, this leap is difficult for many students to make. If they read this expression as they have read the others, they would say, "I have negative 4 groups of 20." This makes sense if we look at the negative as being a direction sign. Four 20s in a negative direction on the number line would be the same as twenty 4s in a negative direction.

Expression 4 is similar to expression 1 except that it contains integers opposite to those in expression 1. Students may say that they know ${}^{-}5 \times 4$ must be ${}^{-}20$ because they know that $4 \times {}^{-}5$ is ${}^{-}20$. Others may say the expression is ${}^{-}20$ because there seems to be a pattern: when two numbers with different signs are multiplied, their product is always negative. If students notice this pattern, ask them why it seems reasonable that the product of a negative and a positive number would be negative.

In discussing the follow-up questions, you may want to have students draw a thermometer and demonstrate the temperature changes and why their solutions make sense. Because question 2 involves decimals, they may choose to mark off a thermometer in 0.5° increments. Question 3 addresses the idea of looking for patterns to help predict products of integers.

4.2 • Studying Multiplication Patterns

As in Problem 3.3, students are given a series of related equations and are asked to look for patterns—this time, patterns that will help them determine the product of any two integers.

Launch

Read the introduction and problem with your students, and have them work in pairs to answer the questions.

Explore

As students work on the problem, listen to the patterns they are noticing. Students may struggle with multiplying a negative by a negative in parts E and F. If so, suggest they think about what each sentence is saying and what seems reasonable.

Summarize

Have pairs share their observations for part A. They should notice that most of the equations are composed of two positive integers and have positive products. The last equation is the product of a positive integer and 0, which gives a product of 0. They should also see that the products become smaller as the size of the groups decreases.

For part B, ask students to share their solutions and explain why they are reasonable and how they fit the patterns they noticed.

For part C, have students give their solutions and tell how they found them and why they are reasonable. In part D, students should notice that all but one equation contain a positive and a negative integer and have a negative product. The last equation is composed of a negative integer and 0 and has a product of 0. They should also see that the products are increasing as fewer groups of negatives are involved. For part E, again have students explain why their solutions are reasonable and how they fit the patterns they noticed.

Have students give their solutions and the reasoning behind them for part F. Ask questions to help them continue to look for patterns that will help them to predict the product of any two integers.

> In these two series of equations, I notice that when 0 is one of the integers in the multiplication expression, the product is 0. Is this always true? When you multiply any number by 0, will 0 always be the product? Explain why or why not.

This is always true. This can be thought of as 0 times any number equals 0, or that we have no groups of this amount. Thus 0×5 means we have no groups of 5.

In the first series of equations, the first five equations involve multiplying two positive integers and result in a positive product. Is that always true? Does a positive integer times a positive integer always give a positive product? Explain why or why not.

This is always true. Multiplying two positive integers can be interpreted as repeated groups of a positive amount. For example, 5×6 can be thought of as 5 groups of 6. As positive amounts are being accumulated, the answer must be positive.

In the second series of equations, the first five equations involve multiplying a positive integer times a negative integer and result in a negative product. Is this always true? Does a positive integer times a negative integer always give a negative product? Explain why or why not.

This is always true. A positive times a negative integer can be interpreted as repeated groups of negative quantities. For example, $12 \times {}^-2$ can be interpreted as 12 groups of $^-2$, which is a negative amount.

If students offer an explanation similar to this, ask what a negative integer times a positive integer gives and why. Students often say that the product will be negative and explain this by informally using the commutative property ($6 \times {}^-3$ is the same as ${}^-3 \times 6$).

In part E, you multiplied two negative integers. What is the sign of the product when two negative integers are multiplied? Explain your reasoning.

The product of two negative integers is always positive. Thinking about multiplying a negative by a negative is abstract and quite difficult to explain for most middle school students' mathematical understanding and language. These ideas need time and reinforcement to make sense. Here are two explanations students have offered.

- Zenelia: "To fit the pattern of the equations in part C, the product of ${}^-1 \times {}^-4$ has to be 4."
- Thomas: "The problem ${}^-1 \times {}^-4$ means that you need to take the opposite of 1 group of $^-4$."

The other thing I have noticed is that when multiplying any two integers—positive by positive, positive by negative, negative by positive, or negative by negative—the numerical value of the solution is always the product of the two integers (disregarding their signs). Therefore, it is the *sign* of the product that I must reason about. Do you think that whenever you multiply two integers, the solution will be the product of the numerals? Explain.

Students may not be able to explain all of their ideas at this time, but help them to notice that the absolute value of the solution is always the product of the absolute values of the integers.

When we added and subtracted positive and negative integers, it was not always possible to just add or subtract the numerical values—the absolute values—of the numbers. Sometimes when we added we ended up with a quantity that looked like the difference. The same was true when subtracting; sometimes we got a quantity that looked like the sum of the integers. Can someone give an example of each of these situations? *(8 – -5 is the same as the sum of the two absolute values, and 8 + -5 is the same as the difference of the two absolute values.)*

Discuss the follow-up questions as part of the summary. The first three follow-up questions ask students to think about which operations are commutative. You may have already discussed the ideas in question 4 in the summary of the problem.

4.3 • Playing the Integer Product Game

This problem helps students practice their multiplication of integers with a version of the Product Game from the *Prime Time* unit. You may want to review, or have students review, the sample games that appear in the *Prime Time* student edition.

Launch

You could start this problem by displaying Transparency 4.3 and asking a member of the class to explain the rules of the game. Or, display the game board, and review the rules that appear in the student edition.

Play the game with the class, or divide the class into two teams and have one group play against the other.

For the Teacher: Game Rules

Suppose you begin the game by placing a paper clip on the factor 4. You do not get to mark a product on the board because it takes two factors to make a product. The class then places a paper clip, say, on the factor -6 and covers the corresponding product, -24, on the board.

1	-1	2	-2	3	-3
4	-4	5	-5	6	-6
8	-8	9	-9	10	-10
12	-12	15	-15	16	-16
18	-18	20	-20	24	-24
25	-25	30	-30	36	-36

Factors:
-6 -5 -4 -3 -2 -1 1 2 3 4 5 6

Now it's your turn to move a paper clip and cover a product. You can move either one of the paper clips. You could move the paper clip from ⁻6 to 6 and cover 24 on the board.

1	⁻1	2	⁻2	3	⁻3
4	⁻4	5	⁻5	6	⁻6
8	⁻8	9	⁻9	10	⁻10
12	⁻12	15	⁻15	16	⁻16
18	⁻18	20	⁻20	24	⁻24
25	⁻25	30	⁻30	36	⁻36

Factors:
⁻6 ⁻5 ⁻4 ⁻3 ⁻2 ⁻1 1 2 3 4 5 6

Now it is the class's turn. They can move either one of the paper clips. They could move the paper clip from 4 to ⁻6 and cover ⁻36.

1	⁻1	2	⁻2	3	⁻3
4	⁻4	5	⁻5	6	⁻6
8	⁻8	9	⁻9	10	⁻10
12	⁻12	15	⁻15	16	⁻16
18	⁻18	20	⁻20	24	⁻24
25	⁻25	30	⁻30	36	⁻36

Factors:
⁻6 ⁻5 ⁻4 ⁻3 ⁻2 ⁻1 1 2 3 4 5 6

Play continues until one team or player has covered four squares in a row—horizontally, vertically, or diagonally.

Explore

This is a two-person game. Have students pair up and play the game a few times. Some teachers find it productive to let teams of two play each other. This allows the teammates to share and discuss strategies. Remind students to write down any patterns or winning strategies that they discover.

Summarize

Discuss any strategies for playing and winning the game that students discovered. Here are some strategies students have found.

- Lyle: "It is better to go second because if you go first you really don't get to make a move on the board."
- Tamara: "There are more ways to get certain numbers than there were in the old games. For example, 6 can be made by 1×6 and 2×3 but it can also be made by $^-1 \times {}^-6$ and $^-2 \times {}^-3$. This version of the game makes you more aware of where the markers are on the board. I needed to carefully check all the possibilities before making my move so that I would have more choices on my next turn or not set my opponent up for a good move."
- Kai: "I tried to get products that would block my opponent."

> Did you discover any new patterns that will help you to find the product of any two integers?

The answer to this will depend on the level of understanding your students have about positive and negative integers. The game may have helped them to generalize the rules for multiplying integers, but it is possible that they did not discover any new patterns.

Use the follow-up questions as part of the summary.

4.4 • Dividing Integers

This problem focuses on the relationship between multiplication and division. In it, students develop rules for dividing integers based on what they know about multiplication.

Launch

Discuss with the class what division means and how it relates to multiplication.

> We have discussed what it means to add, subtract, and multiply. We have talked about addition as the operation of "combining" and subtraction as the operation of "taking away." We have also discussed how addition and subtraction are related. We have referred to these as opposite, or inverse, operations. We can think of them as undoing each other. If we add an integer to another integer, we can undo the addition by subtracting the integer that we added from the sum. If we subtract one integer from another, we can undo the subtraction by adding the integer that we subtracted to the difference.

For example, $6 + 4 = 10$, so $6 = 10 - 4$. And since $5 - 12 = {}^-7$, then $5 = {}^-7 + 12$.

We now want to look at the operation of division. What does it mean to divide two integers? Give an example of a situation that calls for division, and tell how your example shows a way to interpret division.

Division is sometimes referred to as the "sharing" operation. One interpretation of division is breaking an amount into groups of the same size. For example: I have 36 cupcakes. How many should I give to each of my four friends if I want to share the cupcakes equally? To answer this question, we need to group the cupcakes into four sets and find how many are in each set.

Write $36 \div 4 = 9$ on the board.

How do you read this sentence? What does it mean?

The sentence is read "36 divided by 4 equals 9." This equation means that there are 36 things that are put into 4 groups of equal size and that there will be 9 things in each group. Or, it can be thought about as putting 36 things in groups of 4 and finding that there are enough to make 9 groups.

How are the operations of multiplication and division related?

In multiplication, groups of the same size are put together to find the total amount. In division, the total is taken apart or partitioned to make groups of equal size. Multiplication and division are opposite, or inverse, operations; they undo each other. Multiplication puts equal-size groups together to find the total; division partitions the total to find either the size of the groups or the number of groups of a given size.

If multiplication and division are opposite operations that undo each other, how could we write a sentence that would undo the sentence $3 \times 12 = 36$? What would the new sentence mean?

This multiplication sentence says that the total of 3 groups of 12 each is 36. If we start with the total and divide by 3, we will be partitioning the total to find the size of each equal-size group ($36 \div 3 = 12$). If we divide the total by 12, we will be finding how many groups of size 12 we began with ($36 \div 12 = 3$).

If students are making sense of this relationship, explain that they will use their understanding of the relationship between multiplication and division to do the problem and to find patterns that will help them to predict the quotient of the division of any two numbers, including integers. If your class is still confused, work through a few more examples of the two division sentences that are related to any multiplication sentence.

Have students work in pairs on the problem.

Explore

If the class seems to be making sense of the task, have them answer the follow-up questions as well. If they are struggling, discuss the problem in the summary, and then have pairs do the follow-up.

Summarize

You might have students go to the board or overhead projector to share their solutions to the problem. If there are disagreements about any of the solutions, have other students share their solutions and explain why they make sense. Do the same for the follow-up questions if pairs have worked on them.

Facilitate a conversation to help students generalize some rules for dividing positive and negative integers.

> How can I find the quotient when I am dividing a positive integer by a positive integer? For example, how do I find the quotient of $125 \div 5$? Explain why your rule is reasonable.

Students may respond that to divide 125 by 5, two integers are divided as any two whole numbers would be. The quotient must be positive because the division problem can be interpreted as having a total of 125 and wanting to partition this positive total into groups of 5. There will be 25 in each group. We also know this because 5×25 is 125.

> Do you all agree with what has been said? Does anyone have another way of thinking about this?
>
> How can I find the quotient when I am dividing a negative integer by a negative integer? For example, how do I find the quotient of $^-125 \div {}^-5$? Explain why your rule is reasonable.

We can interpret the problem as having a total of $^-125$ and wanting to find how many groups of $^-5$ we can make by partitioning the total into equal-size groups. We can make 25 groups of $^-5$ from $^-125$. Also, the quotient must be positive, because $^-5$ must be multiplied by a positive 25 to have a product of $^-125$.

> Do you all agree with what has been said? Does anyone have another way of thinking about this?
>
> How can I find the quotient when I am dividing a negative integer by a positive integer or a positive integer by a negative integer? For example, how do I find the quotient of $^-125 \div 5$ or $125 \div {}^-5$? Explain why your rules are reasonable.

We can interpret $^-125 \div 5$ as partitioning a total of $^-125$ into 5 groups of equal size. The groups must be negative amounts, since we are partitioning a negative amount, so the quotient will be negative.

We can think of $125 \div {}^-5$ as starting with a total of 125. We want to make groups of $^-5$, but we know that the number in each group multiplied by the number of groups must be a positive number. That means that the number of groups must be negative! This is difficult to imagine. Here it helps to look at division as the inverse of multiplication. If we know that $^-5 \times {}^-25 = 125$, then we know that $125 \div {}^-5$ must be $^-25$ and that $125 \div {}^-25$ must equal $^-5$.

Additional Answers

Answers to Problem 4.3 Follow-Up

1. a. 1 and 5; $^-1$ and $^-5$
   b. 2 and $^-6$, $^-2$ and 6, 3 and $^-4$, $^-3$ and 4
   c. $^-2$ and $^-6$, 2 and 6, $^-3$ and $^-4$, 3 and 4
   d. 5 and $^-5$
2. 4, $^-4$, 8, $^-8$, 12, $^-12$, 16, $^-16$, 20, $^-20$, 24, and $^-24$
3. Move the marker from $^-2$ to 3.
4. Move the marker from $^-3$ to 3 or move the marker from $^-2$ to 2.
5. The product $^-35$ is not on the board because the factor list does not contain 7 or $^-7$.

Mathematical Reflections

2. The quotient will be positive if the two integers have the same sign and negative if the two integers have different signs. Once the sign of the quotient is determined, the "number part" of the quotient can be calculated by dividing the "number parts" of the two integers (disregarding the signs).

2a. $126 \div {}^-9 = {}^-14$

2b. ${}^-36 \div {}^-12 = 3$

2c. ${}^-2592 \div 32 = {}^-81$

2d. $0 \div 18 = 0$

For the Teacher: Zero in Division

The quotient of two nonzero integers can never be 0, because there is no way to undo a division problem that has a quotient of 0. To see this, suppose someone says that he or she divided a nonzero number m by a nonzero number n and got 0: $m \div n = 0$. This would mean that $n \times 0 = m$, which is not true, because $n \times 0 = 0$, and m is known to be a nonzero integer.

If we divide 0 by a nonzero number, such as in part d above, we do get 0 because, in that problem, 18×0 is 0. The other way around does not work. If we try to divide a nonzero number, such as 18, by 0, no answer makes sense. We cannot have 0 as the answer, because that would mean that 0×0 must be 18. If we think the answer is a nonzero number, call it q, then we would have $q \times 0 = 18$, but we know that this product must be 0! Since neither answer can be true, we say that the division is impossible. So division *by* 0 is impossible. We can divide a number *into* 0 and get 0, but we cannot divide a number *by* 0, because no answer makes sense.

INVESTIGATION 5

Coordinate Grids

In previous units, students have graphed in the first quadrant of a coordinate grid. Their work with integers now facilitates the introduction of the complete coordinate grid, and their familiarity with number lines will help them see the x- and y-axes as perpendicular number lines representing positive and negative integers.

Problem 5.1, Extending the Coordinate Grid, introduces students to the expanded coordinate grid. They name and locate points, focusing on positive and negative integers. In Problem 5.2, Breaking Even, they explore a problem by graphing by hand to foreshadow what can be done with a graphing calculator. In Problem 5.3, Using a Calculator to Explore Lines, students begin their work with the graphing calculator. Setting up the coordinate grid requires a familiarity with setting scales and minimum and maximum values for the x- and y-axes. Students explore pairs of equations using the standard window, and they look at relationships between linear equations and their graphs, considering what happens when equations have positive or negative coefficients for x. In Problem 5.4, Exploring Window Settings, they adjust the window to display different parts of the graph. In Problem 5.5, Revisiting Jean's Problem, students compare solutions done by hand in Problem 5.2 to those found using graphing calculators.

Mathematical and Problem-Solving Goals

- *To locate points and lines on a coordinate grid using all four quadrants*
- *To set up a coordinate grid on a graphing calculator by naming the scale and maximum and minimum values of x and y*
- *To graph linear equations using a graphing calculator*
- *To informally observe the effects of opposite coefficients and adding a constant to $y = ax$*
- *To answer questions using equations, tables, and graphs*

Materials

Problem	For students	For the teacher
All	Graphing calculators (with the capacity to display a function as a table), coordinate grids and graphing calculator grids (provided as blackline masters)	Transparencies 5.1A to 5.5 (optional), transparencies of coordinate grids and graphing calculator grids (optional), overhead display model of the student's graphing calculator (optional)
5.4	Grid paper	
ACE	Grid paper, coordinate grids, and graphing calculator grids (optional)	

Student Pages 67–82 | Teaching the Investigation 82a–82o

INVESTIGATION 5

Coordinate Grids

In previous units, you created and studied coordinate graphs. Coordinate graphs let you look at the relationship between two variables and observe how a change in one variable affects the other variable. All the points on the graphs you have worked with so far have had coordinates greater than or equal to 0. In this investigation, you will see how the coordinate grid can be extended in order to plot points with negative coordinates.

5.1 Extending the Coordinate Grid

The x-axis on a coordinate grid is a horizontal number line, and the y-axis is a vertical number line. On the coordinate grids you have worked with so far, all the values on the x- and y-axes have been greater than or equal to 0.

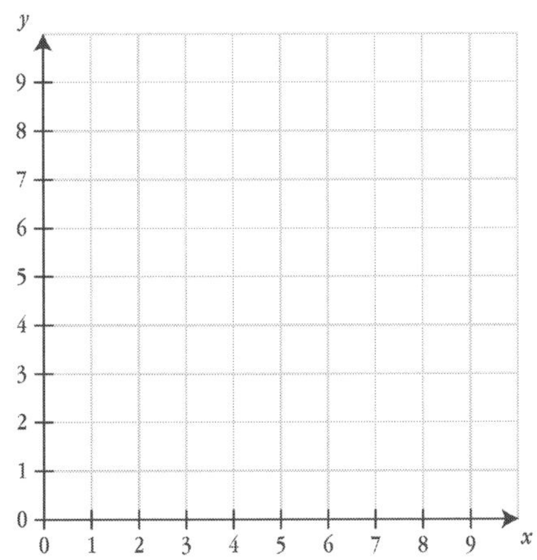

5.1

Extending the Coordinate Grid

At a Glance

Grouping:* *pairs

Launch

- Review the plotting of points in the first quadrant of a coordinate grid.
- Discuss and locate points on the full four-quadrant coordinate grid.

Explore

- As pairs work on the problem and follow-up, make sure they are correctly locating points.
- Ask questions relating point coordinates to grid quadrants.

Summarize

- Discuss students' answers to the problem and follow-up.

Assignment Choices

ACE questions 2–5, 13, and unassigned choices from earlier problems

Just as we extended the number line in Investigation 1 to include negative numbers, we can extend the *x*- and *y*-axes of the coordinate grid to include negative numbers.

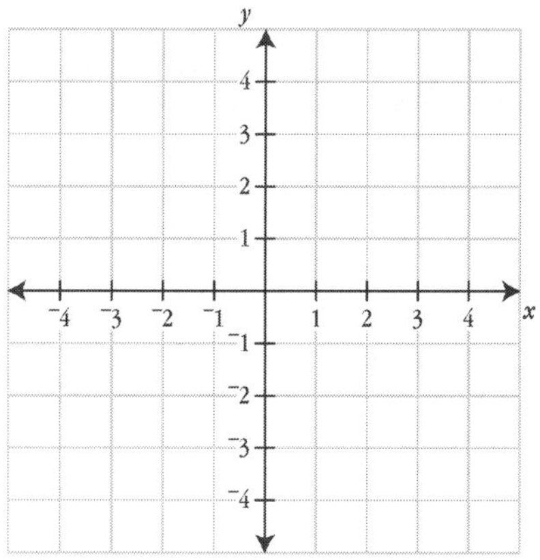

When the axes are extended, they divide the grid into four regions called ***quadrants.*** We can number these quadrants, starting with the region at the upper right and continuing counterclockwise. The quadrants are usually numbered by using roman numerals as shown below.

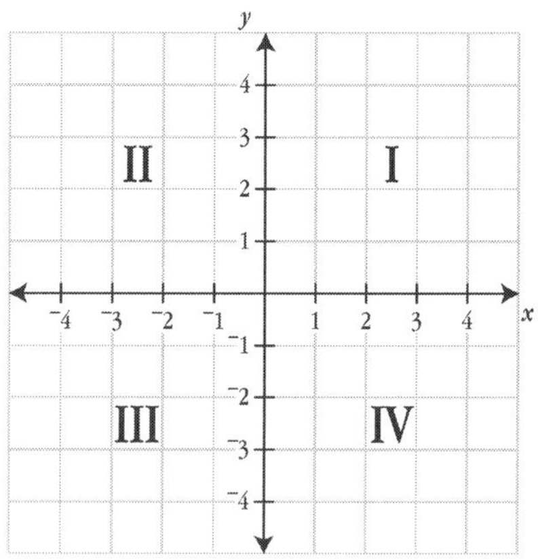

Melina made a coordinate grid and plotted the points (4, 3), (⁻3, 1), (⁻4, ⁻5), and (3, ⁻3). Study her work, and see if you can figure out what she did.

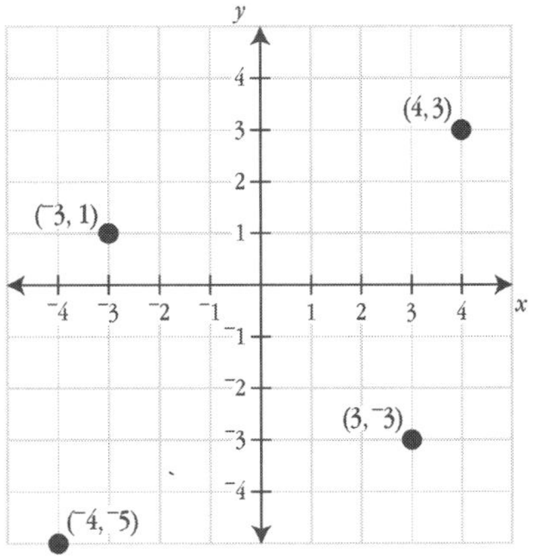

Recall that the two numbers that describe a point are called the *coordinates* of the point. The first number is the *x-coordinate,* and the second number is the *y-coordinate.* For example, the first point Melina plotted has coordinates (4, 3); the *x*-coordinate is 4, and the *y*-coordinate is 3.

Problem 5.1

A. Describe how Melina located each of the four points on the coordinate grid.

B. What polygon could you make by connecting the four points? Justify your answer.

C. On a coordinate grid, plot four points that are the vertices of a square, such that both coordinates of each point are positive integers.

D. On a coordinate grid, plot four points that are the vertices of a square, such that both coordinates of each point are negative integers.

E. On a coordinate grid, plot four points that are the vertices of a square, such that one point has two negative-integer coordinates, one point has two positive-integer coordinates, and each of the other points has one positive-integer coordinate and one negative-integer coordinate.

F. Two vertices of a square are (3, 1) and (⁻1, 1). Find the coordinates for every pair of points that could be the other two vertices.

Answers to Problem 5.1

A. See page 82h.

B. If you connect the four points in the order given, you make a parallelogram, as the opposite sides of the four-sided figure are parallel and of equal length. (Note: Students may not have formal ways to verify that opposite sides are parallel, but they can reason informally using visual clues or by observing that the lines rise and fall in the same way on the grid.)

C. Possible answer: (2, 1), (5, 1), (5, 4), (2, 4)

D. Possible answer: (⁻4, ⁻5), (⁻4, ⁻3), (⁻2, ⁻5), (⁻2, ⁻3)

E. Possible answer: (2, 1), (⁻1, ⁻2), (⁻1, 1), (2, ⁻2)

F. (3, 5) and (⁻1, 5), (3, ⁻3) and (⁻1, ⁻3), (1, 3) and (1, ⁻1) (Note: Students may miss the last pair of points.)

Problem 5.1 Follow-Up

Imagine that you can walk on a coordinate grid. Each integer unit is one step, and you must stay on the grid lines. Suppose you want to walk from point (4, 2) to point (2, 1), taking the least number of steps possible.

You could go 2 steps to the left and then 1 step down.

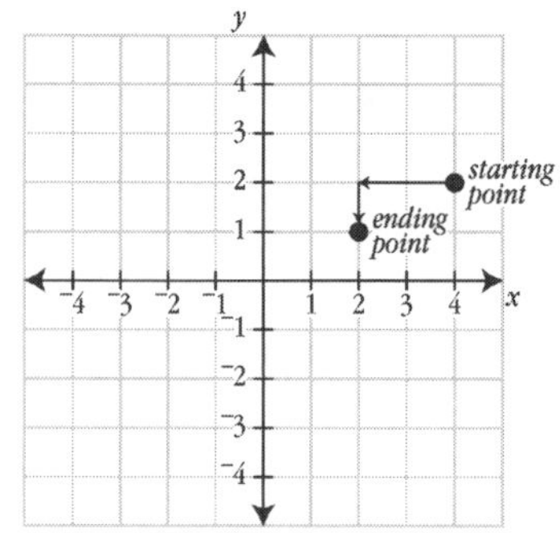

Or you could go 1 step down and then 2 steps to the left.

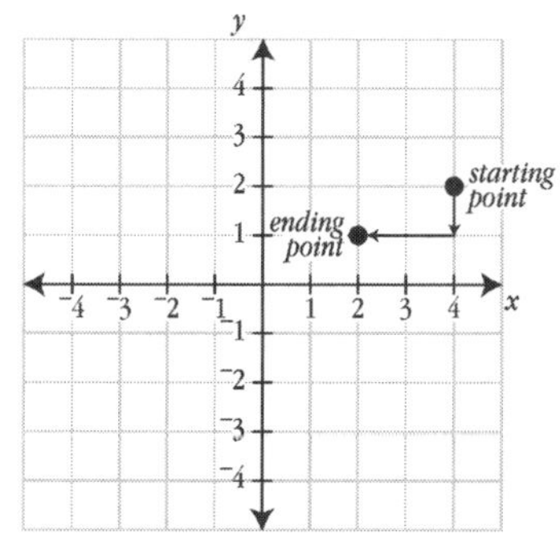

Paths between two points that require the least possible number of steps are called *minimal paths.*

1. For each pairs of points, describe two minimal paths from the first point to the second point.

a. ($^-4$, $^-2$) to (5, 3) **b.** ($^-4$, 3) to (5, 2) **c.** (2, $^-4$) to ($^-1$, $^-2$)

2. a. Locate two points on the coordinate grid such that it will take 12 steps to travel from one of the points to the other on a minimal path.

b. Will every one name the same two points for part a? Why do you think this is so?

Answers to Problem 5.1 Follow-Up

1. a. Possible answer: Go right 9 units and up 5 units. Or, go right 5 units, up 2 units, right 4 units, and up 3 units. Each path is 14 units long.

   b. Possible answer: Go right 9 units and down 1 unit. Or, go right 5 units, down 1 unit, and right 4 units. Each path is 10 units long.

   c. Possible answer: Go left 3 units and up 2 units. Or, go left 1 unit, up 2 units, and left 2 units. Each path is 5 units long.

2. a. Possible answer: A minimal path from ($^-1$, 5) to (5, $^-1$) is 12 units long.

   b. no; There is an infinite number of answers because from any point, many points are 12 steps away.

5.2 Breaking Even

Jean is planning to start a bicycle tune-up business. She figures out that her start-up costs will be \$800 to buy the tools and parts she needs. She decides to charge \$60 for each tune-up. She comes up with the following equation to determine her profit:

$$P = 60t - 800$$

where P is her profit in dollars, and t is the number of tune-ups.

If she does 30 tune-ups ($t = 30$), her profit will be

$$P = (60 \times 30) - 800 = \$1000$$

Jean wants to use her equation to calculate her ***break-even point***. That is, she wants to find out the number of tune-ups she will have to do before she begins to make a profit. Then, she wants to figure out how her profit will change with each tune-up after this break-even point.

Problem 5.2

A. Make a table that shows the profit Jean will earn for 0 through 20 tune-ups.

B. Plot the (tune-ups, profit) data from your table on a coordinate grid. Be sure to label the axes. Explain how you chose the scale for each axis.

C. What will Jean's profit be if she does only four tune-ups? How is this shown on the graph?

D. How many tune-ups will Jean have to do before she breaks even? How is this shown on the graph?

E. How does Jean's profit change with each tune-up she does? How is this shown on the graph?

5.2 Breaking Even

At a Glance

Grouping: individuals, then pairs

Launch

- Read the story of Jean's tune-up business.
- Make sure students understand the equations and variables.
- Review how to make tables and graphs. *(optional)*

Explore

- Let students work individually on the problem and share answers in pairs.
- Ask questions of pairs who are having trouble with the tables or graphs.
- Have pairs work on the follow-up.

Summarize

- Have students share solutions to the problem and follow-up.
- Make sure everyone understands how to find the break-even point in the tables and graphs.

Answers to Problem 5.2

A. See page 82h.

B. See page 82h.

C. Her profit would be $^-$\$560, shown on the graph as the point (4, $^-$560), which is below the *x*-axis. A negative profit of \$560 is really a loss of \$560.

D. She will have to do 14 tune-ups to break even. The graph of the line crosses the *x*-axis just past 13 tune-ups, and at this point the value of the profit is 0—no gain and no loss. However, since Jean can't do part of a tune-up, she would have to do 14 to pass the break-even point.

E. For each tune-up, profit goes up \$60. This shows up in the rise of the graph from left to right. (Students may use the word *slope* to describe this rise in the graph, but they have not yet formally met the word in this curriculum.)

Assignment Choices

ACE questions 6, 11, and unassigned choices from earlier problems

5.3

Using a Calculator to Explore Lines

At a Glance

Grouping:* *pairs

Launch

- Review how to enter equations and display graphs and tables.
- Challenge students to notice how the sign of the coefficient of x affects the graph.
- Have pairs work on the problem and follow-up, one calculator per student if possible.

Explore

- Encourage students to notice what effect changes to the equation have on the graph of the equation.

Summarize

- Have students share their solutions to the problem.
- Ask questions about how changing the equation affects the graph.

Problem 5.2 Follow-Up

1. Jean figures out that she could decrease her start-up cost to $600 by buying used tools. She writes a new equation, $P = 60t - 600$, to determine her profit. What is the break-even point for this profit equation?

2. Jean's friend Chuck thinks Jean should advertise her business in the local paper. This would increase her costs, giving her the profit equation $P = 60t - 1200$. What is the break-even point for this profit equation?

5.3 Using a Calculator to Explore Lines

Jean has several profit equations, each based on a different start-up cost. She borrows her brother's graphing calculator so she can explore the graphs of the equations. Since she has never used the calculator before, she decides to start by experimenting with some simple equations.

Problem 5.3

A. **1.** Enter the equation $y = 4x$ into your graphing calculator as Y_1, and then press GRAPH to see a graph of the equation. Make a sketch of the graph you see.

2. Predict how the graph of $y = {}^-4x$ will differ from the graph of $y = 4x$. Then, enter the equation $y = {}^-4x$ as Y_2, and press GRAPH to see the graphs of both equations in the same window. Add a sketch of $y = {}^-4x$ to your sketch from part 1.

3. How are the graphs alike? How are they different?

B. **1.** Press TABLE to look at the table showing data for both equations ($y = 4x$ and $y = -4x$). You may need to use the ▶ key to see the Y_2 column. Copy part of the table onto your paper.

2. For each value of x in the table, look at the two corresponding values of y (Y_1 and Y_2). How are the two y values for a given x value related? How does this relationship show up in the graph?

C. With your graphing calculator, experiment with each set of equations. Look at the graphs and the tables. Record your observations.

1. $y = 4x + 5$ and $y = {}^-4x + 5$

2. $y = 4x - 5$ and $y = {}^-4x - 5$

Assignment Choices

ACE question 14 and unassigned choices from earlier problems

Answers to Problem 5.2 Follow-Up

1. Jean would need to do 10 tune-ups to break even.
2. Jean would need to do 20 tune-ups to break even.

Answers to Problem 5.3

See page 82h.

■ **Problem 5.3 Follow-Up**

In 1–3, predict what the graphs of the equations will look like. Then test your predictions by using a graphing calculator.

1. $y = 3x$ and $y = {}^-3x$
2. $y = 3x + 3$ and $y = {}^-3x + 3$
3. $y = 3x - 3$ and $y = {}^-3x - 3$
4. Give three other pairs of equations that will have a relationship similar to the pairs above.

5.4 Exploring Window Settings

Jean's brother tells her that she can change the section of the graph displayed on the calculator by using the WINDOW key. Jean decides to experiment with this key, using the equation $y = 3x + 2$.

Below are the window settings Jean used. You will need to refer to these settings as you work on Problem 5.4.

Window settings 1	Window settings 2
WINDOW	WINDOW
XMIN=0	XMIN=⁻10
XMAX=10	XMAX=10
XSCL=1	XSCL=1
YMIN=0	YMIN=⁻10
YMAX=10	YMAX=10
YSCL=1	YSCL=1

5.4 Exploring Window Settings

At a Glance

Grouping: pairs

Launch

- Talk with the class about setting minimum and maximum values for x and y and scales for the axes.
- Have students work in pairs on the problem.

Explore

- Remind students to record their results.
- Ask questions about using other scale settings.

Summarize

- Talk about students' results for each part of the problem.
- Have students compare the graphs of the two equations.
- Discuss the follow-up questions.

Answers to Problem 5.3 Follow-Up

See page 82i.

Assignment Choices

ACE questions 1, 7–10, 12, and unassigned choices from earlier problems (optional: distribute Labsheet 5.ACE for 1 and 7–10)

Problem 5.4

A. On paper, make a table of x and y values for the equation $y = 3x + 2$.

B. On grid paper, sketch a graph of $y = 3x + 2$.

C. Enter the equation $y = 3x + 2$ into your graphing calculator, and press GRAPH. Make a sketch of the graph you see. How does this graph compare with the graph you drew by hand?

D. If you press WINDOW, you will see a screen that allows you to change the section of the graph displayed in the window. Change the settings to those shown in "Window settings 1" on the previous page, and then press GRAPH to see the graph of $y = 3x + 2$ in the new window.

1. Make a sketch of the graph you see.
2. How does this graph compare with the graph you drew by hand in part B?
3. How does this graph compare with the graph you made with your calculator in part C?
4. Explain what you think each entry on the "Window settings 1" screen means.

E. On paper, make a table of x and y values for the equation $y = 2x$.

F. On grid paper, sketch a graph of $y = 2x$.

G. Enter the equation $y = 2x$ into your graphing calculator, and press GRAPH. Make a sketch of the graph you see.

H. Change the window settings to those shown in "Window settings 2" on the previous page, and then press GRAPH to see the graph of $y = 2x$ in the new window.

1. Make a sketch of the graph you see.
2. How does this graph compare with the graph you drew by hand in part F?
3. How does this graph compare with the graph you made with your calculator in part G?
4. Explain what you think each entry on the "Window settings 2" screen means.

Answers to Problem 5.4

See page 82j.

Problem 5.4 Follow-Up

1. In part D of Problem 5.4, what happened to the coordinate grid on your calculator when you changed the window settings? Why?
2. Change the window settings so that only quadrant III of the coordinate grid is displayed. Record the window settings you used.
3. Graph $y = 2x$ in this new window. Make a sketch of the graph you see.
4. Except for the point (0,0), which quadrants contain none of the points on the graph of $y = 2x$?
5. Which window settings would you use to display only quadrant II? Quadrant IV?

5.5 Revisiting Jean's Problem

Jean uses her brother's graphing calculator to display the graph of her original profit equation, $P = 60t - 800$. She lets the number of tune-ups, t, be the x variable and the profit, P, be the y variable. She uses the window settings shown below at the left and gets the display shown below at the right.

```
WINDOW
 XMIN=⁻10
 XMAX=10
 XSCL=1
 YMIN=⁻10
 YMAX=10
 YSCL=1
```

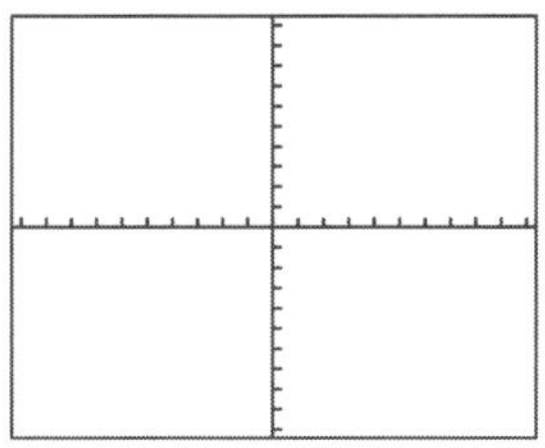

Only the axes appear in the display. There is no sign of the graph anywhere! Jean reasons that the window shown on the screen does not include any of the points on her graph. She needs to change her window settings so that the graph of her equation will show.

Think about this!

What information could Jean use to help her choose an appropriate window setting?

5.5 Revisiting Jean's Problem

At a Glance

Grouping: individuals, then pairs

Launch

- Review students' answers to Problem 5.2.
- Have students enter Jean's equation and press GRAPH.

Explore

- Have students work individually and then compare their work in pairs.
- Ask questions to help students interpret the data realistically.
- Let pairs work on the follow-up.

Summarize

- Have students share their answers to the problem and follow-up.
- As a class, discuss the window settings and how they influence what is displayed.

Answers to Problem 5.4 Follow-Up

1. The window moved from showing all four quadrants to show only the first quadrant. This happened because we changed the minimum values for x and y. Changing the minimum for x moved the window to the right; changing the minimum for y moved the window up.
2. To display only quadrant III, the maximum values for x and y must be 0, and the minimum values for x and y must be negative.
3. See page 82l.
4. None of the points that lie on $y = 2x$, except (0, 0), are in quadrants II and IV.
5. See page 82l.

Assignment Choices

Unassigned choices from earlier problems

Problem5.5

In the following questions, use Jean's profit equation $P = 60t - 800$ and your work from Problem 5.2.

A. 1. In the table of data you made in Problem 5.2, what range of values did you use for the number of tune-ups?

2. What range of values did you use for the profit?

B. Enter Jean's profit equation into your calculator. Use the number of tune-ups as the x variable and the profit as the y variable. Use your answers to part A to help you decide how to adjust the window settings so that you will be able to see the graph of the profit equation. Press GRAPH to display the graph. Make a sketch of the graph you see on the screen.

C. How is the break-even point shown on the graph?

D. Look at the table of data on your calculator. How is the break-even point shown in the table?

Problem 5.5 Follow-Up

1. Recall that Jean wrote the equation $P = 60t - 600$ to represent the profit she would make if she bought used tools instead of new tools. Find an appropriate window for viewing the graph of this profit equation. Graph the equation on a calculator. Make a sketch of what you see.

2. Jean wrote the equation $P = 60t - 1200$ to represent the profit she would make if she advertised in the local paper. Find an appropriate window for viewing the graph of this profit equation. Graph the equation on a calculator. Make a sketch of what you see.

3. Find the break-even points for the equations in 1 and 2.

Answers to Problem 5.5

A. 1. Possible answer: The range of tune-ups was 0 to 20.

2. Possible answer: The range of values for profit was $^{-}800$ to 400.

B–D. See page 82l.

Answers to Problem 5.5 Follow-Up

See page 82m.

Applications • Connections • Extensions

As you work on these ACE questions, use your calculator whenever you need it.

Applications

1. **a.** When the window settings on the left are used, the coordinate axes look like those shown on the right. Copy the axes, and label the tick marks with the appropriate scale values.

```
WINDOW
 XMIN=⁻10
 XMAX=10
 XSCL=2
 YMIN=⁻10
 YMAX=10
 YSCL=5
```

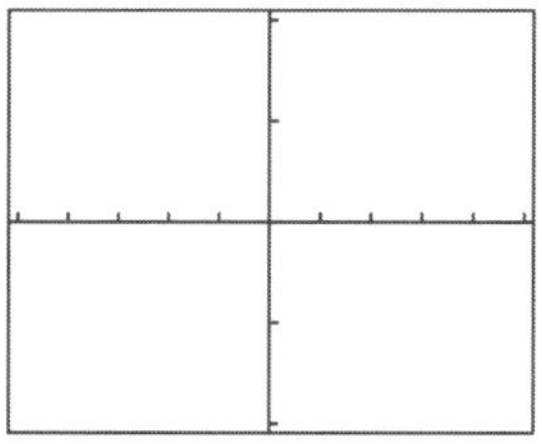

2. **b.** Sketch a graph of the equation $y = {}^{-}2x$ on the axes.

In 2–5, use the coordinates of the points to figure out what scale interval was used on each axis.

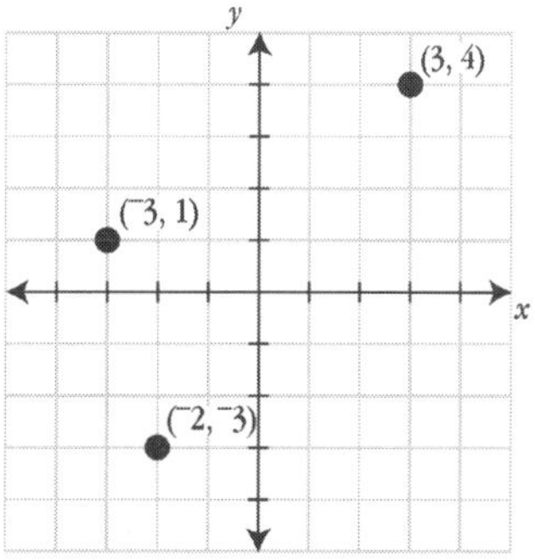

Answers

Applications

1. See below left.
2. x scale = 1, y scale = 1

1a.

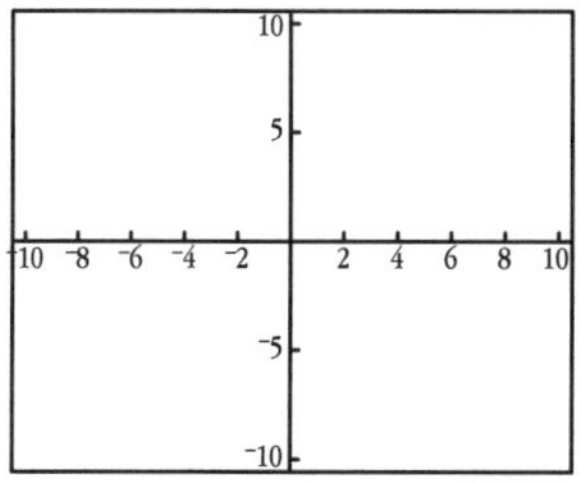

1b.

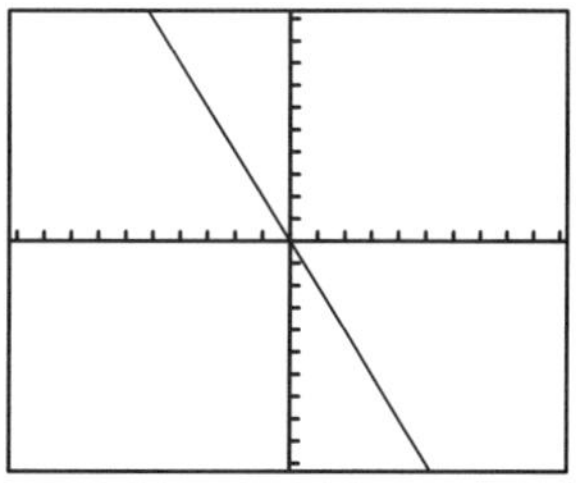

ACE

3. x scale = 1, y scale = 2
4. x scale = 5, y scale = 1
5. x scale = 5, y scale = 5

3.

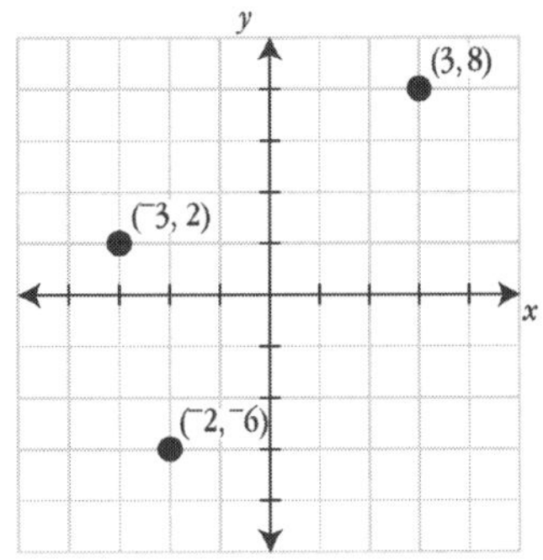

4.

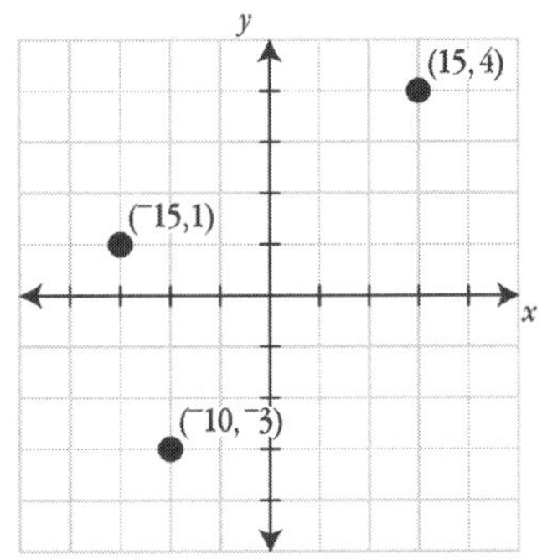

5.

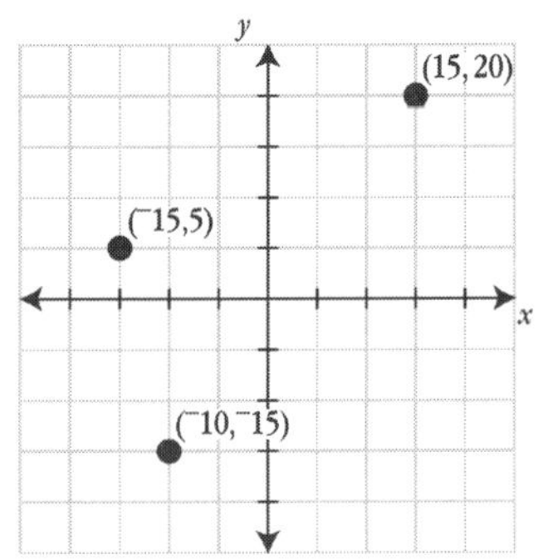

6. The graph at the right shows the relationship between the number of riders on a bike tour and the cost of providing snacks for the riders.

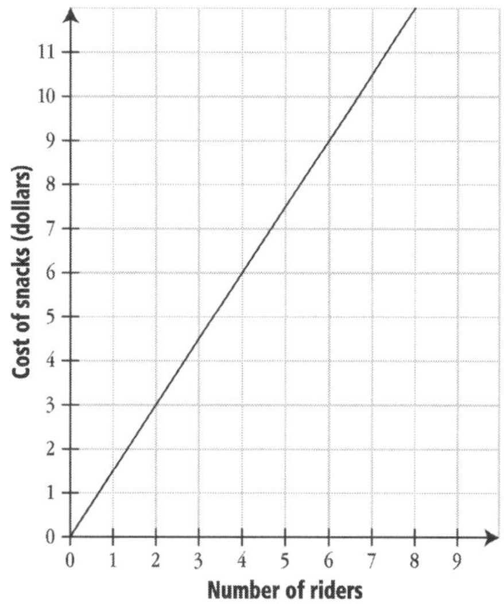

a. What is the cost of a snack for one rider?

b. What is the total cost of snacks for eight riders?

c. If snacks for all the riders cost $18, how many riders are there?

d. If there were 100 riders, what would be the total cost for the snacks? Explain how you got your answer.

In 7–10, tell which graph on the screen on the left below matches the equation, and explain how you know you are right. The screen on the right shows the settings that were used for the display window.

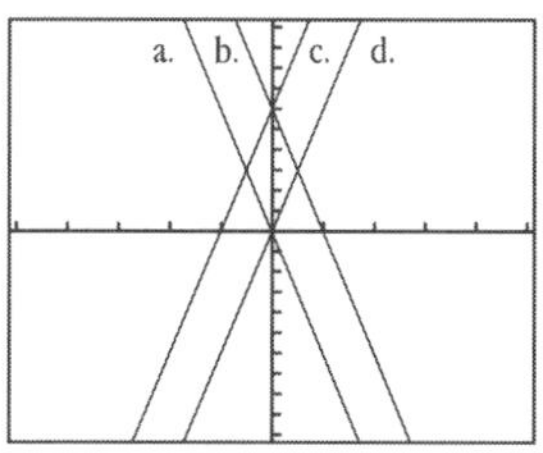


```
WINDOW
 XMIN=-5
 XMAX=5
 XSCL=1
 YMIN=-10
 YMAX=10
 YSCL=1
```

7. $y = 5x$

8. $y = {}^{-}5x$

9. $y = 5x + 6$

10. $y = {}^{-}5x + 6$

6a. $1.50

6b. $12

6c. Snacks cost $1.50 for one rider, so $18 is the cost of snacks for $18 \div 1.50 = 12$ riders.

6d. The graph shows that for each rider the cost of snacks increases by $1.50, so snacks would cost $100 \times \$1.50 = \$150.00$ for 100 riders.

7. $y = 5x$ is graph d

8. $y = {}^{-}5x$ is graph a

9. $y = 5x + 6$ is graph c

10. See page 82n.

Connections

11. Possible answer: On a number line, subtraction is reversing the direction of addition, so by subtracting a positive 73 you move to the left 73 units to the point 12. To add ⁻73 you go to the left 73 units, so the result is the same, 12. On a chip board, 85 – 73 means to take away 73, which can be done by removing 73 black chips; you are left with 12 black chips, so the answer is 12. The sentence 85 + ⁻73 means to add 73 red chips. The 73 red chips can be paired with 73 black chips and removed from the board, and there will be 12 black chips remaining. The net result is to remove 73 black chips, so this is the same as 85 – 73.

12a. If they worked 0 weeks, they would make $0. This is shown on the graph by the line going through the origin (0, 0), the point that represents 0 weeks of work on the *x*-axis and $0 of income on the *y*-axis.

12b. The point (⁻2, ⁻160) does not make sense in the context of this problem, because the ⁻2 means the students would have worked negative 2 weeks and would have lost $160.

Connections

11. Explain why 85 – 73 is equivalent to 85 + ⁻73.

12. Three students—Sami, Manoj, and Aimee—started a lawn-mowing business. They made this table and graph to relate their income in dollars (the *y* values) to the number of weeks worked (the *x* values). The third screen shows the window settings they used for the graph.

X	Y1
1	80
2	160
3	240
4	320
5	400
6	480
X=1	

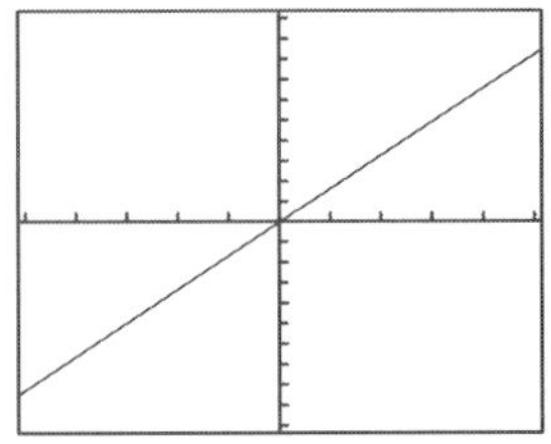

```
WINDOW
 XMIN=⁻10
 XMAX=10
 XSCL=2
 YMIN=⁻1000
 YMAX=1000
 YSCL=100
```

a. How much income would the students make if they worked 0 weeks? How is this shown on the graph?

b. Locate the point (⁻2, ⁻160) on the graph. What does this point represent in the context of the situation presented? Is this situation possible? Explain your thinking.

13. The following table gives the temperature (in °C) in Fairbanks, Alaska, for each month over two consecutive years.

Month	Temperature in year 1 (°C)	Temperature in year 2 (°C)
January	−25	−27
February	−20	−23
March	−13	−12
April	−2	−4
May	+9	+10
June	+15	+12
July	+17	+15
August	+14	+16
September	+7	+9
October	−4	0
November	−16	−16
December	−23	−23

a. Find the median and mean temperatures for these two years.

b. Make a coordinate graph that shows how the temperature changed over these two years.

Extensions

14. a. Name five pairs of numbers with a sum of −3.

b. Plot the pairs of numbers from part a, and connect the points.

c. Find the coordinates of a point on the connecting line. (Choose a point that is different from the points you plotted in part b.) What is the sum of these coordinates? Pick another point on the line and find the sum of its coordinates. If you picked a third point on this line, what do you think the sum of its coordinates would be?

d. What would a graph of pairs of numbers whose sum is +8 look like? Justify your answer.

13b. **Temperature in Fairbanks**

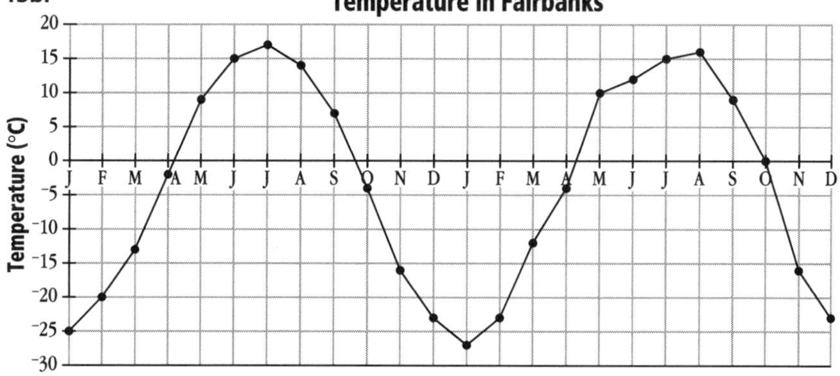

13a. From lowest to highest, the temperatures are −27, −25, −23, −23, −23, −20, −16, −16, −13, −12, −4, −4, −2, 0, 7, 9, 9, 10, 12, 14, 15, 15, 16, 17. The median falls between the twelfth and thirteenth temperatures, or between −4 and −2, which is a median of −3°C. The mean temperature is −84 ÷ 24 = −3.5°C.

13b. See below left.

Extensions

14a. Possible answer: 2 and −5, 0 and −3, −1 and −2, −4 and 1, −6 and 3

14b. See page 82n.

14c. Possible answer: The coordinates of (−3, 0) and (1.5, −4.5) both have a sum of −3. I think this will always be true.

14d. See page 82o.

Possible Answers

1. See 82o.

2. You have to look at the meaning of the variables in the problem. For example, if a variable represents numbers of people, only positive whole numbers make sense. If a variable represents profit, positive and negative numbers make sense because we may make money or we may lose money.

Mathematical Reflections

In this investigation, you extended the coordinate grid to include points with negative coordinates, and you used your graphing calculator to explore graphs of equations. These questions will help you summarize what you have learned:

1. How can you tell which quadrant a point will fall in by looking at its coordinates?
2. You have looked at several problem situations in which you figured out how to make a table of data. You also learned that if you can write an equation to describe how the variables are related, you can use a graphing calculator to graph the equation. How do you figure out what part of the entire graph actually makes sense in the real problem situation? Use an example to help explain.

Think about your answers to these questions, discuss your ideas with other students and your teacher, and then write a summary of your findings in your journal.

Tips for the Linguistically Diverse Classroom

Original Rebus The Original Rebus technique is described in detail in *Getting to Know Connected Mathematics*. Students make a copy of the text before it is discussed. During the discussion, they generate their own rebuses for words they do not understand; the words are made comprehensible through pictures, objects, or demonstrations. Example: Question 1—Key words for which students might make rebuses are *quadrant* (a large + with one quadrant shaded), *point* (•), *coordinates* (x, y).

5.1 • Extending the Coordinate Grid

This problem introduces students to the expanded coordinate grid. You may want to refer to work done in the *Variables and Patterns* and *Stretching and Shrinking* units to help students remember where they have used coordinate grids before.

Launch

Introduce the problem. First, display only quadrant I of the transparent coordinate grid. With the class, label the tick marks in the positive direction on the two axes. Then, make sure students know how to locate points in this quadrant.

> We have used this kind of grid to make graphs before. How do we locate points on this grid?

When you are satisfied that students know how to locate points in the first quadrant, introduce the extension of the x- and y-axes by revealing the other three quadrants.

> You have seen the number line extended to represent numbers that are less than 0. The two axes on the coordinate grid are number lines too. They are perpendicular to each other and can show both positive and negative numbers.

Work with your students to finish labeling the tick marks on each axis using negative integers. Then, have them locate Melina's four points as discussed in the student edition. Label the four quadrants on the transparent grid to reinforce this idea. When students have an idea of how to locate points on the grid, let them work in pairs on the problem and follow-up.

Explore

Circulate to make sure students understand how to locate points. Ask students to tell which quadrant a particular point is in, and vice versa.

> What are the coordinates of a point that will fall in quadrant III? What about quadrant IV? Quadrant II?

Summarize

For each part of the problem, call on more than one pair of students to share their solution. A good way to share solutions is to have students plot points on a transparent coordinate grid.

Problem 5.1 is basically a get-to-know-the-coordinate-grid problem. However, parts C–E provide a context in which students must think hard about what is being asked and the relationships between coordinate pairs. An infinite number of solutions are possible for these questions. The key here is to encourage students to generalize about how the coordinates that define a square are related.

Most students will miss the third pair of coordinates possible for part F, in which the two points are the opposite, rather than adjacent, vertices of a square.

Discuss the follow-up questions, for which multiple solutions are possible. Two goals for these tasks are for students to become comfortable with a variety of answers and with finding their way around the coordinate grid.

5.2 • Breaking Even

The big idea in this problem is the concept of a break-even point. Be sure that students know what it means to break even. Be sure they can articulate that this is when expenditures and income are equal (or balance each other).

Launch

This problem is similar to one students explored in the *Variables and Patterns* unit. Go over the problem situation. Discuss the equations and the meaning of the variables. Review how to make a table and a graph if you think students need the instruction. Model the first couple of values for t.

If $t = 0$, then $P = 60(0) - 800 = ^-800$.
If $t = 1$, then $P = 60(1) - 800 = ^-740$.
If $t = 2$, then $P = 60(2) - 800 = ^-680$.

t	P
0	$^-800$
1	$^-740$
2	$^-680$

Explore

Let students work individually for a few minutes, then put them in pairs to share their ideas. When each pair has resolved their differences and answered the questions, they should move on to the follow-up questions.

As you monitor the class, look for pairs who are having trouble making tables and graphs. Ask questions to help them to focus on their work.

What should the labels in your table be?

Which variable will you put on the x-axis? How did you decide which variable should be used as the independent variable?

How can you use an x value to find a y value?

How are you scaling the axes?

Summarize

Let pairs share their solutions and thinking for each part of the problem and follow-up. Be sure they understand how to find the break-even point in the table and the graph for each version of the profit equation.

5.3 • Using a Calculator to Explore Lines

Students used graphing calculators in the *Variables and Patterns* unit to graph lines in the standard window. This problem will review their earlier work as well as raise the question of how graphs with opposite coefficients for the x variable are related—for example, how the graph of $y = 5x$ is related to the graph of $y = {}^{-}5x$.

Launch

Review how to enter an equation by pressing [Y=], how to press [GRAPH] to display the graph, and how to press [TABLE] to display the table.

Explain that in the problem, students will graph pairs of linear equations so that they can compare the graphs. Be sure everyone remembers how to enter a second equation as Y_2. The equations will be graphed on the same set of axes when [GRAPH] is pressed.

Remind students that they can always graph the lines on separate screens if they want to focus on a particular graph. It can become confusing when several graphs are displayed on the same screen. Remind students to record a sketch of their graphs.

Challenge the class to notice the difference between graphs when the coefficient of x is positive and when it is negative.

Have students work in pairs to explore the problem and follow-up. If you have enough calculators, give each person his or her own even though they are working with partners.

Explore

Encourage students to develop hypotheses about what will change a graph and to make up other equations in addition to those provided in order to test their hypotheses. Some of the things they might notice are the following:

- Changing the coefficient of x to its opposite changes the direction of the line.
- Adding a constant moves the line up or down on the y-axis.
- Changing the coefficient of x to a greater or smaller whole number changes the slope of the line.

Summarize

Have students share solutions to each part of the problem. Ask questions to help them summarize what they have learned.

> What effect does a negative coefficient for x have on the graph?

A typical response is that the graph of an equation with a positive coefficient for x goes up, and the graph of an equation with a negative coefficient for x goes down. (Since slope will be studied in a later unit, it is not important to require precise language here.)

> What influence on the graph does adding or subtracting a number (a constant) have?

Many students will be able to say that the line is shifted up or down by the amount of the constant number that is added. They may also connect the constant with the y-intercept of the equation, but it is not necessary to push for this understanding at this time.

For the Teacher: Numerical Values on the Graph

The equations in problem 1 of part C both cross the y-axis at 5. This point is the constant or b value (we are not suggesting that you introduce this concept to your class). The sign of the coefficient of x determines whether the graph rises or falls as you look from left to right across the graph. Positive indicates a rise in the graph; negative indicates a fall.

5.4 • Exploring Window Settings

This problem focuses students' attention on scaling the x- and y-axes. Graphing calculators do not label the axes, so students need to understand how the window settings allow these values to be set on the graphing calculator to display the section of the graph that is of interest. This is a simple introduction, as students will be using their graphing calculators to explore linearity in succeeding units. This problem just gets students thinking about the possibilities.

Launch

If you have an overhead display for a graphing calculator, use it to display a coordinate grid using the standard window. To access this window, press [ZOOM] [6]. The x-values range from $^-10$ to 10, and the y-values range from $^-10$ to 10. You can see this by pressing [WINDOW]. Otherwise, you may want to use a transparent graphing calculator grid.

> Where is the point (0, 0) on this grid? If the axes are marked with a scale of 1, how would the tick marks be labeled?
>
> What are the minimum and maximum values for x and for y that can be shown on this grid?

The minimum and maximum values depend on the grid and are found by counting the tick marks in each direction from (0, 0).

> Suppose the scales for the x-axis and y-axis were both 2 units per tick. How would the tick marks on the axis be labeled? What are the minimum and maximum values for x and y that can be shown on this grid with a scale of 2? *(double what they were for a scale of 1)*

It is a good idea to pace the class through finding the window screen. Ask students what they think the current values in the window screen mean and what will happen on the graph.

> Will the graph show all four quadrants or only one or two quadrants?

Ask why they think their answers are correct, but don't stress this. The point is to allow them to make conjectures and let the calculator provide evidence that they can use to check their ideas.

Talk students through changing the window from the standard settings (ZOOM 6) to set the x and y minimums to 0 and the x and y maximums to 10. Ask the students what happens when they do this. (The graph will have an x-axis scaled in units of 1, a maximum value of x set at 10, and a minimum value of x set at 0. The values for the y-axis will be the same. This means that we will see the graph for values of x between 0 and $^{+}10$ and y between 0 and $^{+}10$.) Ask students to return their windows to the standard settings.

> If we change the scale for the axes, we can change how much and what we show of our graphs. In this problem, you are going to explore how to change the scale of the axes and thus what portion of an equation that your calculator displays.
>
> Before we use the calculator, the first part of Problem 5.4 asks you to make a table and sketch a graph for $y = 3x + 2$ by hand. This gives you something to check your work on the graphing calculator against. Then you will experiment with your graphing calculator to observe what happens when you change the window settings to different minimum and maximum values of x and y and different scales.

Have students explore the problem in pairs.

Explore

Be sure students are recording what they try and what the result is in each case. Save the follow-up questions to do as part of the summary.

As pairs complete the problem, ask what would happen if they tried other scales for the x- and y-axes.

> Is it possible for the x-axis to be scaled by 1s and the y-axis to be scaled by 10s? What does this do to the graph?

Ask questions to encourage students to go beyond the problem and explore other window settings.

Summarize

The main idea you want to highlight in this summary is that students have control over the grid on which the graph will be displayed by adjusting the settings for the graph window. Every graphing calculator has these kinds of choices for the display.

In the process of discussing Problem 5.4, you will have opportunities to ask questions and to add comments that will help students think about the impact of the window settings on the graph.

Parts A and B are done by hand. Students will likely have made different choices about values for x and y pairs that they calculated for their tables. Some will probably have avoided negative values for x, and some may have only graphed in the first quadrant. Look for several different tables and graphs to make the point that our choices for our tables affect what our graphs look like. All of our graphs may be correct and yet look different.

Students will have done part C on the standard window, which (on Texas Instruments graphing calculators) shows all four quadrants and only the part of the grid between $^-10$ and $^+10$ in each direction.

Tell me about the differences between the graphs for parts C and D. How can you explain those differences?

In part D, the window settings have been changed to show only the first quadrant.

How does the information given in the window tell you that this is only the first quadrant? How do you know what part of the first quadrant will be showing?

Parts E–H ask students to repeat the sequence of questions with a different equation. Ask the same kinds of probing questions about what is showing on the graph and why this is what shows.

Ask students to compare the graphs of the two equations $y = 3x + 2$ and $y = 2x$ (using the same window) and discuss how are they alike and how are they different. Here are some observations students have made.

- Linda: "The graph of $y = 2x$ goes through the center of the grid, (0, 0), and the graph of $y = 3x + 2$ does not."
- Darcy: "The graph of $y = 3x + 2$ is higher on the y-axis above the point where the two graphs cross."
- Pedro: "The graph of $y = 3x + 2$ crosses the y-axis at $^+2$, which is related to the $^+2$ that is added to every value of $3x$ to get the value of y."
- Wesley: "The graph of $y = 3x + 2$ is steeper than the graph of $y = 2x$ as you look at the graph from left to right."

Discuss the follow-up questions, which explore moving the window around to view different quadrants. Have some students share their ideas. Different settings are possible, but all settings that show only quadrant III must have the maximums of x and y equal to 0 and the minimums set to negative numbers. Ask questions to check students' understanding.

Set your windows to show only the part of the graph of $y = x - 20$ that is in quadrants I and II.

Tell me your window settings. What parts of the window setting must be the same for all of us? What parts can be different and still show only quadrants I and II?

To show both quadrants, the x-axis must be set to show positive and negative values, so x minimum must be negative and x maximum must be positive. Every student should have set the minimum value for y to 0, and y maximum must be positive.

5.5 • Revisiting Jean's Problem

Students will now compare their paper-and-pencil methods to the graphing calculator method for solving the same problem.

Launch

Have students take out their solutions to Problem 5.2, which were done by hand. Explain that they will now look at a graphing calculator version of the problem. Reread Problem 5.2 with the class. You might want to review the answers students found for part A of Problem 5.2 and note the range of values in their tables.

Have students set their calculators to the standard window settings and graph the equation so that they can see Jean's dilemma.

> What you need to find is a window setting that will show the portion of the graph needed to answer the question, "What is the break-even point?

Explore

Have students work alone for a few minutes and then pair up to compare ideas. When they are satisfied that they have answered the questions correctly, they can move on to the follow-up.

As you circulate, look for students who are having difficulty with the window settings. Encourage them to experiment with different settings but to think about what settings would be reasonable. The table of values should be a starting point, but some students may need to expand their table of values to see what part of the graph is needed. Ask questions to encourage them to think about interpreting the data realistically.

> What range of values for x shows the most interesting part of the graph? What range of values for y goes with this range of values for x?
>
> In this equation, what does x stand for? *(the number of tune-ups)* Do negative values of x make sense?

The answers to questions like these will influence students' choices for the window settings.

Summarize

Discuss the problem and follow-up. Have several students share their answers and how they thought about the problem. You want the class to realize that there are many options for the window settings and that we must be careful to get the part of the graph that we want to see. Looking at the table can give us an idea of what range of values we want to display in the window. Also, you want to begin to help students make the connection between a point on the graph and the corresponding entry in the table and to values in the equation and vice versa.

> What do the coordinates of the point (10, $^{-}$200) mean in this problem? How does this point relate to the table? How does it relate to the equation?

Additional Answers

Answers to Problem 5.1

A. Melina used the first number in each pair to locate a point on the *x*-axis that represents that number, moving to the left of 0 for a negative number and to the right for a positive number. From that point on the *x*-axis, she went up (for a positive number) or down (for a negative number) the distance indicated by the second number, which relates to the *y*-axis.

Answers to Problem 5.2

A.

t	P
0	$^-800$
1	$^-740$
2	$^-680$
3	$^-620$
4	$^-560$
5	$^-500$
6	$^-440$
7	$^-380$
8	$^-320$
9	$^-260$
10	$^-200$

t	P
11	$^-140$
12	$^-80$
13	$^-20$
14	40
15	100
16	160
17	220
18	280
19	340
20	400

B. Possible explanation: The profit seems to go from $^-800$ to 400, so I divided the vertical axis into intervals of 200. Smaller intervals will also work. The number of tune-ups goes from 0 to 20, so intervals of 2 for the horizontal axis will work, as well as smaller intervals.

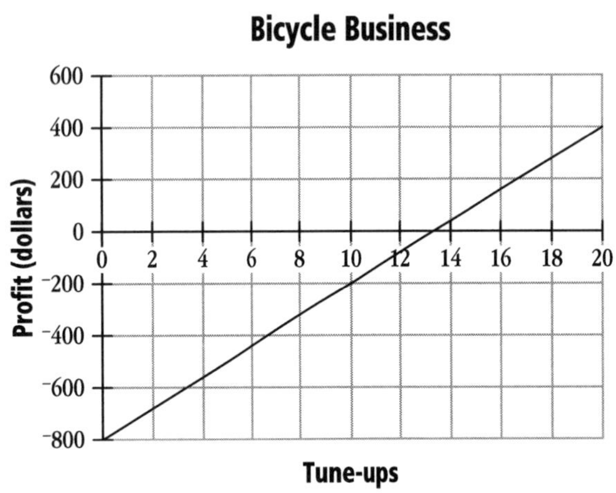

Answers to Problem 5.3

A. 1. $y = 4x$

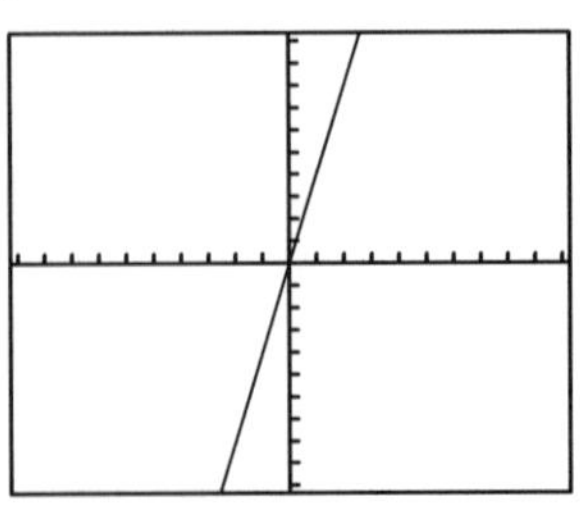

2. $y = 4x$ and $y = {}^{-}4x$

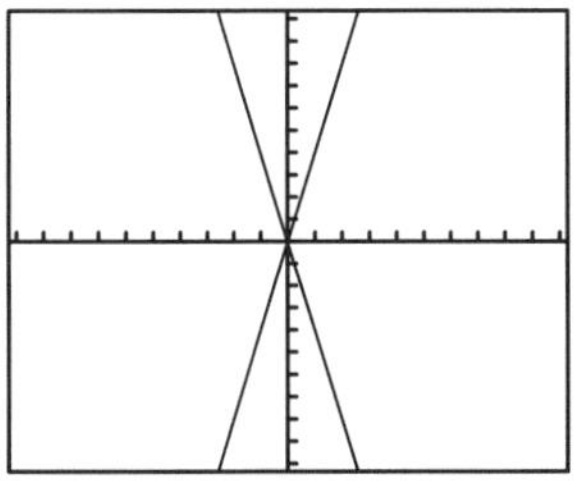

3. Both graphs go through (0, 0), but the graph of $y = 4x$ is going up (rising from left to right) while the graph of $y = {}^{-}4x$ is going down (falling from left to right).

B. 1. (Note: If students have only positive values for *x* and *y*, demonstrate how to use the arrow keys to show other table values.)

X	Y1	Y2
-3	-12	12
-2	-8	8
-1	-4	4
0	0	0
1	4	-4
2	8	-8
3	12	-12
X=-3		

2. The values of *y* for a particular value of *x* in the two equations are opposites of each other. If the coefficient of the *x* variable is positive, the graph rises from left to right. If it is negative, the graph falls from left to right.

C. 1. $y = 4x + 5$ and $y = {}^{-}4x + 5$

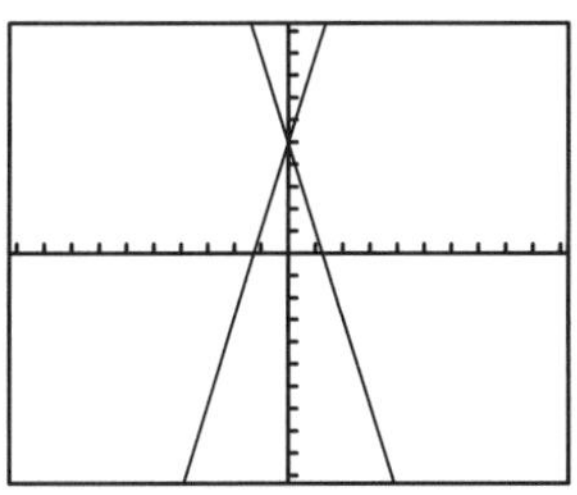

X	Y1	Y2
-2	-3	13
-1	1	9
0	5	5
1	9	1
2	13	-3
3	17	-7
4	21	-11
X=-2		

2. $y = 4x - 5$ and $y = {}^{-}4x - 5$

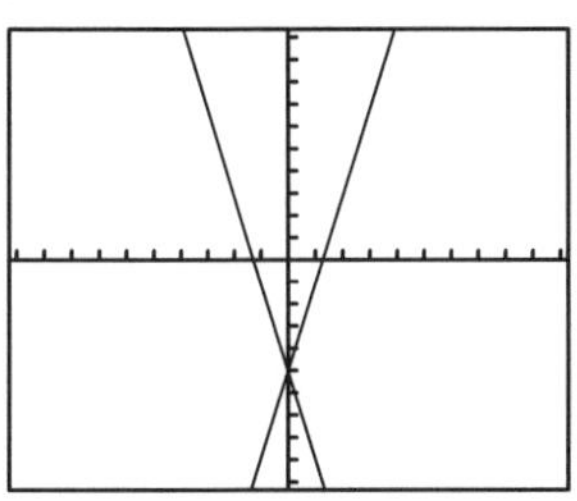

X	Y1	Y2
-2	-13	3
-1	-9	-1
0	-5	-5
1	-1	-9
2	3	-13
3	7	-17
4	11	-21
X=-2		

Answers to Problem 5.3 Follow-Up

1. $y = 3x$ and $y = {}^{-}3x$

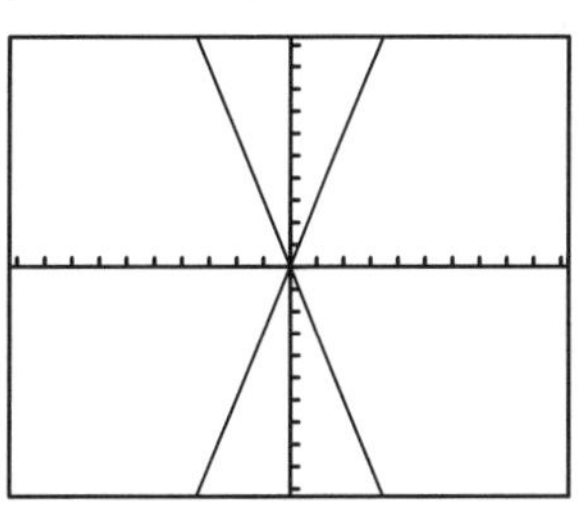

2. $y = 3x + 3$ and $y = {}^-3x + 3$

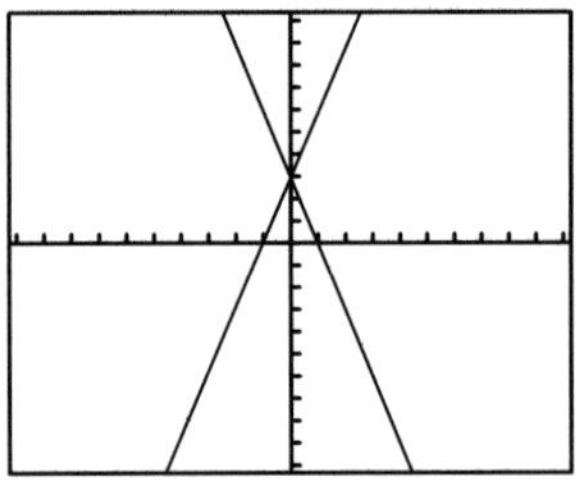

3. $y = 3x - 3$ and $y = {}^-3x - 3$

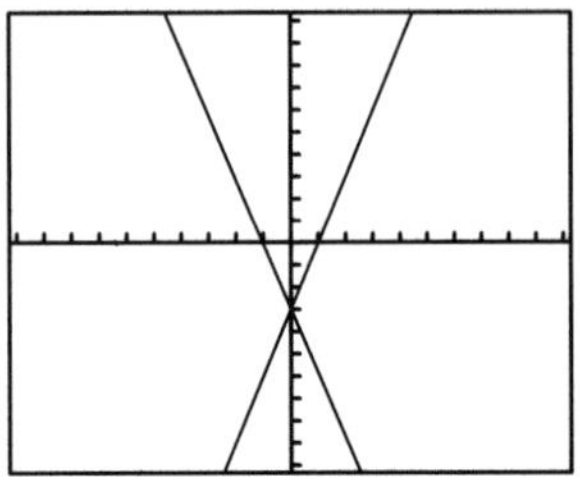

For the Teacher: Six Graphs at Once

Here are the six graphs in questions 1–3 displayed all together. You may want to suggest that students try this on their calculators. (Note: Graphing calculators differ in how many functions they allow you to graph at once. The TI-80 allows only four functions.)

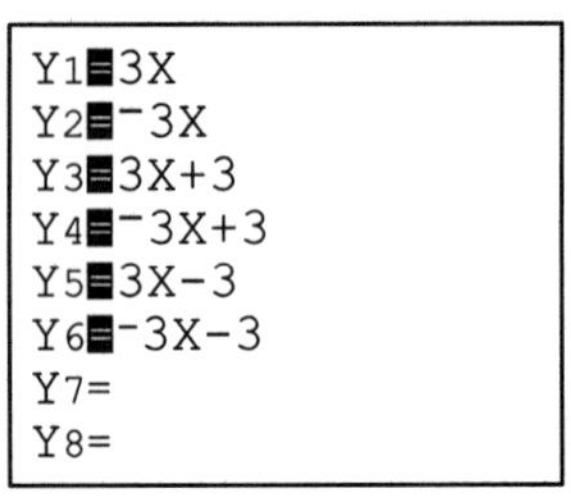

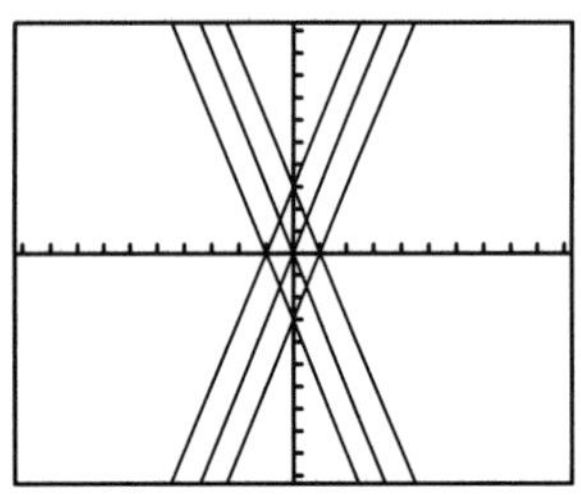

---

4. Possible answer: $y = 0.5x$ and $y = {}^-0.5x$, $y = 0.5x - 4$ and $y = {}^-0.5x - 4$, $y = 0.5x + 4$ and $y = {}^-0.5x + 4$

Answers to Problem 5.4

A. Possible table:

x	0	1	2	3	4	5	6	7	8	9
y	2	5	8	11	14	17	20	23	26	29

B. $y = 3x + 2$

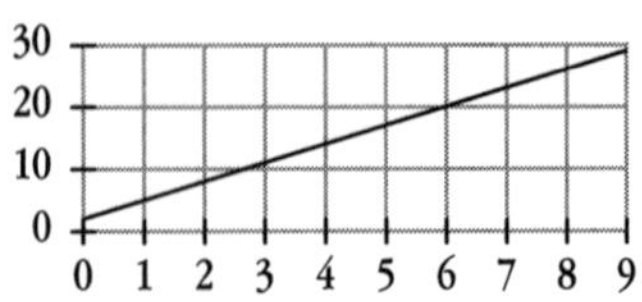

C. $y = 3x + 2$

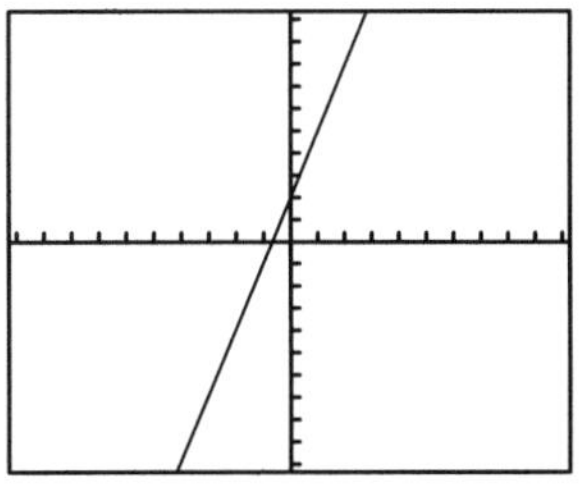

Possible answer: This graph looks different from mine, because it shows negative values and is not stretched out like my graph is.

D. 1. $y = 3x + 2$

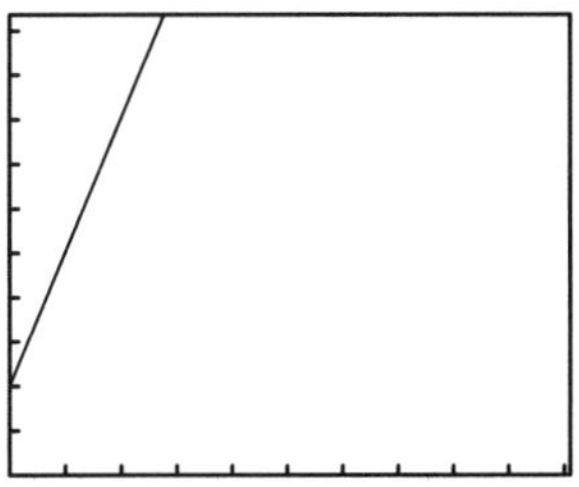

2. Possible answer: It shows just the first quadrant, like my graph does, but my graph is more stretched out.
3. The two calculator graphs look different, because one shows all four quadrants and one shows only the first quadrant.
4. XMIN = 0 means that the smallest value of x shown on the grid is 0.
XMAX = 10 means that the greatest value of x shown on the grid is 10.
XSCL = 1 means that the scale used to label the tick marks on the x-axis is 1 unit per tick.
YMIN = 0 means that the smallest value of y shown on the grid is 0.
YMAX = 10 means that the greatest value of y shown on the grid is 10.
YSCL = 1 means that the scale used to label the tick marks on the y-axis is 1 unit per tick.

E. Possible table:

x	0	1	2	3	4	5	6	7	8	9
y	0	2	4	6	8	10	12	14	16	18

F. $y = 2x$

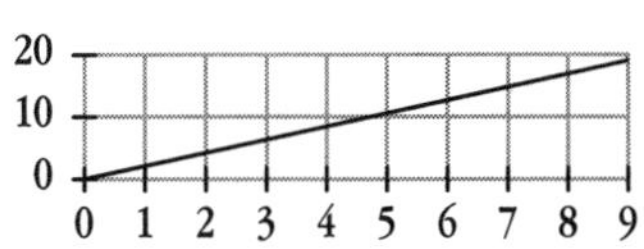

G. $y = 2x$

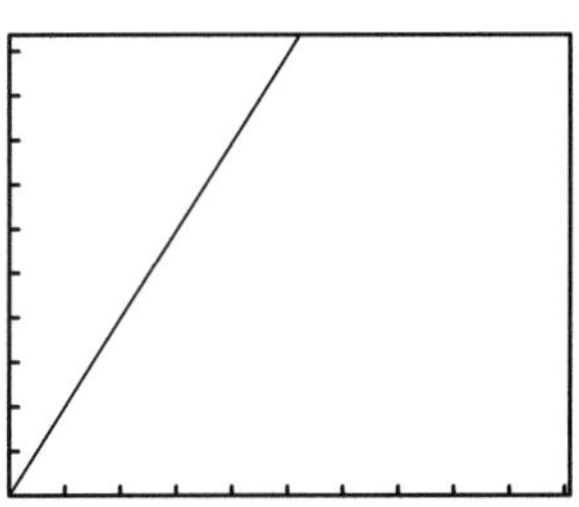

H. 1. $y = 2x$

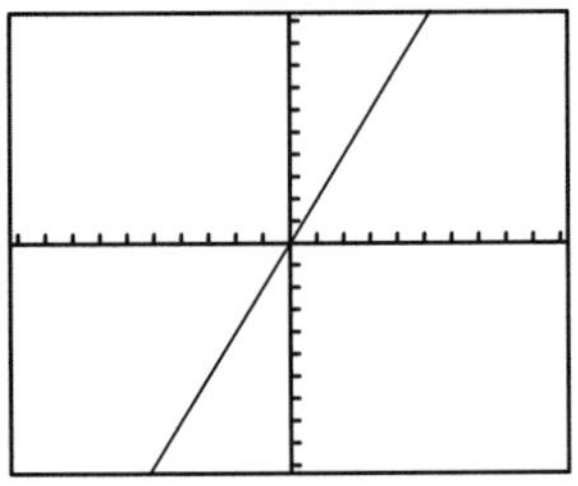

2. Possible answer: My graph shows only the first quadrant, and the calculator graph shows all four quadrants.

3. The two calculator graphs look different because one shows all four quadrants and one shows only the first quadrant.

4. XMIN = $^{-}10$ means that the smallest value of x shown on the grid is $^{-}10$.
XMAX = 10 means that the greatest value of x shown on the grid is 10.
XSCL = 1 means that the scale used to label the tick marks on the x-axis is 1 unit per tick.
YMIN = $^{-}10$ means that the smallest value of y shown on the grid is $^{-}10$.
YMAX = 10 means that the greatest value of y shown on the grid is 10.
YSCL = 1 means that the scale used to label the tick marks on the y-axis is 1 unit per tick.

Answers to Problem 5.4 Follow-Up

3. $y = 2x$

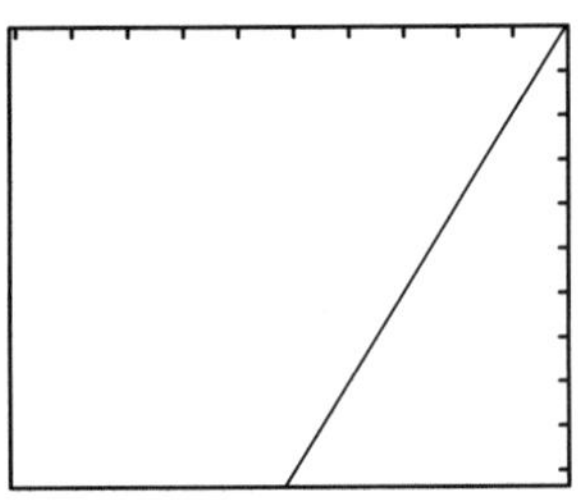

5. To display only quadrant II, the maximum value for x and the minimum value for y must be 0, the minimum value for x must be negative, and the maximum value for y must be positive. To display only quadrant IV, the minimum value for x and the maximum value for y must be 0, the maximum value for x must be positive, and the minimum value for y must be negative.

Answers to Problem 5.5

B. Possible answer: Use the values for tune-ups to set the scale (by 1s or 2s) with XMIN = 0 and XMAX = 20. Use the values for profit to set the scale (by 50s or 100s) and YMIN = $^{-}800$ or smaller and YMAX = some reasonable positive number.

```
WINDOW
 XMIN=0
 XMAX=20
 XSCL=2
 YMIN=⁻1200
 YMAX=1200
 YSCL=100
```

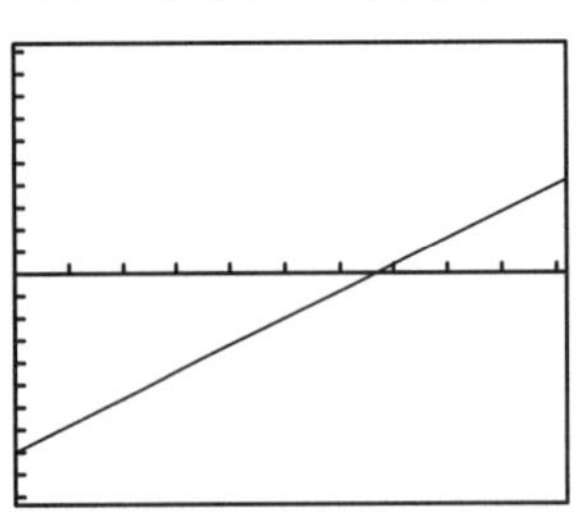

C. The break-even point is where the graph crosses the x-axis. At this point, the number of tune-ups generates an income equal to \$800. At that point, the profit, or y value, is 0.

D. The mathematical model says that the break-even point occurs when the number of tune-ups is $13\frac{1}{3}$, but since we cannot realistically have a part of a tune-up, it is reasonable to say 14 tune-ups. (In the table, we are looking for the point at which the number of tune-ups gives a y value of 0. Since the table uses a scale of 1, the solution will not appear on the table. The solution will be between tune-ups. You may want to talk to students about what makes sense in the real problem and what the mathematical model says.)

Answers to Problem 5.5 Follow-Up

1. Possible answer:

```
WINDOW
  XMIN=0
  XMAX=20
  XSCL=2
  YMIN=⁻600
  YMAX=800
  YSCL=100
```

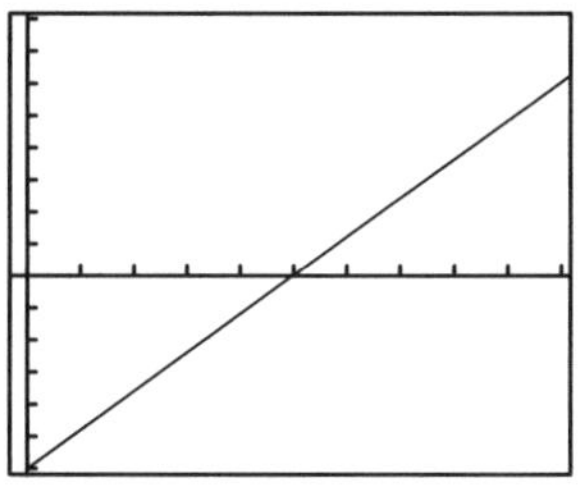

2. Possible answer:

```
WINDOW
  XMIN=0
  XMAX=50
  XSCL=5
  YMIN=⁻1500
  YMAX=300
  YSCL=100
```

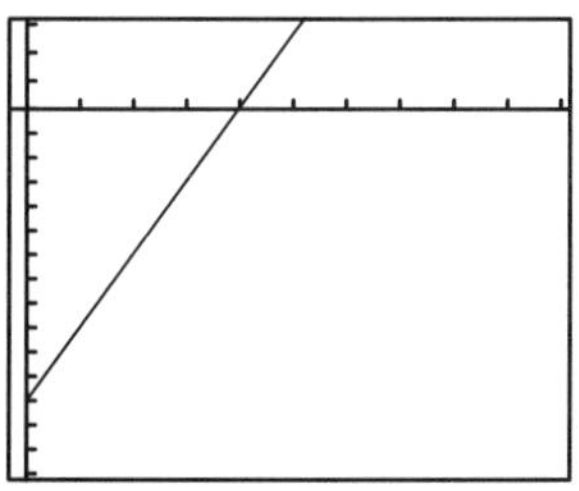

3. The break-even point for $P = 60t - 600$ is 10 tune-ups. The break-even point for $P = 60t - 1200$ is 20 tune-ups.

ACE Answers

Applications

10. $y = {}^-5x + 6$ is graph b

For the Teacher: Locating Points

Questions 7–10 can be solved by locating points. By choosing a point that satisfies the equation $y = 5x$—for example (1, 5)—and locating it on the grid, you can see which line contains that point and is therefore the graph of $y = 5x$. The same can be done for $y = {}^-5x$, picking the point (1, ⁻5) and finding the line that contains that point.

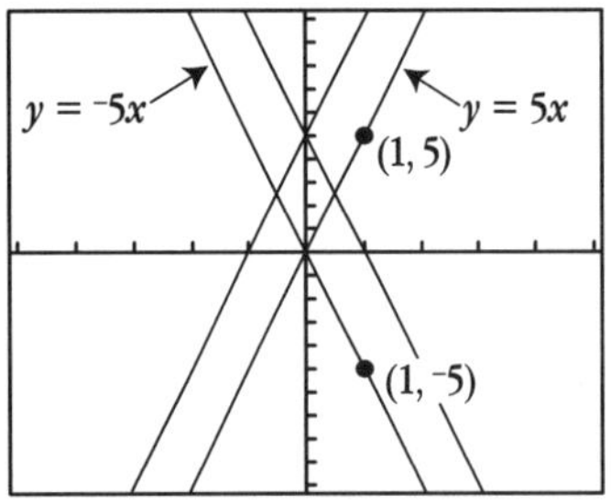

One point that satisfies $y = 5x + 6$ is (⁻2, ⁻4), and one point that satisfies $y = {}^-5x + 6$ is (1, 1). Some points, however, are not useful for identifying the graphs. For example, (0, 6) falls on both of these lines.

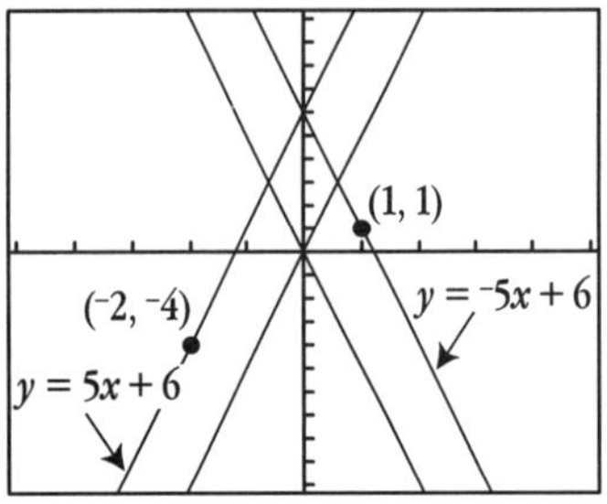

Extensions

14b.

Sums of ⁻3

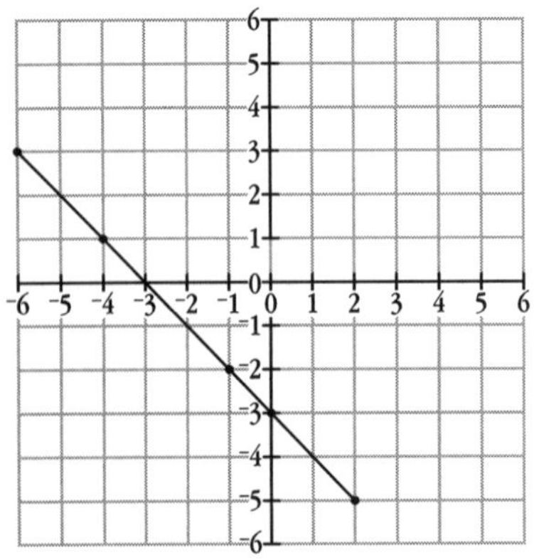

14d. Just as the last graph passed through both axes at $^-3$, this graph would pass through both axes at 8.

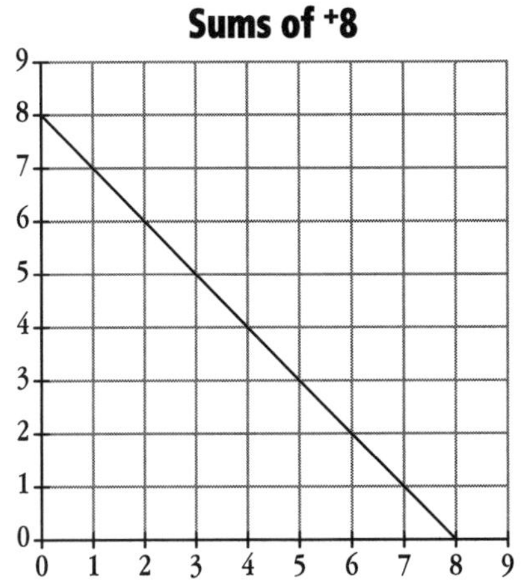

Mathematical Reflections

1. The signs of the *x*- and *y*-coordinates tell you where a point will land.

- Any point with both *x* and *y* positive (+, +) will be in quadrant I, because you move right and up from (0, 0) to locate the point.
- Any point with both *x* and *y* negative (–, –) will be in quadrant III, because you move left and down from (0, 0) to locate the point.
- Any point with *x* positive and *y* negative (+, –) will be in quadrant IV, because you move right and down from (0, 0) to locate the point.
- Any point with *x* negative and *y* positive (–, +) will be in quadrant II, because you move left and up from (0, 0) to locate the point.
- Any point with $x = 0$ and $y =$ anything will have the form (0, *y*) and will be on the *y*-axis, because you only move up or down from (0, 0) to locate the point.
- Any point with $x =$ anything and $y = 0$ will have the form (*x*, 0) and will be on the *x*-axis, because you move right or left from (0, 0) to locate the point.

Looking Back and Looking Ahead

Unit Reflections

While working on problems in this unit, you investigated properties, operations, and applications of *positive* and *negative* numbers and zero. The numbers {... , −3, −2, −1, 0, 1, 2, 3, ... } are called the *integers*. You learned how to represent integers on a number line and how to add, subtract, multiply, and divide integers. Answering questions about thermometers, distance on a number line, elevations, and scoring games focused your attention on important uses of integers.

Using Your Understanding of Integers — To test your understanding and skill in use of integers, consider the questions that arise in the following games and problem situations.

1. *Kaylee and Cassie designed a board game that involves a number line. In their game, players take turns flipping a penny and moving a marker to the left or the right on a number line like this one.*

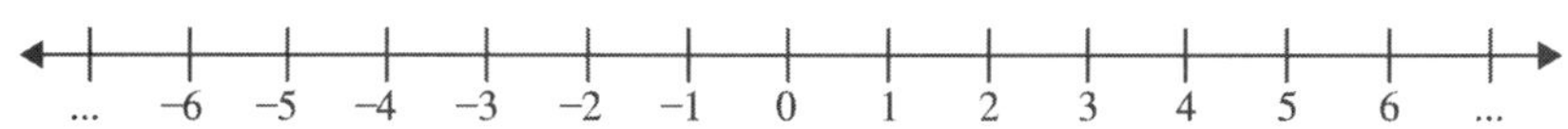

These are the rules of the game.

- *At the start of the game each player puts a marker on the point labeled 0.*
- *In round one each player flips a coin and moves 2 spaces to the left if the penny shows a tail (T) or two spaces to the right if the penny shows a head (H).*
- *In round two, each player flips the coin but moves 5 spaces left (T) or right (H).*
- *In round three, each player flips the coin but moves 10 spaces left (T) or right (H).*
- *At the end of three rounds, the player whose marker is on the greater number wins.*

a. Where will Jose's marker end up if he flips HHT on his three turns?

b. Where will Maria's marker end up if she flips THT on her three turns?

c. Consider the possible outcomes of this game and their probabilities.

How to Use *Looking Back and Looking Ahead: Unit Reflections*

The first part of this section includes problems that allow students to demonstrate their mathematical understandings and skills. The second part gives them an opportunity to explain their reasoning. This section can be used as a review to help students stand back and reflect on the "big" ideas and connections in the unit. This section may be assigned as homework, followed up with class discussion the next day. Focus on the *Explaining Your Reasoning* section in the discussion. Encourage the students to refer to the problems to illustrate their reasoning.

i. Make a list showing all possible final numbers in the game.

ii. Write number sentences using integer addition to confirm your answers.

iii. Find the probability of ending on each possible final number.

d. Repeat the directions of part c. to show what will happen if the moves in each round are 2, 4, and 6 spaces to the left or right.

2 *Write number sentences involving integer operations that answer the following questions.*

a. In four plays of a football game, one team gained 12 yards, lost 8 yards, lost 3 yards, and gained 7 yards. What was the team's net gain or loss for those four plays?

b. Bill and Susan were comparing the depths of two submarines. One was 890 feet below sea level, and the other was 1425 feet below sea level.

i. Which submarine was at the greater depth?

ii. What change in the first submarine's depth would put it at the same depth as the other submarine?

c. The Blue Devil Booster Club sells snacks at Duke Middle School activities. To get a good price on supplies, the club ordered food worth $125 for each of eight major events and paid in full at the start of the year. After the first four events, the club's total income was $745. How much profit or loss did they have at that time?

d. In Mooseville, the high temperature on one Monday in January was 40°F. It rose 12°F on Tuesday, dropped 10°F on Wednesday, dropped another 6°F on Thursday, and rose 12°F on Friday. What was the high temperature on Friday?

e. Sunday was a cold day in Wolfville. Then the low temperature dropped an average of 8°F per day for the next five days. On Friday, the low temperature was −30°F. What had the low temperature been on Sunday?

3 **a.** Copy and complete the pyramid below so that each number represents the sum of the two numbers directly beneath it.

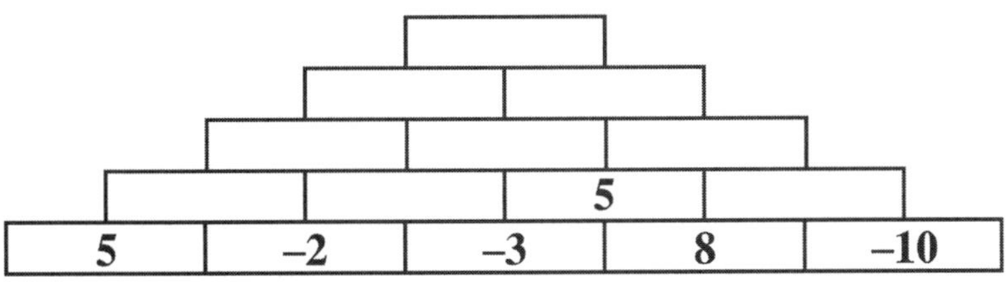

Answers

Using Your Understanding of Integers

1a. Jose's marker will land on −3.

b. Maria's marker will land on −7.

c. See below.

d. See the bottom of page 82r.

2a. +12 − 8 − 3 + 7 = 8 yard gain

b. i. Distance is positive. The second submarine that is 1425 feet below sea level is at a greater depth.

ii. The first submarine should descend 535 feet.

c. −8 × 125 + 745 = −255 or 745 − 9 × 125 = −255. They still owe $255.

d. 40 + 12 − 10 − 6 + 12 = 64 − 16 = 48°F

e. −30 − (−8 × 5) = 10°F.

1c.

i. Possible Outcomes	ii. Corresponding Number Sentence	iii. Probability of ending on number
HHH: 17	2 + 5 + 10 = 17	$\frac{1}{8}$
HHT: −3	2 + 5 − 10 = −3	$\frac{1}{8}$
HTH: 7	2 − 5 + 10 = 7	$\frac{1}{8}$
THH: 13	−2 + 5 + 10 = 13	$\frac{1}{8}$
HTT: 13	2 − 5 − 10 = −13	$\frac{1}{8}$
THT: −7	−2 + 5 − 10 = −7	$\frac{1}{8}$
TTH: 3	−2 − 5 + 10 = 3	$\frac{1}{8}$
TTT: −17	−2 − 5 − 10 = −17	$\frac{1}{8}$

3a.

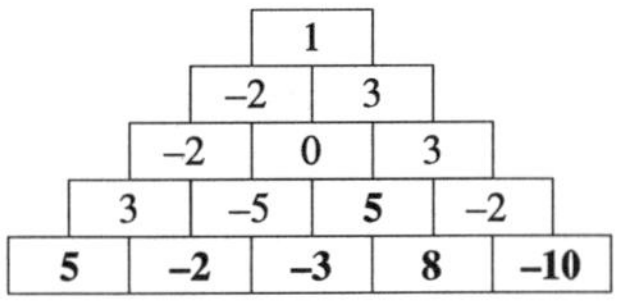

b.

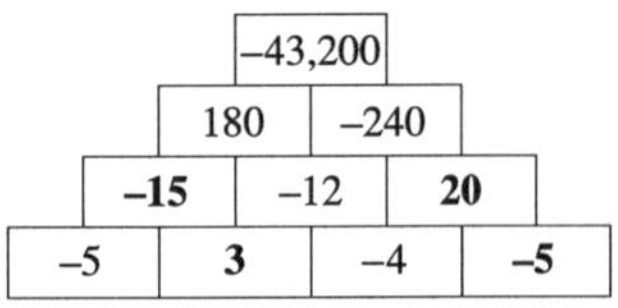

Explaining Your Reasoning

1. Possible answer: In the set of integers, if any two integers are subtracted, the resulting difference is also an integer. For example, in the set of integers $3 - 5 = -2$, and 3, 5, and -2 are all integers. However, in the set of whole numbers $5 - 3 = 2$ and 5, 3, and 2 are all whole numbers, but $3 - 5$ is not a whole number. In mathematics, the set of whole numbers is not closed under subtraction, but the set of integers is closed under subtraction.

2. $-55, -20, 0, 15, 30$

3, 4. See page 82s.

b. Copy and complete the pyramid below so that each number represents the product of the two numbers directly beneath it.

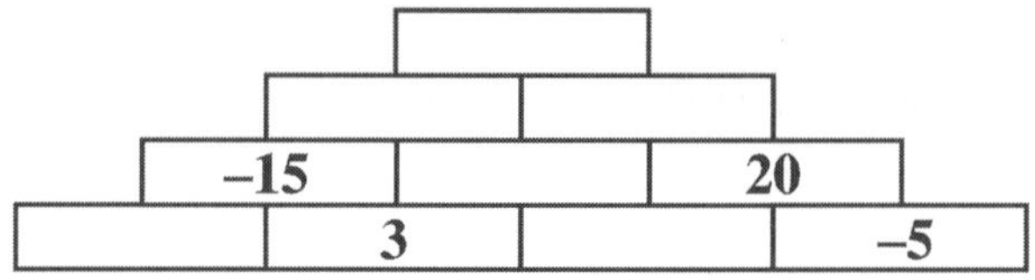

Explaining Your Reasoning—Prior to this unit, you worked only with whole numbers and positive fractions and decimals. Answering the questions in Problems 1–3 required knowledge of integers and operations with integers. You should be able to justify the ways that you used that knowledge in each problem.

1. What operation(s) can you do with the set of integers that you could not do with just the set of whole numbers?
2. Arrange the following numbers from least to greatest and be prepared to justify your answer.
   $-20, \quad 15, \quad -55, \quad 30, \quad 0$
3. Use sketches of number line or chip models to demonstrate each of these calculations:
   a. $5 + (-7) = -2$ **b.** $(-2) + (-9) = -11$ **c.** $3 \times (-2) = -6$
   d. $(-3) \times (-2) = 6$
4. If you are given two integers, how do you find the sign of their
   a. sum?
   b. difference?
   c. product?
   d. quotient?

Positive and negative numbers are useful in solving a variety of problems that involve losses and gains. They also provide coordinates for points on an extended number line and coordinate plane. These ideas will be useful when you study graphs of functions in future *Connected Mathematics* units like *Moving Straight Ahead*, *Thinking with Mathematical Models*, and *Growing, Growing, Growing*. You will also use negative and positive numbers when you solve equations in these units and in the algebraic reasoning of *Say It with Symbols*.

1d.

i. Possible Outcomes	**ii.** Corresponding Number Sentence	**iii.** Probability of ending on number
HHH: 12	$2 + 4 + 6 = 12$	$\frac{1}{8}$
HHT: 0	$2 + 4 - 6 = 0$	$\frac{1}{8}$
HTH: 4	$2 - 4 + 6 = 4$	$\frac{1}{8}$
THH: 8	$-2 + 4 + 6 = 8$	$\frac{1}{8}$
HTT: −8	$2 - 4 - 6 = -8$	$\frac{1}{8}$
THT: −4	$-2 + 4 - 6 = -4$	$\frac{1}{8}$
TTH: 0	$-2 - 4 + 6 = 0$	$\frac{1}{8}$
TTT: −12	$-2 - 4 - 6 = -12$	$\frac{1}{8}$

Note the probability of landing on 0 is $\frac{2}{8}$ or $\frac{1}{4}$.

Looking Back and Looking Ahead

Answers

3a. $5 + (-7) = -2$

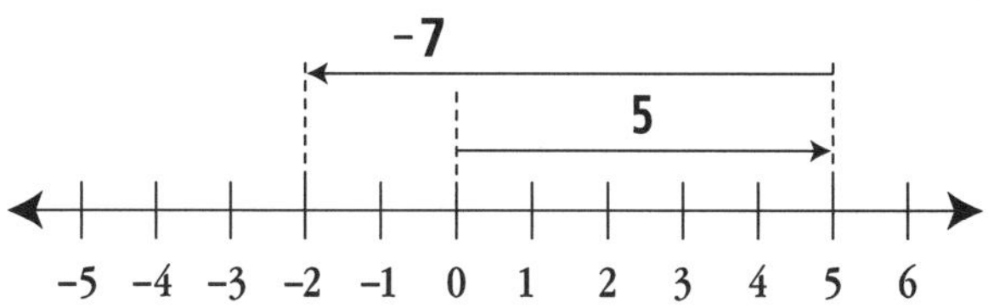

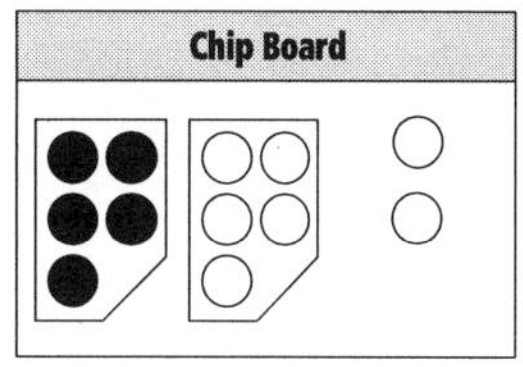

b. $(-2) + (-9) = -11$

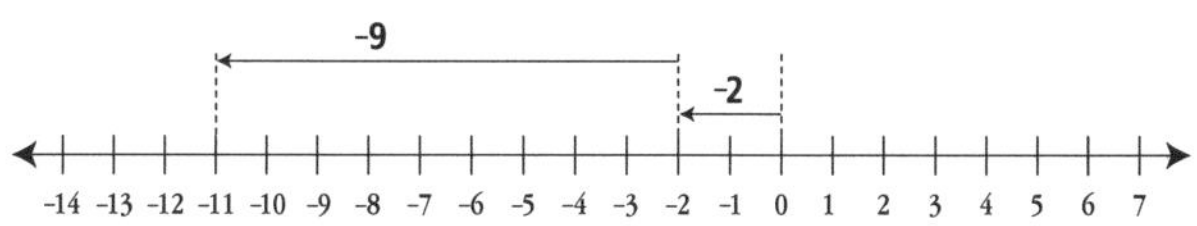

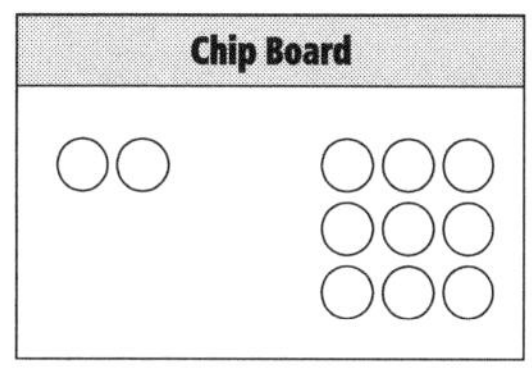

c. $3 \times (-2) = -6$

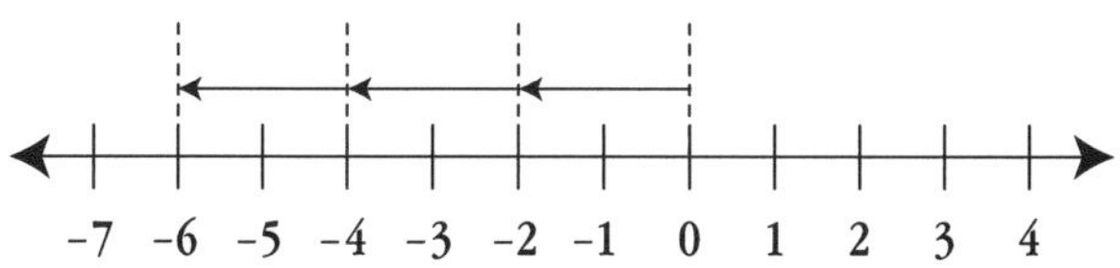

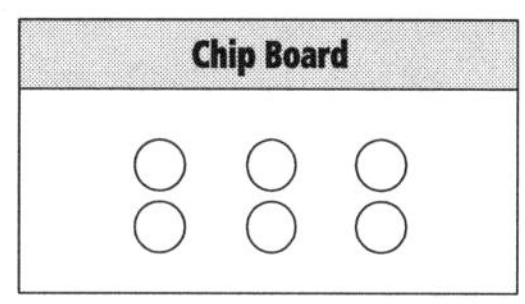

Note that no chip model for this situation is presented in the student book. Students may present a model similar to the one shown.

d. $(-3) \times (-2) = 6$

No chip model nor number line is presented. A pattern approach is used in the student materials.

4a. If the two integers have the same sign, then their sum has the same sign.

If the two integers have different signs, then the sign of the sum of those two integers is the sign of the integer that has the greater absolute value.

b. To determine the sign of the difference of two integers, write the subtraction sentence as an addition sentence and then follow the rules for integer addition.

c. If the signs of two integers are different, then the sign of the product is negative. If the signs of the two integers are the same, then the sign of the product is positive.

d. If the signs of two integers are different, then the sign of the quotient is negative. If the signs of the two integers are the same, then the sign of the quotient is positive.

Assessment Resources

Name ______________________________ Date ______________

Check-Up 1

1. Construct a number line using the line below. Locate the numbers in parts a–c on your number line.

   a. $^{-}10$ **b.** 0 **c.** $\frac{1}{3}$

   d. In a different color, locate the opposite of each number in parts a–c.

2. Rewrite these temperature readings from lowest to highest.

   $^{-}9°$ $14°$ $^{-}2°$ $0°$ $8°$ $^{-}1°$ $1°$

3. **a.** Suppose the temperature is 6°. What will the temperature be if it rises 22°? ________

   b. Suppose the temperature is 6°. What will the temperature be if it falls 7°? ________

4. **a.** Suppose the temperature is $^{-}6°$ (6° below 0°). What will the temperature be if it rises 13°? ________

   b. Suppose the temperature is –6°. What will the temperature be if it falls 15°? ________

In 5–8, solve the problem.

5. $^{+}32 + {}^{-}12 =$

6. $^{-}14 + {}^{-}15 =$

7. $^{-}32 + {}^{+}12 =$

8. $^{-}24 + {}^{-}9 + {}^{-}16 =$

Name ______________________ Date ____________

Check-Up 1

9. Suppose that time is measured in days and that 0 stands for today.

   a. What number stands for tomorrow? ________

   b. What number stands for yesterday? ________

   c. What number stands for a week ago? ________

   d. What number stands for a year from today? ________

10. Barry plays fullback on his high school football team. Sometimes he gains yardage ($^{+}5$ means a 5-yard gain). Sometimes he loses yardage ($^{-}3$ means a 3-yard loss). Determine Barry's total yardage in each game below.

    a. Game 1: $^{+}4$ $^{+}6$ $^{+}7$ $^{+}1$ $^{-}8$

    b. Game 2: $^{+}6$ $^{-}3$ 0 $^{+}15$ $^{-}1$ $^{+}8$ $^{+}11$ $^{-}6$

11. Suppose the Rocky Mountains have 72 centimeters of snow. Warmer weather is melting the snow at a rate of 5.8 centimeters a day. If the snow continues to melt at this rate, after seven days of the warm weather, how much snow will be left?

12. Write a number less than $^{-}1000$. ________

Name ______________________________ Date ______________

Check-Up 2

1. After several minutes of playing MathMania, three teams have the following scores:

SuperSmarties	DynaBrains	MegaMinds
650	–150	200

   a. The SuperSmarties are how many points ahead of the MegaMinds? ______
   Write a number sentence that could be used to find this amount.

   b. The SuperSmarties are how many points ahead of the DynaBrains? ______
   Write a number sentence that could be used to find this amount.

   c. The MegaMinds are how many points ahead of the DynaBrains? ______
   Write a number sentence that could be used to find this amount.

In 2–4, tell how far apart the two numbers are on a number line.

2. $^{-}15$ and $^{+}20$

3. 35 and 17

4. $^{-}5$ and $^{-}12$

In 5–12, solve the problem.

5. $18 - 27 =$

6. $27 - 18 =$

7. $14 - {}^{-}8 =$

8. $^{-}14 - {}^{+}8 =$

9. $^{-}150 - {}^{+}24 =$

10. $90 - {}^{-}99 =$

11. $16 + {}^{-}12 + {}^{-}4 =$

12. ______ $+ 21 = 13$

13. Alexis says she is thinking about a number whose absolute value is 19. What are all the possible numbers she could be thinking about?

14. Batai says he is thinking about a number whose absolute value is 6.5. What are all the possible numbers he could be thinking about?

Assign these questions as additional homework, or use them as review, quiz, or test questions.

In 1–3, use this information: In the fifteenth century, European flour merchants used positive and negative numbers. If the merchants wrote $^{+}5$ on a flour barrel, it meant that the barrel was 5 pounds overweight; $^{-}5$ meant that a barrel was 5 pounds underweight.

1. Suppose five 100-pound flour barrels are labeled as shown below.

a. Do the five barrels contain more or less than 500 pounds altogether?

b. How much more or less?

2. Suppose these numbers are on eight 100-pound barrels:

$^{-}6$ $\quad$ $^{-}8$ $\quad$ $^{+}7$ $\quad$ $^{+}2$ $\quad$ $^{-}10$ $\quad$ $^{+}6$ $\quad$ $^{+}3$ $\quad$ $^{+}1$

a. Do the barrels contain more or less than 800 pounds altogether?

b. How much more or less?

3. The drawings below show six 100-pound barrels. The total weight in the barrels is 11 pounds under 600 pounds. Suppose each barrel is marked with a different number. Show a way that the barrels could be marked. Keep your numbers between $^{-}10$ and $^{+}10$.

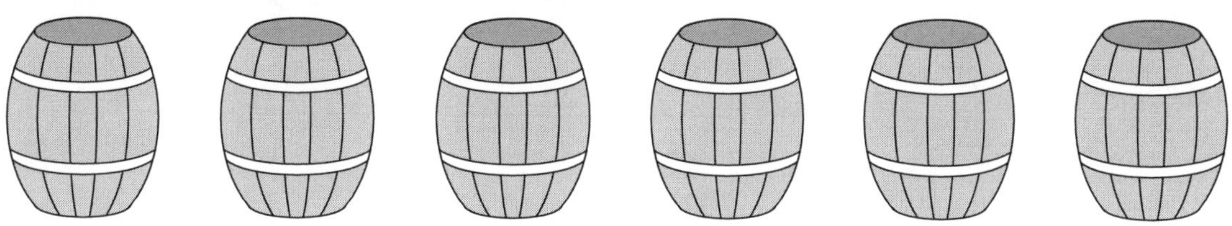

4. Teri made up a game of darts for a party. To play the game, you throw three darts at the board and then total your points. The highest score wins. Everyone at the party played the game several times. List all possible scores for three darts if all three hit the target.

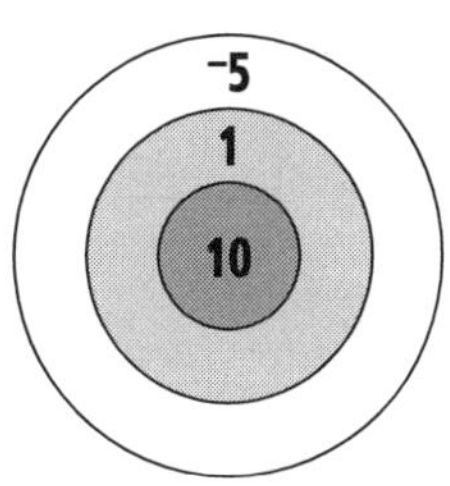

Question Bank

In 5–8, answer true or false, and *explain* your answer.

5. The sum of two negative integers is always negative.

6. The product of two negative integers is always negative.

7. The sum of a negative integer and a positive integer is always positive.

8. The product of a negative integer and a positive integer is always negative.

9. One integer added to another integer gives a sum of $^-9$. When the smaller integer is subtracted from the greater integer, the difference is 1. What could the two integers be?

10. **a.** Below is a grid with four quadrants. Plot the following points, and connect them with line segments.

Point A (1, 0) Point B (3, 4) Point C (4, 0)

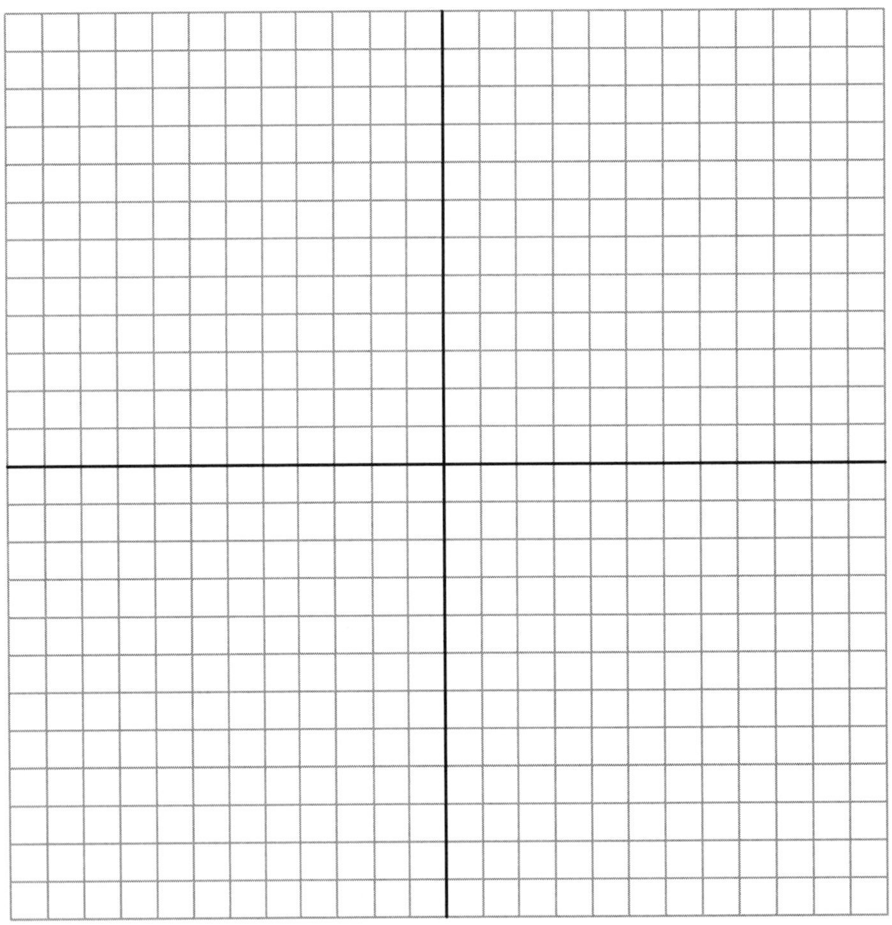

b. On the same grid paper, transform your figure *ABC* using the rule $(2x, 2y)$.

c. On the same grid paper, transform *ABC* using the rule $(^-2x, ^-2y)$.

d. On the same grid paper, transform *ABC* using the rule $(^-2x, 2y)$.

e. On the same grid paper, transform *ABC* using the rule $(2x, ^-3y)$.

f. Without drawing, predict what will happen to *ABC* using the rule $(3x, 3y)$.

g. Without drawing, predict what will happen to *ABC* using the rule $(^-3x, ^-3y)$.

h. Without drawing, predict what will happen to *ABC* using the rule $(^-3x, 3y)$.

Name ______________________ Date ______________

Unit Test

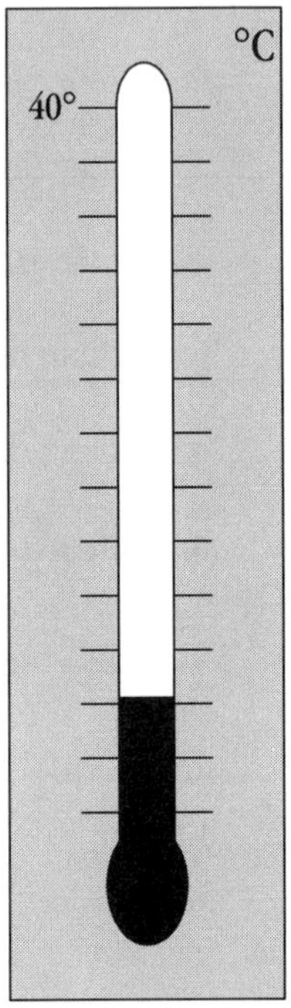

A Celsius thermometer is shown at the right. The marks are in 5° intervals. Label the remaining marks. Then, use the thermometer to help you answer the questions below.

1. What temperature reading is halfway between −15° and 5°? ______

2. What temperature reading is halfway between 4° and −11°? ______

3. The table contains data for temperatures in Portland, Maine, during the month of January. Complete the table.

Temperature at 8:00 A.M.	Temperature at 8:00 P.M.	Change in temperature from 8 A.M. to 8 P.M.
−8°	3°	
−2°	−13°	
−13°		11°
−1°		15°
	−2°	−8°
	−5°	4°

4. The temperature for the past 8 hours has been changing at the rate of −1.5° each hour. The meteorologist predicts that the temperature will continue changing like this for the next 6 hours. The present reading is 0°.
   a. What was the temperature reading 7 hours ago? ______
   b. What temperature is predicted for 6 hours from now? ______
   c. When was the temperature reading 6°? ______
   d. When is the temperature expected to be −8°? ______

Name ______________________________ Date ______________

Unit Test

In 5–7, use this information: Suppose you are in a building in which the floors are numbered from 0 to 15. The building has an underground parking garage with 10 levels, which are numbered from $^{-}1$ to $^{-}10$. Which floor is *farther from* floor $^{-}2$? (Drawing a picture may help you solve this problem.)

5. floor 7 or floor $^{-}10$

6. floor 2 or floor $^{-}8$

7. floor 1 or floor $^{-}5$

8. A bakery bought 225 pounds of baking powder. It used 6.8 pounds per day. How much did the bakery have left after three days?

9. Ray is in debt \$32. He was further in debt, but he has been paying \$6 a month on his debt for the last five months.

a. How much was Ray in debt five months ago? ________

b. At his present rate, how much longer will it take Ray to pay off his debt? Explain your reasoning.

In 10–17, solve the problem.

10. $7 - 10 =$

11. $^{-}7 + {}^{+}10 =$

12. $^{-}12 - {}^{-}11 =$

13. $11 - {}^{-}8 =$

14. $^{-}24 \div {}^{-}6 =$

15. $25 \times {}^{-}6 =$

16. $^{-}12 \times {}^{-}5 =$

17. $^{-}10 \times {}^{-}10 \times {}^{-}10 =$

Name ______________________________ Date ______________

Unit Test

In 18–21, use the following table, which lists the lowest daily temperatures in Marquette, Michigan, for the first two weeks of January 1995.

Date	Lowest temperature (°F)
1	10
2	7
3	-8
4	-12
5	-1
6	12
7	9
8	2
9	-6
10	-9
11	17
12	30
13	30
14	21

18. What is the range of daily temperatures?

19. What is the median temperature?

20. What is the mean temperature?

21. On the grid, plot the temperatures for the data. Label the horizontal axis "Date" and the vertical axis "Temperature (°F)."

Name ______________________________ Date ______________

Notebook Checklist

Journal Organization

_____ Problems and Mathematical Reflections are labeled and dated.

_____ Work is neat and is easy to find and follow.

Vocabulary

_____ All words are listed. _____ All words are defined or described.

Check-Ups

_____ Check-Up 1

_____ Check-Up 2

Homework Assignments

_____ ______________________________

_____ ______________________________

_____ ______________________________

_____ ______________________________

_____ ______________________________

_____ ______________________________

_____ ______________________________

_____ ______________________________

_____ ______________________________

_____ ______________________________

_____ ______________________________

_____ ______________________________

_____ ______________________________

_____ ______________________________

_____ ______________________________

Name ______________________________ Date ______________

Self-Assessment

Vocabulary

Of the vocabulary words I defined or described in my journal, the word ______________ best demonstrates my ability to give a clear definition or description.

Of the vocabulary words I defined or described in my journal, the word ______________ best demonstrates my ability to use an example to help explain or describe an idea.

Mathematical Ideas

Situations that involve positive and negative integers are part of everyday life—for example, games, temperature readings, profit, and debts.

1. a. After studying the mathematics in *Accentuate the Negative,* I learned the following things about how to determine whether one number is greater than, less than, or equal to another number and how to operate (add, subtract, multiply, and divide) with positive and negative numbers:

   b. Here are page numbers of journal entries that give evidence of what I have learned, along with descriptions of what each entry shows:

2. a. These are the mathematical ideas I am still struggling with:

   b. This is why I think these ideas are difficult for me:

   c. Here are page numbers of journal entries that give evidence of what I am struggling with, along with descriptions of what each entry shows:

Class Participation

I contributed to the class discussion and understanding of *Accentuate the Negative* when I . . . (Give examples.)

Answer Keys

Answers to Check-Up 1

1.

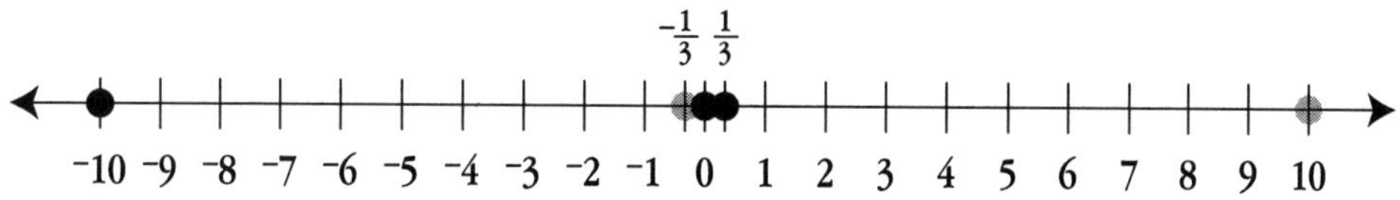

(Zero is an interesting case, as it is the only number that is its own opposite.)

2. $^-9°, ^-2°, ^-1°, 0°, 1°, 8°, 14°$
3. a. $6 + 22 = 28°$
   b. $6 - 7 = {}^-1°$
4. a. $^-6 + 13 = 7°$
   b. $^-6 - 15 = {}^-21°$
5. 20
6. $^-29$
7. $^-20$
8. $^-49$
9. a. 1
   b. $^-1$
   c. $^-7$
   d. 365
10. a. 10 yards gained ($^+10$)
    b. 30 yards gained ($^+30$)
11. $5.8 \times 7 = 40.6$; $72 - 40.6 = 31.4$ cm of snow
12. Possible answers: $^-1001$, $^-1003$, $^-1000.2$

Answers to Check-Up 2

1. a. 450 points; $650 - 200 = 450$
   b. 800 points; $650 - {}^-150 = 800$
   c. 350 points; $200 - {}^-150 = 350$
2. 35 units
3. 18 units
4. 7 units
5. $^-9$
6. 9
7. 22
8. $^-22$
9. $^-174$

10. 189

11. 0

12. $^{-}8$

13. $^{+}19$ and $^{-}19$

14. $^{+}6.5$ and $^{-}6.5$

Answers to the Question Bank

1. a. less than 500 pounds
   b. 2 pounds less (or $^{-}2$ pounds)
2. a. less than 800 pounds
   b. 5 pounds less (or $^{-}5$ pounds)
3. (Note: Numbers should be from $^{-}10$ to 10, no number should be repeated, and the numbers must total $^{-}11$). Possible answers: $^{-}1, ^{-}2, ^{-}3, ^{-}4, ^{-}6, ^{+}5$ or $^{-}10, ^{-}9, ^{-}1, ^{+}2, ^{+}3, ^{+}4$
4. | | |
   |---|---|
   | $10 + 10 + 10 = 30$ | $10 + {^{-}5} + {^{-}5} = 0$ |
   | $10 + 10 + 1 = 21$ | $1 + 1 + 1 = 3$ |
   | $10 + 10 + -5 = 15$ | $1 + 1 + {^{-}5} = {^{-}3}$ |
   | $10 + 1 + 1 = 12$ | $1 + {^{-}5} + {^{-}5} = {^{-}9}$ |
   | $10 + 1 + {^{-}5} = 6$ | ${^{-}5} + {^{-}5} + {^{-}5} = {^{-}15}$ |
5. true; Possible explanation: If you have a negative amount and add a greater negative value to it, the result will be negative.
6. false; Possible explanation: When you multiply two negative integers, the answer is always positive.
7. false; Possible explanation: Whether the sum is positive or negative depends on which of the two numbers has the greater absolute value.
8. true; Possible explanation: You can think of multiplying a negative by a positive as adding the same negative integer together the number of times indicated by the positive integer.
9. $^{-}4$ and $^{-}5$ (${^{-}4} + {^{-}5} = {^{-}9}$ and ${^{-}4} - {^{-}5} = 1$)
10. a.

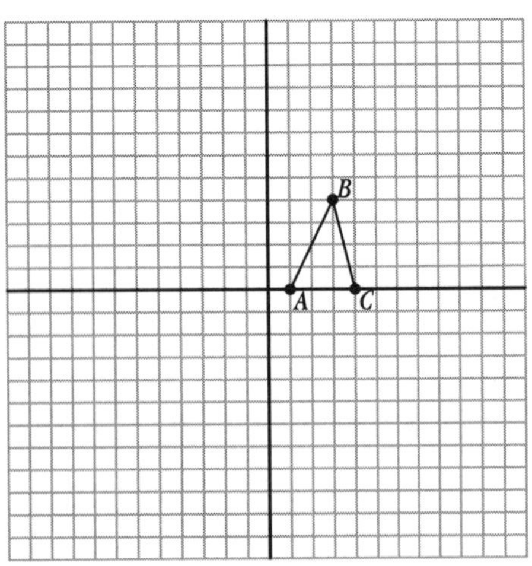

b, c.

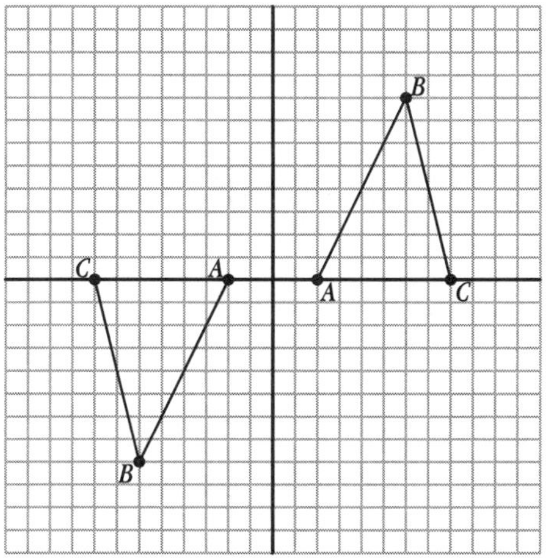

d, e.

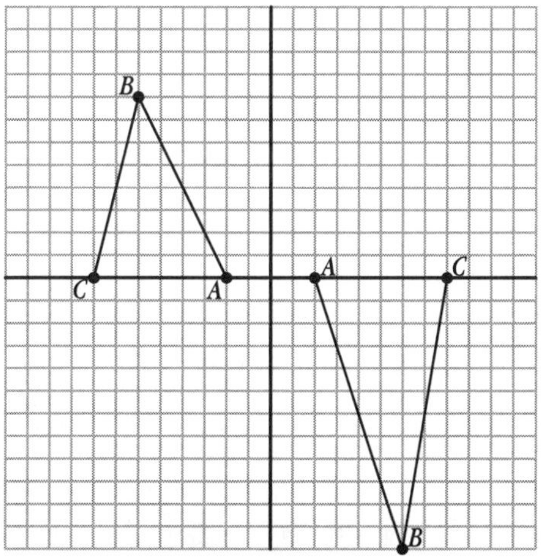

f. This triangle will have the same orientation as the original, but the side lengths will be three times as long.

g. This triangle will have lengths three times as long as the original's but will be in quadrant III. (Note: This could also be called a 180° rotation.)

h. This triangle will have lengths three times as long as the original's but will be in quadrant II. (Note: This is a reflection across the *y*-axis.)

Answers to the Unit Test

1. $^{-}5°$
2. $^{-}3.5°$
3.

Temperature at 8:00 A.M.	Temperature at 8:00 P.M.	Change in temperature from 8 A.M. to 8 P.M.
$^{-}8°$	$3°$	**$11°$**
$^{-}2°$	$^{-}13°$	**$^{-}11°$**
$^{-}13°$	**$^{-}2°$**	$11°$
$^{-}1°$	**$14°$**	$15°$
$6°$	$^{-}2°$	$^{-}8°$
$^{-}9°$	$^{-}5°$	$4°$

4. a. $^-7 \times {^-1.5} = 10.5°$
   b. $6 \times {^-1.5} = {^-9}°$
   c. $6 \div 1.5 = 4$ hours ago
   d. $8 \div 1.5 = 5\frac{1}{3}$ hours; or between 5 and 6 hours from now; or 5 hours, 20 minutes from now
5. floor 7
6. floor $^-8$
7. They are both 3 floors from floor $^-2$.
8. Since $^-6.8 \times 3 = {^-20.4}$, the bakery had $225 - 20.4 = 204.6$ pounds left at the end of three days.
9. a. $32 + 6 \times 5 = \$62$ in debt
   b. $32 \div 6 = 5\frac{1}{3}$ months; or 5 months, 10 days
10. $^-3$
11. 3
12. $^-1$
13. 19
14. 4
15. $^-150$
16. 60
17. $^-1000$
18. The range is from $^-12°$ to $30°$, or a spread of $42°$.
19. In order, the temperatures are $^-12$, $^-9$, $^-8$, $^-6$, $^-1$, 2, 7, 9, 10, 12, 17, 21, 30, 30. The median is between 7 and 9, or 8°F.
20. The temperatures add to 102°, and $102 \div 14 = 7.29$°F or 7°F.
21. Temperatures in January 1995

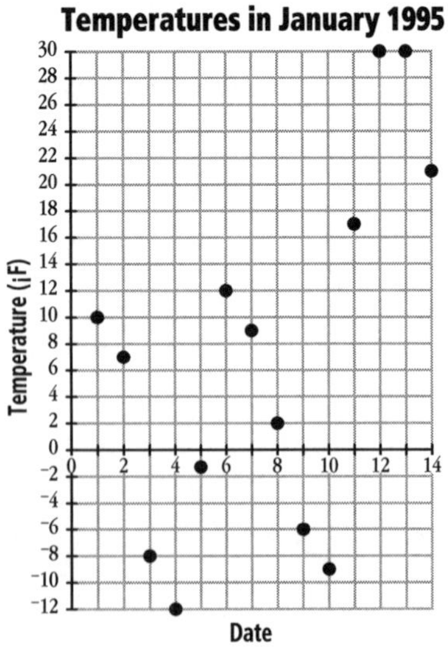

Working with the Unit Vocabulary

Vocabulary lists are provided in the teacher's edition of each Connected Mathematics unit. Here is how one teacher uses these vocabulary lists.

A Teacher's Comments

In my class, I use the vocabulary lists to help me organize for instruction. I make note of the terms that have been identified as essential. This is a signal to me that I need to include these terms in our class conversations as much as possible. I feel students need to understand how these words are used and how they can use them.

I do not hand out the vocabulary lists to my students. Instead, at the start of each unit, I hang a large sheet of paper on the front bulletin board and title it, in this case, *Vocabulary for Accentuate the Negative.* Throughout the unit, the students generate their own class vocabulary list. I make sure that all the essential vocabulary terms are included in the class list. My students often include more words than those given in the teacher's edition.

Each student is to record the class's unit vocabulary terms in the vocabulary section of his or her notebook. I do not have my students look up the words and record formal definitions. Instead, as we talk about and use the vocabulary terms, I suggest that they record what we have said in class, summarizing the main ideas and descriptions, and that they give examples of when and how we have used each term. I suggest that they leave four or five lines between each term so that they can add to their descriptions or change what they have written as they learn more.

My students tend to end up with general descriptions of the vocabulary terms and examples of the words being used. For instance, for the word *integer,* several of my students included statements such as "Integers are numbers like $^-2$, 2, $^-5$, 5, and 0." They do not generate many formal mathematical definitions of the terms. My goal is that my students know enough about the words to use them and to understand what others—people beyond our classroom, including other students and other mathematics teachers—are talking about when they use them.

Shown here are two pages from one of my student's vocabulary sections. She defines the words *integers, positive numbers, negative numbers,* and *opposite.* Students do not always spell the terms correctly; this is not that important to me. What I am looking for when I review my students' vocabulary sections is what sense they are making of the terms. Their vocabulary section is primarily for their own use as a reference during our work in the unit and in future units.

Working with the Unit Vocabulary

I Intergers - Amount of things such as possitive or negitive or zero. They don't include fractions
Example — +1, -1

II Positive number- place value over 0- can have fractions such as +5 +15 +25

III Negitive numbers - place value under 0- can have fractions such as -20 -30 -32

IV Oppisite- The numbers that und. each other. It's the number the same number that is on the opposite intergers- positive and negative such as -7, +7.
Example: +15, -15 = 0, +30, -30 = 0.
Your number added to its opposite to get 0
n + -n = 0.

How to set up a graph:

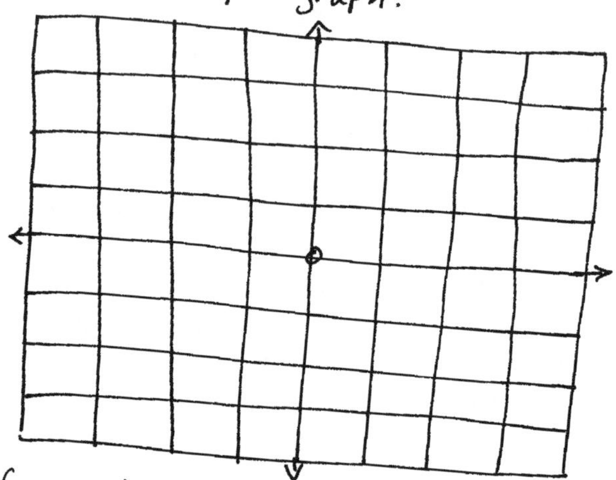

Communitive Property Doesn't matter what order you put the numbers in they come out the same answer. Works with adding also multiplication.

same { 5+ -3 = +2
5 - 3 = +2

Blackline Masters

Labsheets

Transparencies

Additional Resources

Labsheet 4.3

Integer Product Game Boards

1	⁻1	2	⁻2	3	⁻3
4	⁻4	5	⁻5	6	⁻6
8	⁻8	9	⁻9	10	⁻10
12	⁻12	15	⁻15	16	⁻16
18	⁻18	20	⁻20	24	⁻24
25	⁻25	30	⁻30	36	⁻36

Factors:
⁻6 ⁻5 ⁻4 ⁻3 ⁻2 ⁻1 1 2 3 4 5 6

1	⁻1	2	⁻2	3	⁻3
4	⁻4	5	⁻5	6	⁻6
8	⁻8	9	⁻9	10	⁻10
12	⁻12	15	⁻15	16	⁻16
18	⁻18	20	⁻20	24	⁻24
25	⁻25	30	⁻30	36	⁻36

Factors:
⁻6 ⁻5 ⁻4 ⁻3 ⁻2 ⁻1 1 2 3 4 5 6

1	⁻1	2	⁻2	3	⁻3
4	⁻4	5	⁻5	6	⁻6
8	⁻8	9	⁻9	10	⁻10
12	⁻12	15	⁻15	16	⁻16
18	⁻18	20	⁻20	24	⁻24
25	⁻25	30	⁻30	36	⁻36

Factors:
⁻6 ⁻5 ⁻4 ⁻3 ⁻2 ⁻1 1 2 3 4 5 6

1	⁻1	2	⁻2	3	⁻3
4	⁻4	5	⁻5	6	⁻6
8	⁻8	9	⁻9	10	⁻10
12	⁻12	15	⁻15	16	⁻16
18	⁻18	20	⁻20	24	⁻24
25	⁻25	30	⁻30	36	⁻36

Factors:
⁻6 ⁻5 ⁻4 ⁻3 ⁻2 ⁻1 1 2 3 4 5 6

ACE Questions 1 and 7–10

Use these calculator screens for ACE question 1.

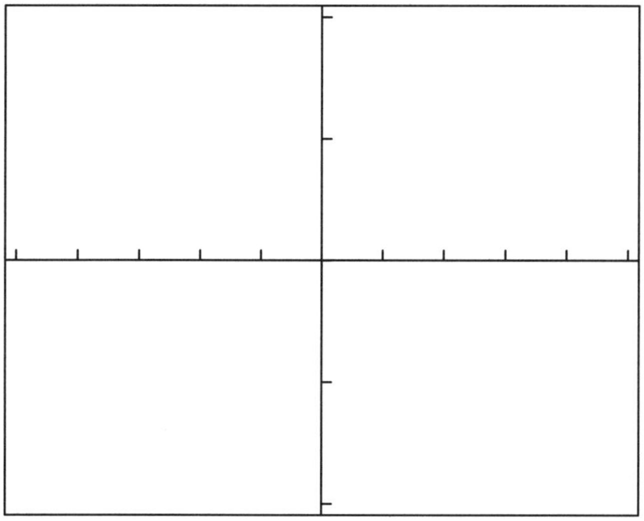

WINDOW
XMIN=$^-10$
XMAX=10
XSCL=2
YMIN=$^-10$
YMAX=10
YSCL=5

Use these calculator screens for ACE questions 7–10.

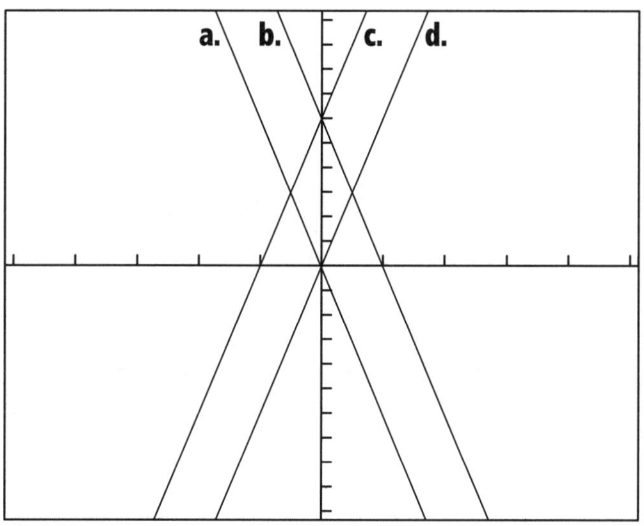

WINDOW
XMIN=$^-5$
XMAX=5
XSCL=1
YMIN=$^-10$
YMAX=10
YSCL=1

At one point in the MathMania game, the scores are as follows:

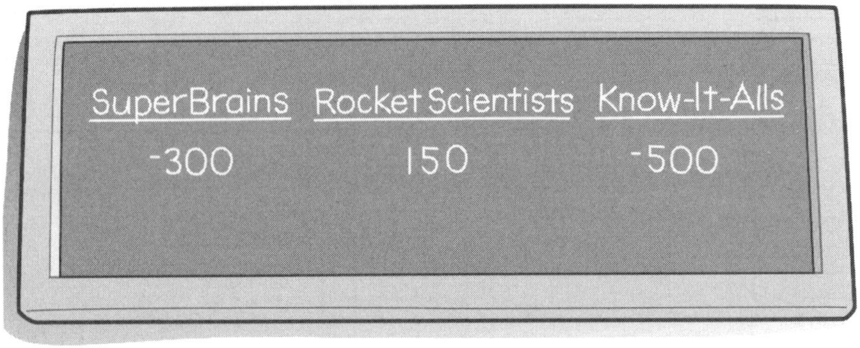

A. Which team has the highest score? Which team has the lowest score? Explain how you know your answers are correct.

B. How many points separate the highest score and the lowest score?

C. To earn their 150 points, the Rocket Scientists may have answered a 100-point question and a 50-point question correctly, or they may have answered a 200-point question correctly and then missed a 50-point question. Describe another possible way they may have reached their score. For each of the other two teams, give one possible way the team could have reached their score.

At one point in the game, the scores are as follows:

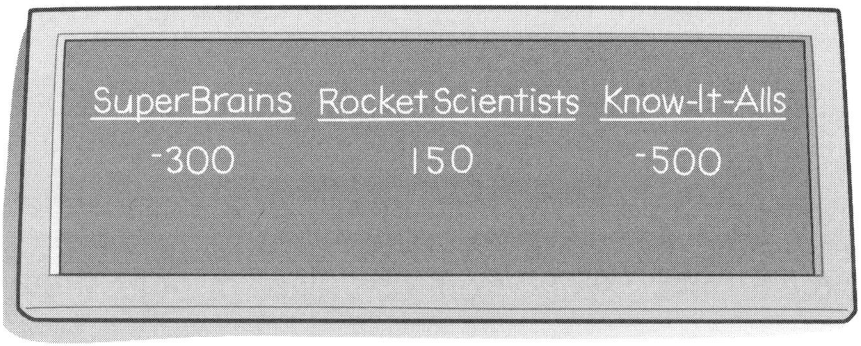

After achieving the scores shown above, the teams continue to play the game. Here is what happens:

- The SuperBrains answer a 200-point question correctly, a 150-point question incorrectly, a 50-point question correctly, and a 50-point question correctly.
- The Rocket Scientists answer a 50-point question incorrectly, a 200-point question incorrectly, a 100-point question correctly, and a 150-point question incorrectly.
- The Know-It-Alls answer a 100-point question incorrectly, a 200-point question correctly, a 150-point question correctly, and a 50-point question incorrectly.

D. What is each team's score now?

E. Which team is in last place? How far behind each of the other two teams is this team?

Mr. Hazan plays MathMania with his class. He divides the class into five teams. At the end of the game, the scores are as follows:

Team A: 200 Team B: -250
Team C: -400 Team D: 350 Team E: -100

A. Order the teams by score, from first place through fifth place.

B. By how many points is the first-place team ahead of the second-place team?

C. By how many points is the first-place team ahead of the third-place team?

D. By how many points is the second-place team ahead of the fourth-place team?

E. By how many points is the third-place team ahead of the fifth-place team?

A. Arrange the following temperatures in order from lowest to highest: −8°, 4°, 12°, −2°, 0°, −15°

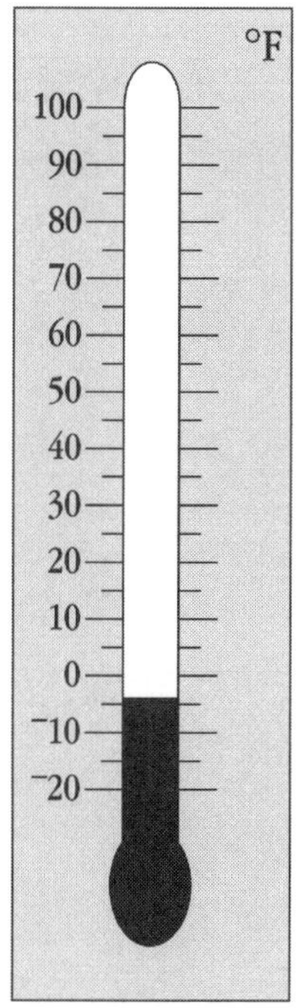

B. The temperature reading on a thermometer is 5°F. Tell what the new reading will be if the temperature

1. rises 10° **2.** falls 2°

3. falls 10° **4.** rises 7°

C. The temperature reading on a thermometer is −5°F. Tell what the new reading will be if the temperature

1. falls 3° **2.** rises 3°

3. falls 10° **4.** rises 10°

D. In 1–6, give the temperature halfway between the two given temperatures.

1. 0° and 10° **2.** −5° and 15°

3. 5° and −15° **4.** 0° and −20°

5. −8° and 8° **6.** −6° and −16°

E. In 1–4, tell which temperature reading is farther from −2°.

1. −6° or 6° **2.** −7° or 3°

3. 2° or −5° **4.** −10° or 5°

F. Explain how you determined your answer for part 4 of question E.

A. Write the addition sentence illustrated by each figure.

1.

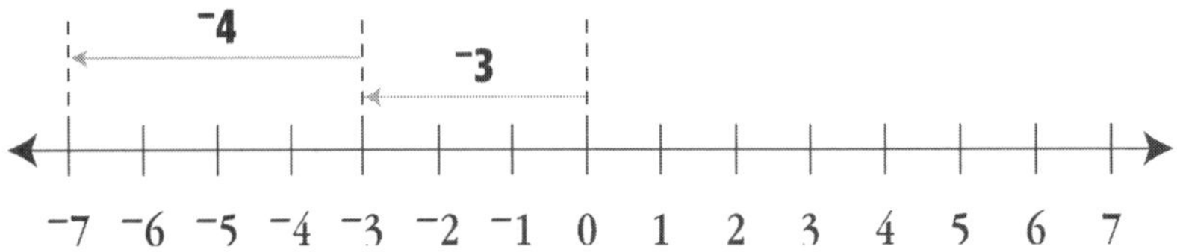

2.

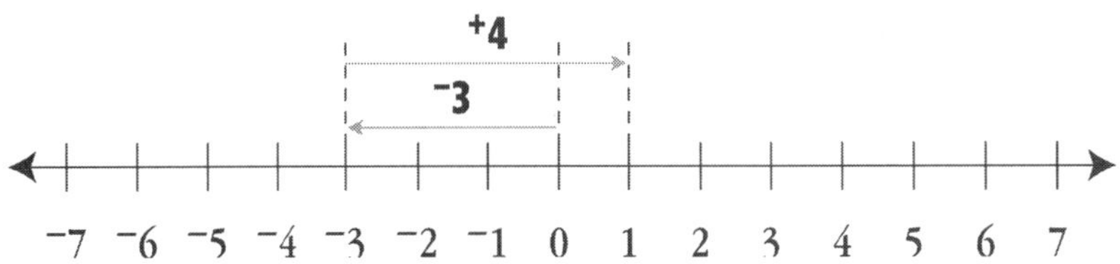

3.

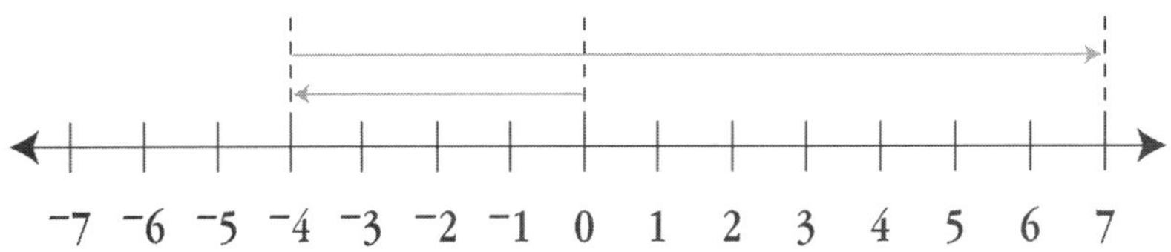

4.

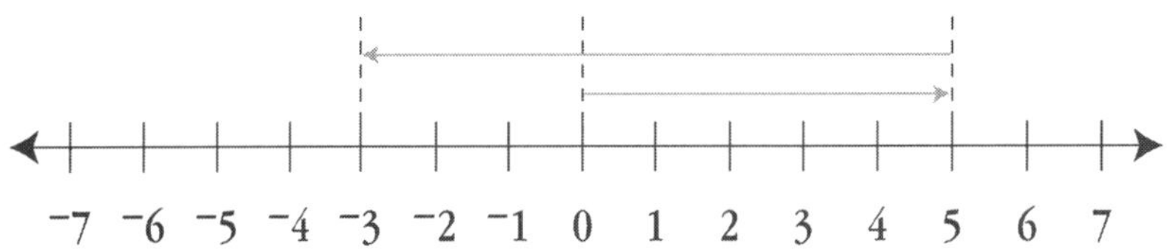

B. Illustrate each addition problem on a number line, and give the answer.

1. ${}^{-}5 + {}^{+}8$ **2.** ${}^{-}4 + {}^{-}3$ **3.** ${}^{-}2 + {}^{-}3 + {}^{+}10$

C. When you add two integers, does the order of the numbers make a difference? Illustrate your answer by showing each of these pairs of sums on a number line.

1. ${}^{-}5 + {}^{+}10$ and ${}^{+}10 + {}^{-}5$ **2.** ${}^{-}4 + {}^{-}6$ and ${}^{-}6 + {}^{-}4$

3. ${}^{+}8 + {}^{-}8$ and ${}^{-}8 + {}^{+}8$ **4.** ${}^{+}6 + {}^{-}7$ and ${}^{-}7 + {}^{+}6$

A. Use a chip board and black and red chips to find each sum. Draw a series of chip boards to illustrate your work.

1. $^-8 + {}^-7$

2. $^-8 + {}^+7$

3. $^+8 + {}^-7$

4. $^+8 + {}^+7$

B. Find two combinations of black and red chips that will simplify to represent the given integer. Draw a series of chip boards to prove that each combination works.

1. $^-3$

2. $^+5$

C. Write each combination you found in part B as an addition sentence.

A. Use a chip board and black and red chips to find each sum or difference.

1. $^-8 - ^-7$ **2.** $^+8 + ^-7$

3. $^-6 - ^-2$ **4.** $^+6 + ^-2$

B. In Problem 2.2, you simplified chip boards to find the number represented. For example, each chip board below represents $^+3$.

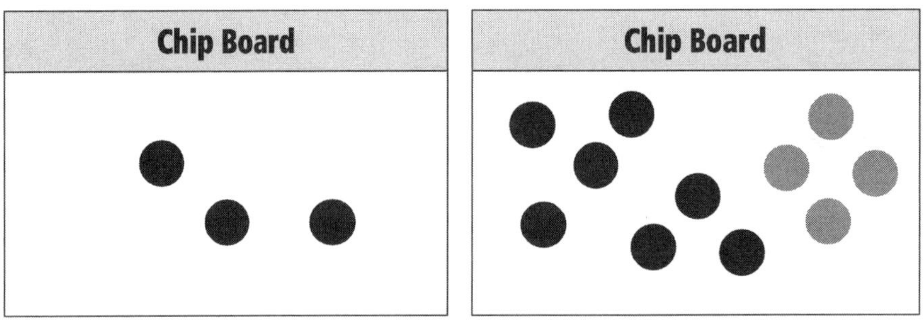

Find three ways to represent $^-8$ on a chip board.

C. Jing-mei wants to find $^-8 - {}^-10$ by using a chip board. She puts eight red chips on the board to represent $^-8$ but then gets stuck because she cannot remove ten red chips to represent subtracting $^-10$. How can Jing-mei show $^-8$ on a chip board so that she can remove ten red chips? What is $^-8 - {}^-10$? Explain how you determined your answer.

D. Drew wants to find $^+5 - {}^+7$ by using a chip board. How can he show $^+5$ on a chip board so that he can remove seven black chips to represent subtracting $^+7$? What is $^+5 - {}^+7$? Explain how you determined your answer.

E. Use a chip board and black and red chips to find each difference. For each difference, tell how many chips of each color you used to represent the first integer so that you could take away chips to represent subtracting the second integer.

1. $10 - 12$

2. $7 - {}^-2$

3. $^-5 - 6$

4. $^-3 - {}^-7$

A. Use a number line to find each difference. Use a chip board to check your work.

1. $^{+}7 - {}^{+}9$

2. $^{-}7 - {}^{+}9$

3. $^{+}7 - {}^{-}9$

4. $^{-}7 - {}^{-}9$

B. Use a number line to find each sum or difference.

1. $^{+}12 - {}^{+}3$

2. $^{+}12 + {}^{-}3$

3. $^{-}10 - {}^{-}7$

4. $^{-}10 + {}^{+}7$

C. Find the distance between each pair of numbers on a number line. In each case, tell how the distance is related to the difference between the two numbers.

1. 1 and 5

2. $^{-}1$ and 5

3. $^{-}5$ and $^{-}9$

4. $^{-}3$ and 3

D. Write two number sentences illustrated by this figure.

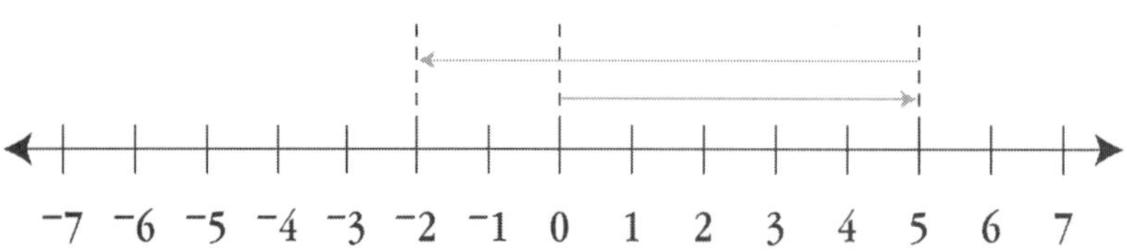

Study the patterns in the equations below.

$$15 - 5 = 10$$
$$15 - 4 = 11$$
$$15 - 3 = 12$$
$$15 - 2 = 13$$
$$15 - 1 = 14$$
$$15 - 0 = 15$$

A. Describe any patterns you observe in the way the differences change as the integers subtracted from 15 get smaller.

B. Use the patterns you observed to predict the answer to $15 - {}^{-}1$. Check your prediction by using a chip board or number line.

C. Predict the answer to $15 - {}^{-}4$. Explain your reasoning.

Transparency 3.4

A. **1.** Complete the addition sentence $^-17 + 13 = ?$.

2. Write a subtraction sentence that "undoes" the addition sentence you found in part 1.

B. **1.** Complete the addition sentence $^-4 + {}^-18 = ?$.

2. Write a subtraction sentence that undoes the addition sentence you found in part 1.

C. Write a subtraction sentence that solves each problem.

1. $? + {}^-18 = 6$

2. $? + {}^-13 = {}^-41$

3. $? + 6.1 = {}^-3.2$

4. $? + {}^-\frac{1}{3} = \frac{1}{3}$

D. Write an addition sentence that solves each problem.

1. $? - {}^-6 = {}^-6$

2. $? - {}^-2 = 3$

3. $? - 5.3 = {}^-7.1$

4. $? - {}^-\frac{1}{4} = {}^-\frac{3}{4}$

A. **1.** Suppose the temperature changed by an average of $^{+}3°$ per hour for a 10-hour period. Copy and complete the table below, and use it to find the total temperature change for the first 5 hours.

Number of hours	1	2	3	4	5
Total temperature change	$^{+}3°$	$^{+}6°$			

2. Write a multiplication sentence that represents the total change in temperature for the first 5 hours. Write a multiplication sentence that represents the total change in temperature for the entire 10-hour period.

B. **1.** Suppose the temperature changed by an average of $^{-}3°$ per hour for a 10-hour period. Copy and complete the table below, and use it to find the total temperature change for the first 5 hours.

Number of hours	1	2	3	4	5
Total temperature change	$^{-}3°$	$^{-}6°$			

2. Write a multiplication sentence that represents the total change in temperature for the first 5 hours. Write a multiplication sentence that represents the total change in temperature for the entire 10-hour period.

C. **1.** Write the addition sentence illustrated by each diagram below.

2. Write the multiplication sentence illustrated by each diagram below.

a.

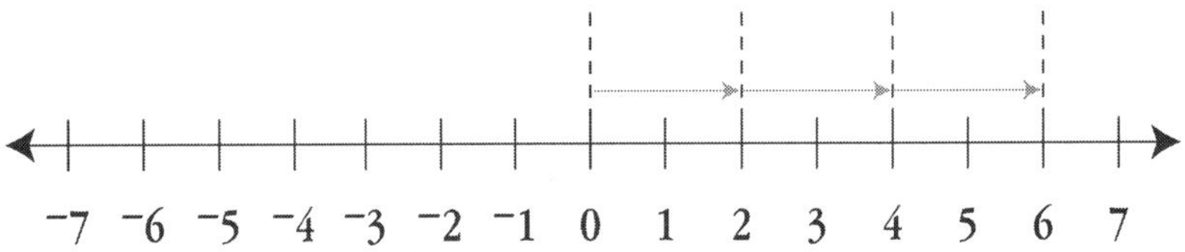

b.

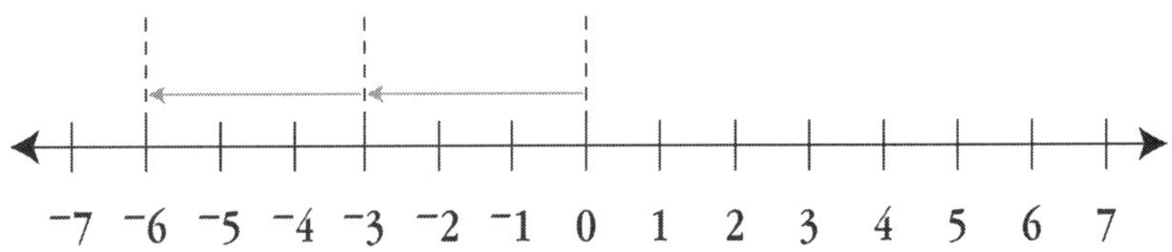

c.

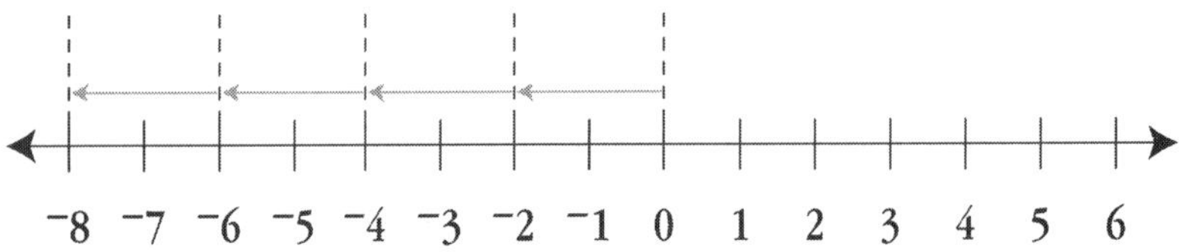

D. Make up a situation about temperatures that can be expressed as $4 \times {}^{-}10$.

E. Find each product.

1. $5 \times {}^{-}4$

2. $20 \times {}^{-}4$

3. -4×20

4. -5×4

A. Describe any patterns you observe in the way the products change as the integers multiplied by 5 get smaller.

$$\begin{aligned} 5 \times 5 &= 25 \\ 5 \times 4 &= 20 \\ 5 \times 3 &= 15 \\ 5 \times 2 &= 10 \\ 5 \times 1 &= 5 \\ 5 \times 0 &= 0 \end{aligned}$$

B. **1.** Use the patterns you observed to predict $5 \times {}^{-}1$. Explain your reasoning.

2. Write the next four equations in the pattern.

C. Complete the equations, and use them to help you answer parts D and E.

$$\begin{aligned} 5 \times {}^{-}4 &= ? \\ 4 \times {}^{-}4 &= ? \\ 3 \times {}^{-}4 &= ? \\ 2 \times {}^{-}4 &= ? \\ 1 \times {}^{-}4 &= ? \\ 0 \times {}^{-}4 &= ? \end{aligned}$$

D. Describe any patterns you observe in the way the products change as the integers multiplied by $^{-}4$ get smaller.

E. **1.** Use the patterns you observed to predict ${}^{-}1 \times {}^{-}4$. Explain your reasoning.

2. Write the next four equations in the pattern.

F. Find the following products.

1. ${}^{-}3 \times 7$ **2.** $5 \times {}^{-}8$ **3.** ${}^{-}11 \times {}^{-}12$ **4.** ${}^{-}3.6 \times 2.7$

Transparency 4.3

Problem 4.3

Play the Integer Product Game with a partner. Look for interesting patterns and ideas that might help you devise a winning strategy. Make notes of your observations.

The Integer Product Game

1	$^{-}1$	2	$^{-}2$	3	$^{-}3$
4	$^{-}4$	5	$^{-}5$	6	$^{-}6$
8	$^{-}8$	9	$^{-}9$	10	$^{-}10$
12	$^{-}12$	15	$^{-}15$	16	$^{-}16$
18	$^{-}18$	20	$^{-}20$	24	$^{-}24$
25	$^{-}25$	30	$^{-}30$	36	$^{-}36$

Factors:

$^{-}6$ $^{-}5$ $^{-}4$ $^{-}3$ $^{-}2$ $^{-}1$ 1 2 3 4 5 6

Transparency 4.4

A. 1. Complete the multiplication sentence $^-5 \times 6 = ?$.

2. Write two division sentences that are equivalent to the multiplication sentence you found in part 1.

B. 1. Complete the multiplication sentence $^-8 \times {}^-4 = ?$.

2. Write two division sentences that are equivalent to the multiplication sentence you found in part 1.

C. Write a division sentence that solves each problem.

1. $? \times 12 = {}^-132$

2. $^-8 \times ? = {}^-56$

3. $? \times {}^-4 = 132$

4. $5.2 \times ? = {}^-8.84$

D. Write a division or a multiplication sentence that solves each problem.

1. $? \div {}^-3 = {}^-8$

2. $91 \div ? = {}^-7$

3. $? \div 11 = {}^-17$

4. $^-19.95 \div ? = 9.5$

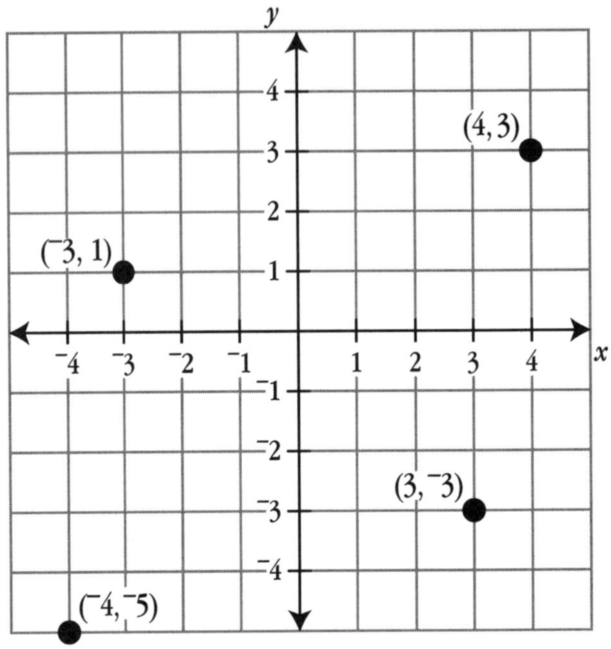

A. Describe how Melina located each of the four points on the coordinate grid.

B. What polygon could you make by connecting the four points? Justify your answer.

C. On a coordinate grid, plot four points that are the vertices of a square, such that both coordinates of each point are positive integers.

D. On a coordinate grid, plot four points that are the vertices of a square, such that both coordinates of each point are negative integers.

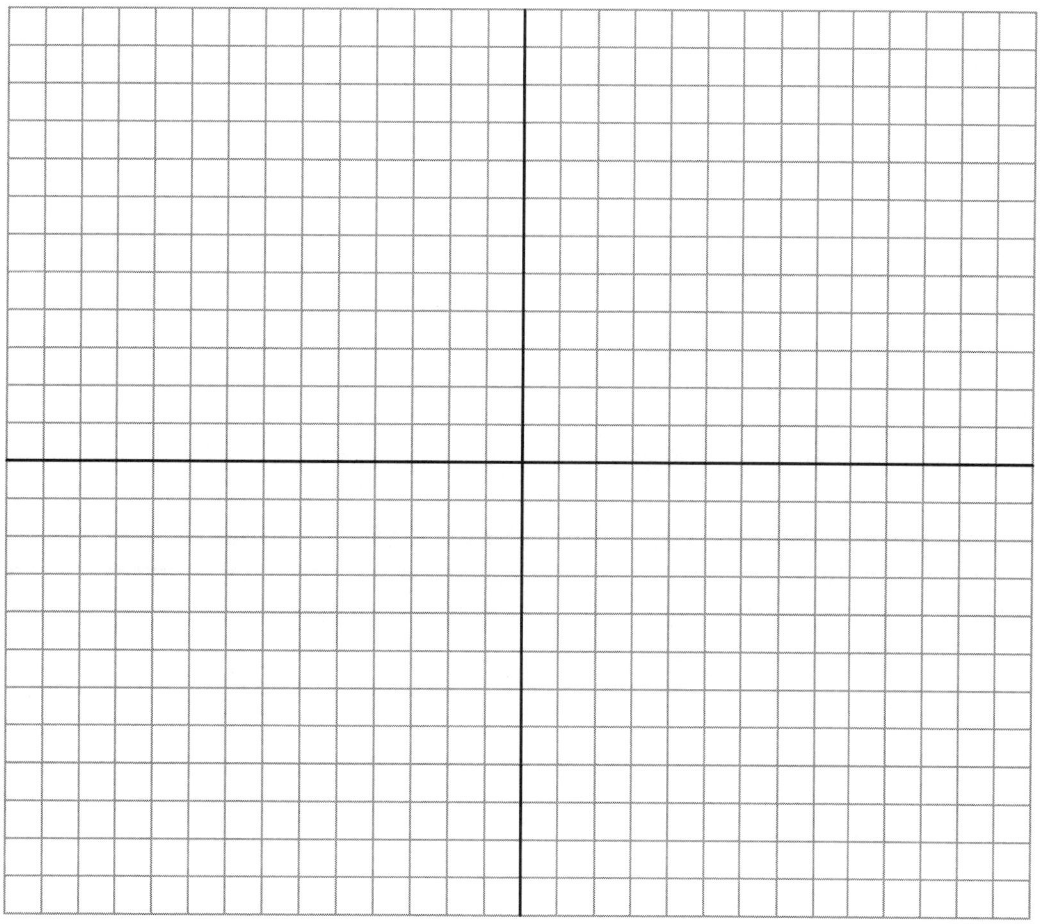

E. On a coordinate grid, plot four points that are the vertices of a square, such that one point has two negative-integer coordinates, one point has two positive-integer coordinates, and each of the other points has one positive-integer coordinate and one negative-integer coordinate.

F. Two vertices of a square are (3, 1) and ($^-$1, 1). Find the coordinates for every pair of points that could be the other two vertices.

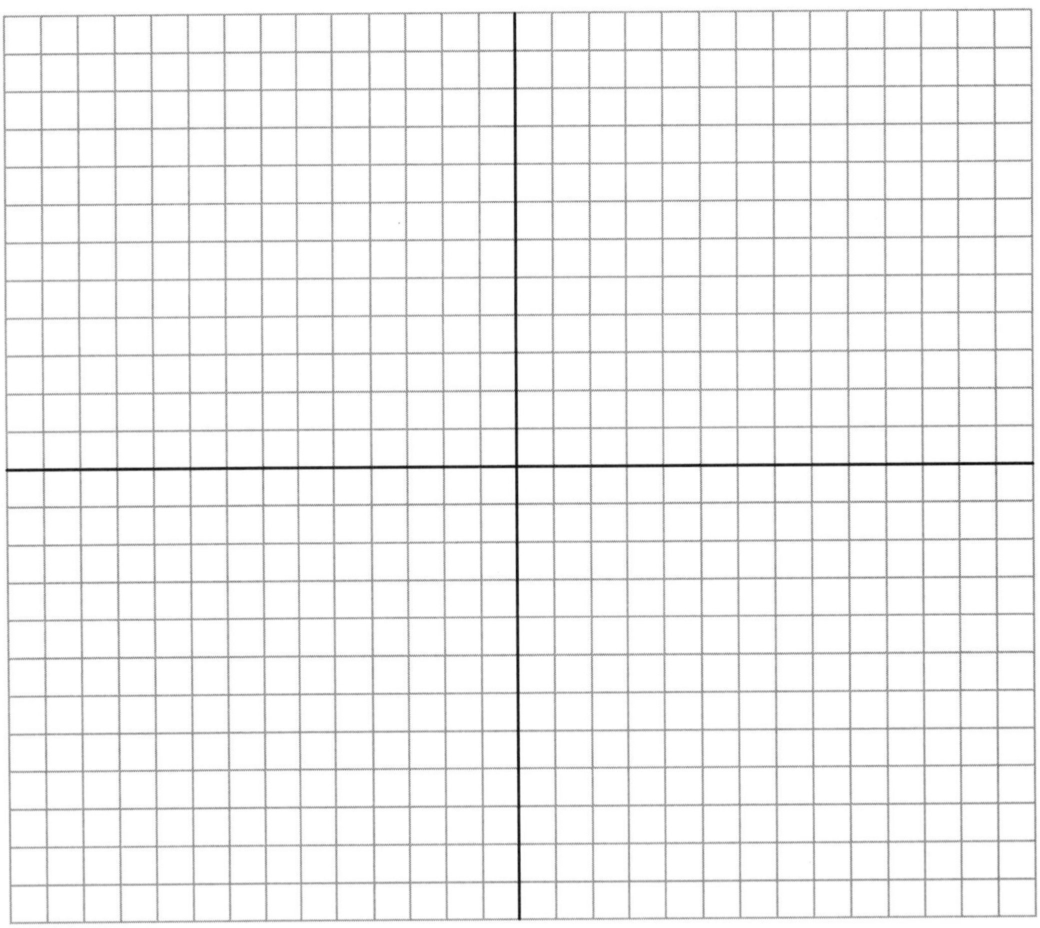

Transparency 5.2

A. Make a table that shows the profit Jean will earn for 0 through 20 tune-ups.

B. Plot the (tune-ups, profit) data from your table on a coordinate grid. Be sure to label the axes. Explain how you chose the scale for each axis.

C. What will Jean's profit be if she does only four tune-ups? How is this shown on the graph?

D. How many tune-ups will Jean have to do before she breaks even? How is this shown on the graph?

E. How does Jean's profit change with each tune-up she does? How is this shown on the graph?

A. **1.** Enter the equation $y = 4x$ into your graphing calculator as Y_1, and then press GRAPH to see a graph of the equation. Make a sketch of the graph you see.

2. Predict how the graph of $y = -4x$ will differ from the graph of $y = 4x$. Then, enter the equation $y = -4x$ as Y_2, and press GRAPH to see the graphs of both equations in the same window. Add a sketch of $y = -4x$ to your sketch from part 1.

3. How are the graphs alike? How are they different?

B. 1. Press TABLE to look at the table showing data for both equations ($y = 4x$ and $y = -4x$). You may need to use the ▶ key to see the Y_2 column. Copy part of the table onto your paper.

X	Y1	Y2

2. For each value of x in the table, look at the two corresponding values of y (Y_1 and Y_2). How are the two y values for a given x value related? How does this relationship show up in the graph?

C. With your graphing calculator, experiment with each set of equations. Look at the graphs and the tables. Record your observations.

1. $y = 4x + 5$ and $y = -4x + 5$

2. $y = 4x - 5$ and $y = -4x - 5$

A. On paper, make a table of x and y values for the equation $y = 3x + 2$.

x										
y										

B. On grid paper, sketch a graph of $y = 3x + 2$.

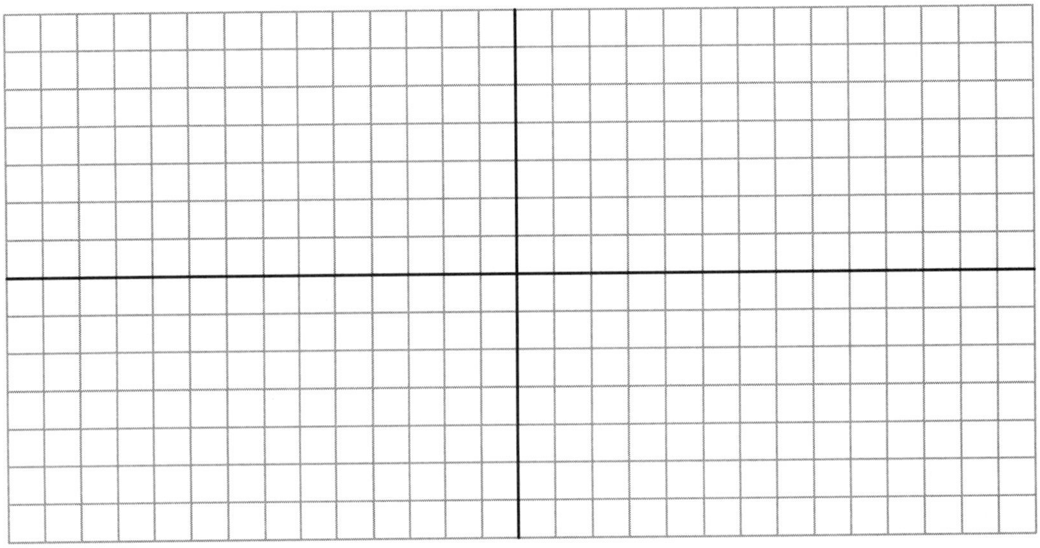

C. Enter the equation $y = 3x + 2$ into your graphing calculator, and press GRAPH. Make a sketch of the graph you see. How does this graph compare with the graph you drew by hand?

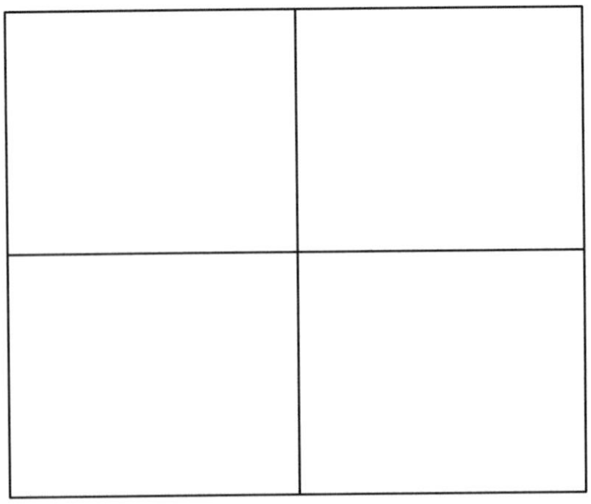

D. If you press [WINDOW], you will see a screen that allows you to change the section of the graph displayed in the window. Change the settings to those shown in “Window settings 1” on the previous page, and then press [GRAPH] to see the graph of $y = 3x + 2$ in the new window.

1. Make a sketch of the graph you see.

2. How does this graph compare with the graph you drew by hand in part B?

3. How does this graph compare with the graph you made with your calculator in part C?

4. Explain what you think each entry on the “Window settings 1” screen means.

E. On paper, make a table of x and y values for the equation $y = 2x$.

x										
y										

F. On grid paper, sketch a graph of $y = 2x$.

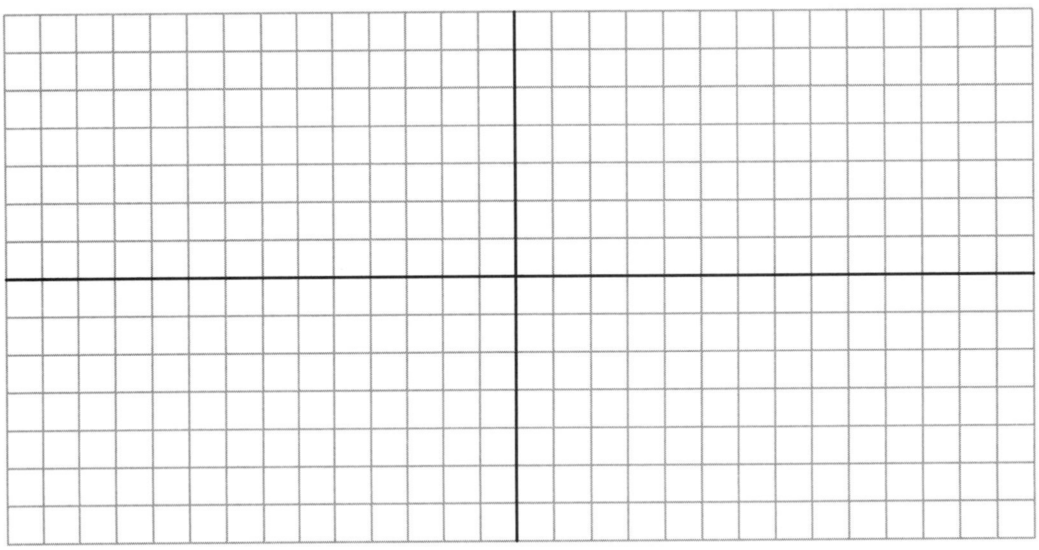

G. Enter the equation $y = 2x$ into your graphing calculator, and press GRAPH. Make a sketch of the graph you see.

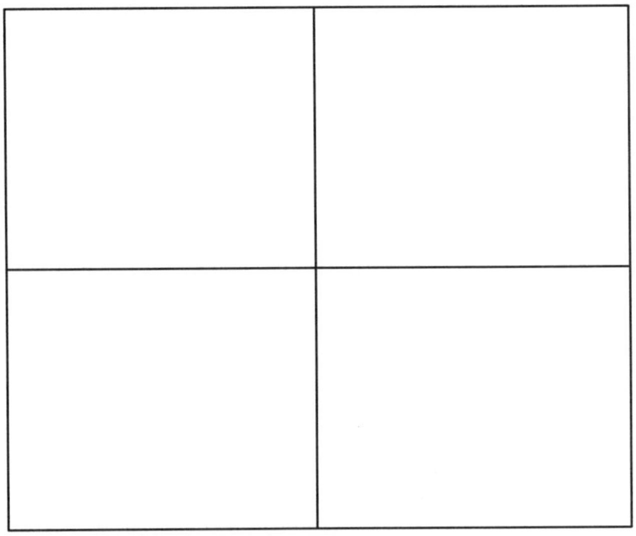

H. Change the window settings to those shown in "Window settings 2" on the previous page, and then press GRAPH to see the graph of $y = 2x$ in the new window.

1. Make a sketch of the graph you see.

2. How does this graph compare with the graph you drew by hand in part F?

3. How does this graph compare with the graph you made with your calculator in part G?

4. Explain what you think each entry on the "Window settings 2" screen means.

In the following questions, use Jean's profit equation $P = 60t - 800$ and your work from Problem 5.2.

A. **1.** In the table of data you made in Problem 5.2, what range of values did you use for the number of tune-ups?

2. What range of values did you use for the profit?

B. Enter Jean's profit equation into your calculator. Use the number of tune-ups as the x variable and the profit as the y variable. Use your answers to part A to help you decide how to adjust the window settings so that you will be able to see the graph of the profit equation. Press GRAPH to display the graph. Make a sketch of the graph you see on the screen.

C. How is the break-even point shown on the graph?

D. Look at the table of data on your calculator. How is the break-even point shown in the table?

Family Letter (English)

Dear Family,

The next unit in your child's course of study in mathematics class this year is *Accentuate the Negative.* This unit will introduce students to positive and negative numbers (integers). Your child will work on problems involving many contexts and learn how to compare integers; to add, subtract, multiply, and divide integers; and to use integers to solve problems. The variety of settings will help your child understand positive and negative integers. The class will begin by looking at a game (similar to the game show *Jeopardy!*®) in which some scores are negative and others are positive. They will work with temperature readings, both above and below 0, on a thermometer. They will also look at business-type situations that speak of being "in the red" or "in the black" and use colored chips to model operations with integers.

Here are some strategies for helping your child work with the ideas in this unit:

- Ask your child to describe some real-world situations in which integers are used. You can help by noting the daily temperature or talking about changes in temperature during the day. If your child talks to you about being "in the red" or "in the black," you may relate this idea to earnings or savings he or she has.
- Look at your child's mathematics notebook. You may want to read some of the explanations that have been written and, if they aren't clear, talk with your child about why you think they may need more explanation.
- Encourage your child's efforts in completing all homework assignments. Look over your child's work, and help your child make sure all questions have been answered and that all explanations are clear.

As always, if you have any questions or concerns about this unit or your child's progress in the class, please feel free to call. We are interested in your child's success in mathematics and want to ensure that this year's mathematics experiences are enjoyable.

Sincerely,

Family Letter (Spanish)

Estimada familia,

La próxima unidad del programa de matemáticas de su hijo o hija para este curso se llama *Accentuate the Negative* (La importancia de lo negativo). En ella los alumnos estudiarán los números positivos y negativos (los números enteros). Realizarán problemas relacionados con una diversidad de contextos y aprenderán a comparar números enteros, a sumarlos, restarlos, multiplicarlos y dividirlos y a emplearlos en la resolución de problemas. La amplia variedad de contextos ayudarán a su hijo o hija a entender esos números, tanto los positivos como los negativos. Así, se iniciará la unidad con un juego (parecido al concurso televisivo *Jeopardy!*®) en el que algunas puntuaciones son positivas y otras negativas. Los alumnos también trabajarán con el termómetro haciendo lecturas de temperaturas superiores e inferiores a 0. Además, examinarán situaciones del mundo de los negocios en las cuales se trata sobre los "números rojos" y los "números negros" y utilizarán fichas de colores para representar operaciones con números enteros.

He aquì algunas estrategias que ustedes pueden emplear para ayudar a su hijo o hija con el trabajo de esta unidad:

- Pìdanle que describa algunas situaciones del mundo real en las que se utilicen números enteros. Como ayuda, ustedes pueden señalar la temperatura diaria o hablar sobre los cambios registrados en la temperatura a lo largo del día. Si su hijo o hija menciona la idea de los "números rojos" o de los "números negros", será interesante tratar de relacionar la misma con sus ganancias o ahorros.
- Repasen su cuaderno de matemáticas. Es recomendable que lean algunas de sus explicaciones y, de resultar poco claras, que comenten con su hijo o hija las razones a favor de ampliar dichas explicaciones.
- Anímenle a esforzarse para que complete toda la tarea. Repasen la misma y comprueben juntos que todas las preguntas han sido contestadas y que todas las explicaciones han sido escritas con claridad.

Y como de costumbre, si ustedes necesitan más detalles o aclaraciones respecto a la unidad o sobre los progresos de su hijo o hija en esta clase, no duden en llamarnos. Nos interesa que su hijo o hija avance en el estudio de las matemáticas y queremos asegurarnos de que las experiencias matemáticas que tenga este año sean lo más amenas posibles.

Atentamente,

Number Lines

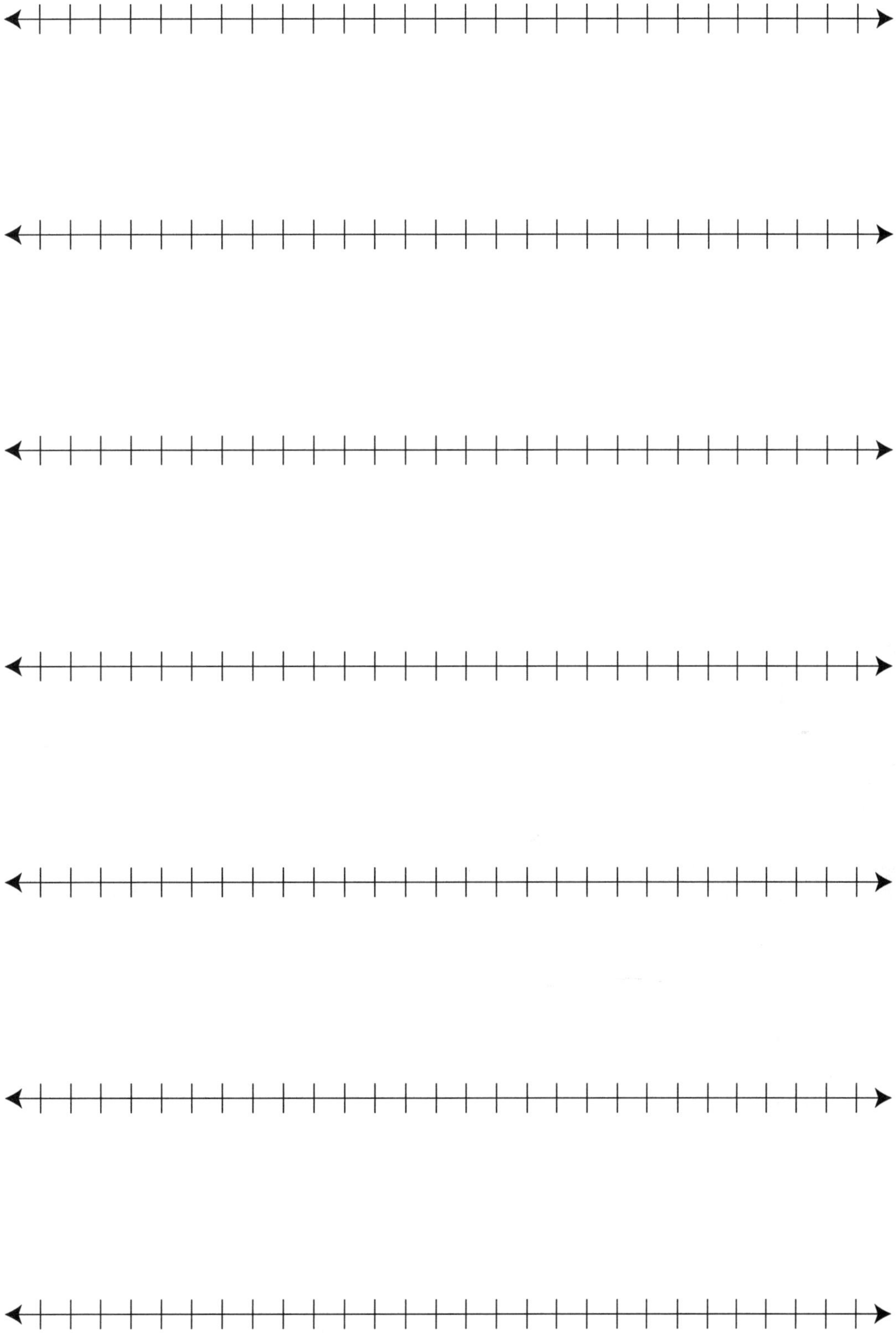

Chip Board

Chip Board

Chip Board

Chip Board

Chip Board

Chip Board

Chip Board

Chip Board

Chip Board

Chip Board

Coordinate Grids

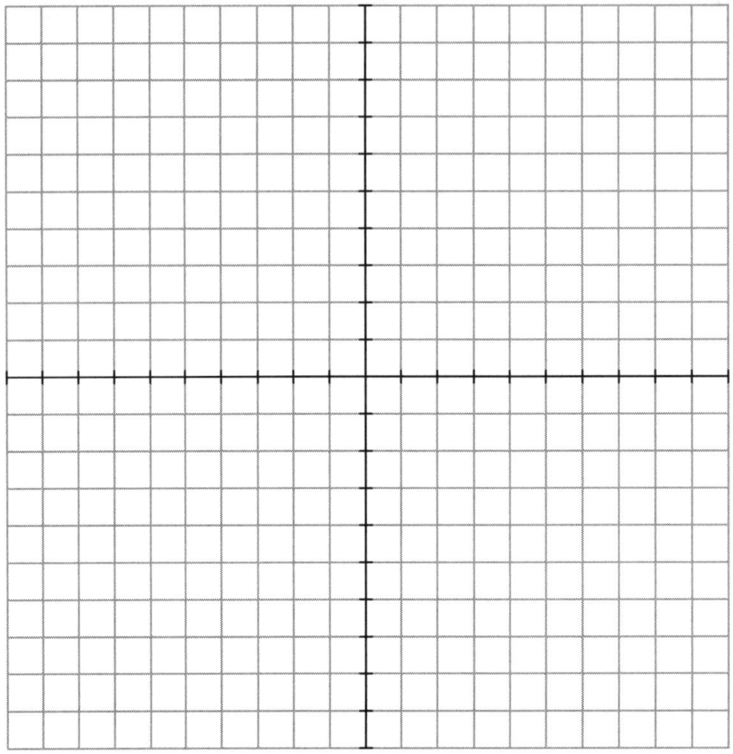

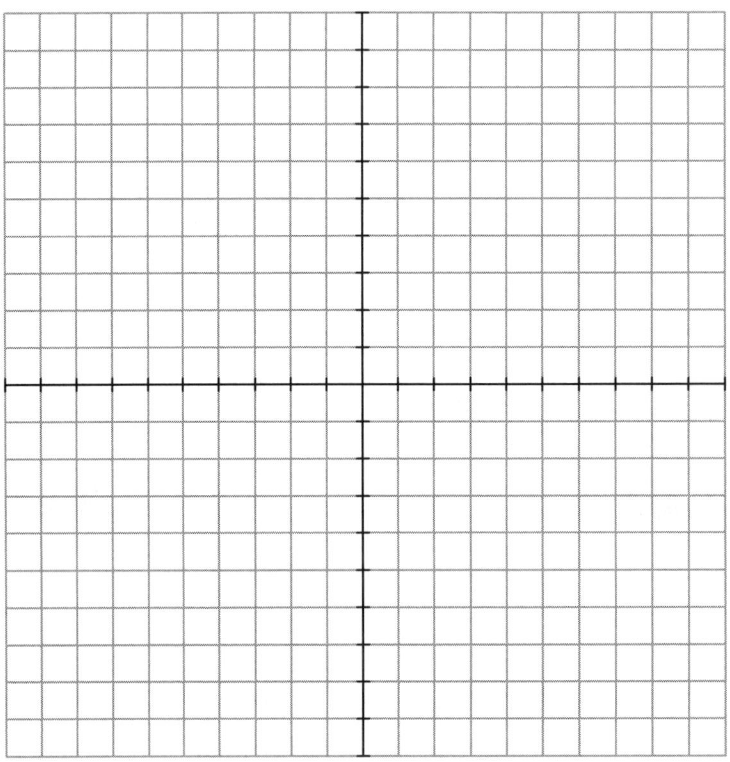

Graphing Calculator Grids

Calculator Grids and Tables

WINDOW
XMIN=
XMAX=
XSCL=
YMIN=
YMAX=
YSCL=

WINDOW
XMIN=
XMAX=
XSCL=
YMIN=
YMAX=
YSCL=

WINDOW
XMIN=
XMAX=
XSCL=
YMIN=
YMAX=
YSCL=

Grid Paper

Additional Practice

Investigation 1

Use these problems for additional practice after Investigation 1.

The teams in questions 1–5 each answered five questions. The score for four of the questions and the final score are given for each team. Give the point value of the fifth question and tell whether the team answered it correctly.

1. The Smarts answered a 150-point question correctly, a 200-point question correctly, a 50-point question incorrectly, and a 250-point question incorrectly. Their final score was 250 points.

2. The Brains answered a 150-point question incorrectly, a 200-point question correctly, a 150-point question correctly, and a 50-point question incorrectly. Their final score was 0 points.

3. The Minds answered a 200-point question incorrectly, a 50-point question correctly, a 100-point question incorrectly, and a 250-point question correctly. Their final score was 150 points.

4. The MegaBrains answered a 150-point question correctly, a 100-point question correctly, a 100-point question incorrectly, and a 250-point question correctly. Their final score was 150 points.

5. The SoSmarts answered a 50-point question incorrectly, a 150-point question correctly, a 100-point question incorrectly, and a 50-point question correctly. Their final score was $^{-}200$.

In 6–10, find two numbers that meet the given conditions.

6. Both numbers are less than 10.
   The distance between the two numbers on the number line is 14.

7. Both numbers are greater than $^{-}15$ and less than 5.
   One number is 6 greater than the other number.

8. One number is $^{-}35$.
   The distance between the two numbers on the number line is 20.

9. The numbers are opposites.
   The distance between the two numbers on the number line is 18.

10. The first number is the opposite of $^{-}17$.
    The second number is less than the first number.
    The distance between the two numbers on the number line is 9.

In 11–15, use the following information: At 10:00 A.M. on a winter day in Fairbanks, Alaska, the temperature was $^{-}12^{\circ}$F. Find the temperature after each of the following temperature changes.

11. Between 10:00 A.M and noon, the temperature rose 10°F.

12. Between noon and 3:00 P.M., the temperature rose 15°F.

13. Between 3:00 P.M. and 6:00 P.M., the temperature dropped 13°F.

14. Between 6:00 P.M. and 9:00 P.M., the temperature dropped 26°F.

15. Between 9:00 P.M. and midnight, the temperature changed by $^-19$°F.

In 16–20, use the sketch below, which shows a submarine cruising at a depth of 100 m. In your answers, express an increase in depth as a positive number and a decrease in depth as a negative number.

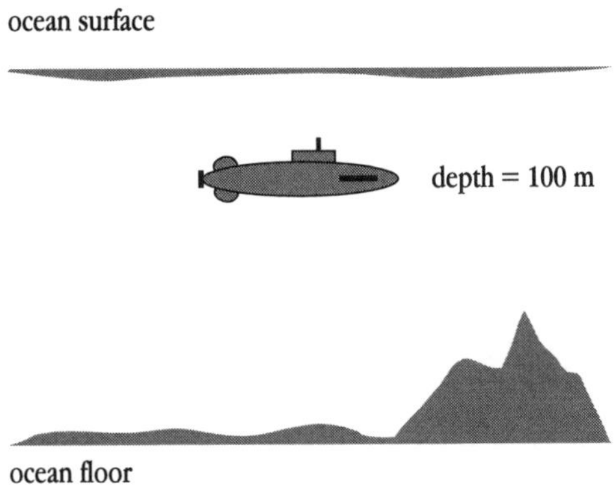

16. If the submarine moves from its depth of 100 m to a depth of 75 m, what is the change in its depth?

17. If the submarine dives from a depth of 100 m to a depth of 180 m, what is the change in its depth?

18. If the submarine surfaces from a depth of 180 m, what is the change in its depth?

19. The submarine is cruising at a depth of 50 m, then dives 75 m, then ascends (moves in the direction of the surface) 60 m, and then dives 45 m. What is submarine's final depth?

20. The submarine is cruising at a depth of 65 m. Then it dives 15 m, ascends 55 m, and then dives 75 m. At this final position, what is the change in depth from its initial position?

Additional Practice

Investigation 2

Use these problems for additional practice after Investigation 2.

In 1–5, show the addition on a number line, and give the sum.

1. ${}^{+}8 + {}^{-}8$

2. ${}^{-}2 + {}^{-}5 + {}^{-}4$

3. ${}^{+}8 + {}^{-}9 + {}^{-}2$

4. ${}^{-}8 + {}^{+}8 + {}^{-}3$

5. ${}^{-}10 + {}^{+}5 + {}^{+}4 + 1$

In 6–10, write the addition sentence illustrated by each figure.

6.

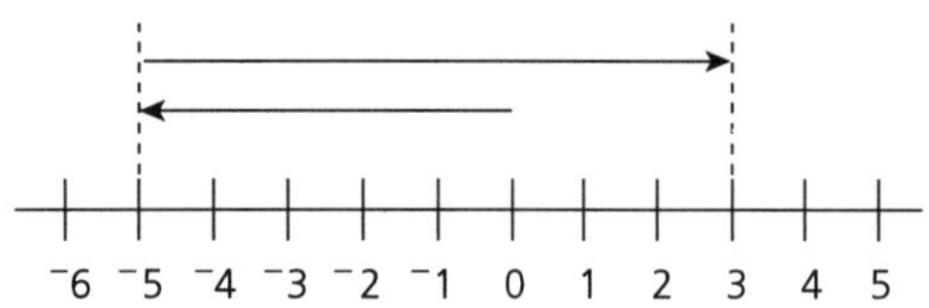

7.

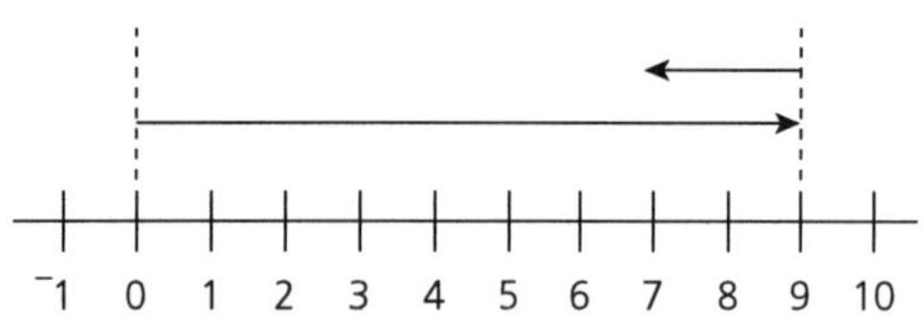

8.

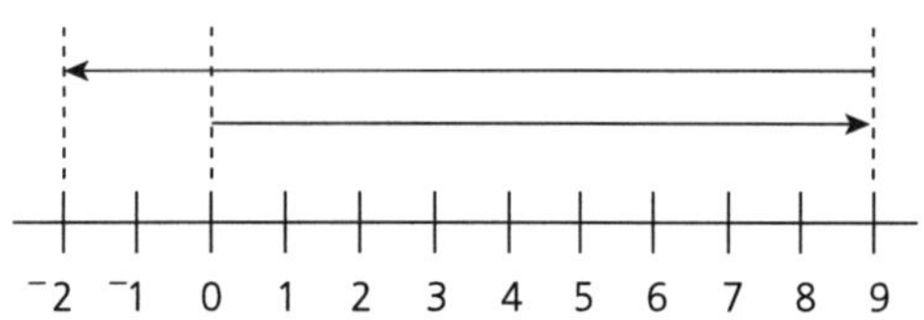

9.

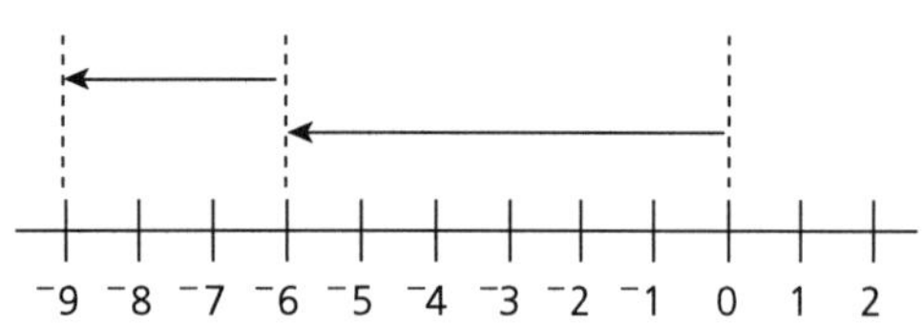

10.

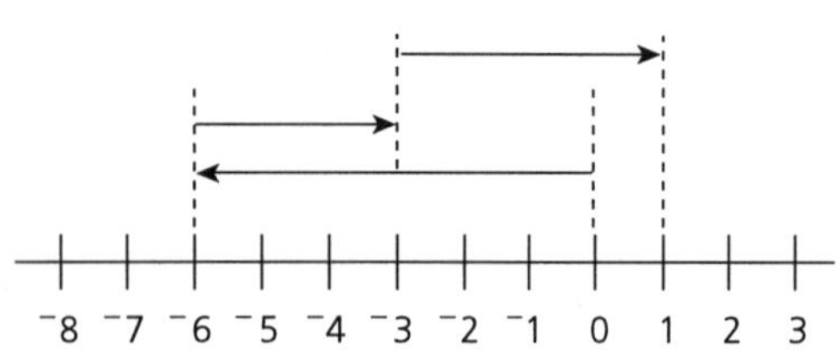

In 11–15, describe the chips that were on the chip board *before* the given action took place. Then write an addition sentence that describes the value of the original board, the value of the chips that are added, and the new value of the board.

11. 7 black chips are added. Now there are 8 black chips and 3 red chips on the board.

12. 5 red chips are added. Now there are 8 black chips and 12 red chips on the board.

13. 2 black chips and 2 red chips are added. Now there are 5 black chips and 3 red chips on the board.

14. 5 black chips and 8 red chips are added. Now there are 7 black chips and 8 red chips on the board.

15. 6 black chips and 8 red chips are added. Now there are 6 black chips and 11 red chips on the board.

16. **a.** Find two combinations of black and red chips that represent $^{-}5$.

b. Draw a chip board to represent each combination from part a.

c. Write an addition sentence to represent each combination from part a.

17. Bill said that $^{-}7 + {}^{+}4$ and $^{+}7 + {}^{-}10$ both represent the same number.

a. Draw a chip board to represent each combination.

b. Do both combinations of chips represent the same number? Explain your reasoning.

18. Tell which one of the following sums is different from the others, and explain your reasoning: $^{-}3 + {}^{+}5$, $^{+}8 + {}^{-}5$, $^{+}7 + {}^{-}5$, and $^{+}12 + {}^{-}10$.

19. On Friday, Anessa has \$5. Over the weekend, she buys a granola bar for \$0.75, sees a movie for \$3.50, gets \$2 from her brother who is repaying a loan, and then spends \$1.25 at the arcade. How much money does Anessa have at the end of the weekend?

20. Scientists sometimes use a temperature scale called the *Kelvin scale*. The relationship between the Kelvin temperature scale and the Celsius temperature scale is expressed by the equation $K = C + 273$ where K is degrees Kelvin and C is degrees Celsius.

a. What is $^{-}45$°C in degrees Kelvin?

b. What is 71°K in degrees Celsius?

c. If the temperature of a substance ranges from 102°K to 230°K, what is the temperature range in degrees Celsius?

Additional Practice

Investigation 3

Use these problems for additional practice after Investigation 3.

1. An amount paid to a business for goods or services is a *credit*, and an amount the business pays for goods, services, or debts is a *debit*. The chart below shows the total monthly credits and debits for the Hailey Middle School Student Store for the first six months of the school year. Use the chart to answer the following questions.

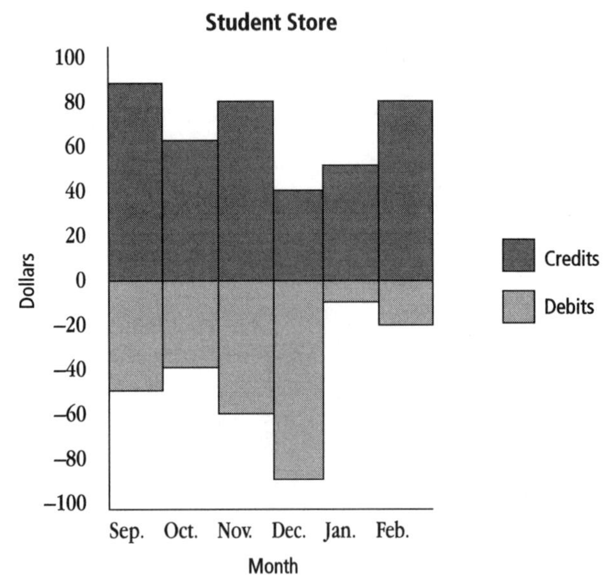

   a. What is the total of the credits for September through February?

   b. What is the total of the debits for September through February?

   c. Did the store make or lose money over this time period? Explain your reasoning.

   d. Adding the credits and debits gives the profit or loss for a given period of time. Tell which months the store showed a loss and which months the store showed a profit. Explain your reasoning.

In 2–5, explain how you could use chips and a chip board to find the difference. Then, find the difference.

2. $^-8 - 5$ 3. $3 - 9$ 4. $^-6 - {}^-12$

Additional Practice

In 5 and 6, write both an addition sentence and a subtraction sentence to represent what is shown on the number line.

5.

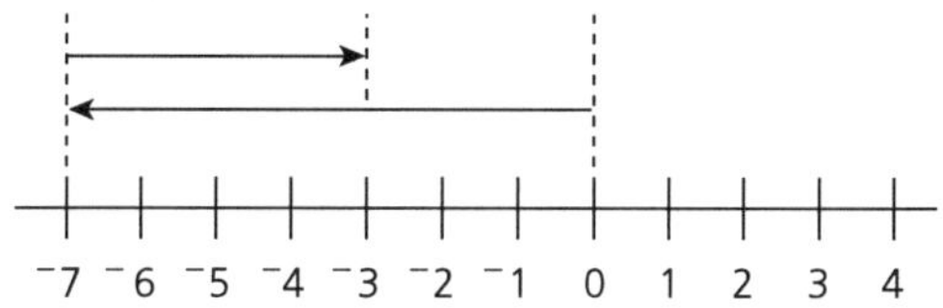

6.

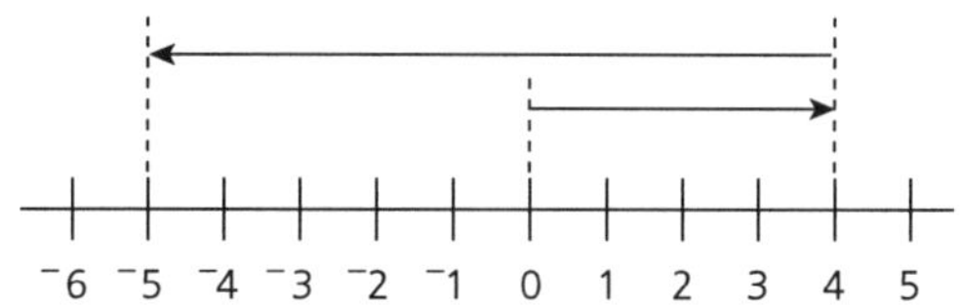

7. A chip board has 10 red chips and 10 black chips.

a. What value is represented by this board?

b. If 2 red chips and 2 black chips are removed, what value do the remaining chips represent?

c. If 20 red chips and 20 black chips are added, what value do the chips represent?

In 8–22, find the value of "?".

8. $? + 5 = 7$

9. $5 + ? = {}^-3$

10. $? + {}^-3 = {}^-9$

11. $7 - ? = 3$

12. $? - 10 = {}^-6$

13. $7 - ? = 12$

14. ${}^-6 - ? = 7$

15. ${}^-3.4 - ? = {}^-5.6$

16. $\frac{2}{3} - ? = 1$

17. $? - 12 = {}^-5$

18. ${}^-4.5 - \frac{9}{2} = ?$

19. $3\frac{2}{5} + ? = \frac{2}{5}$

20. $? + 7.6 = 3\frac{3}{5}$

21. $? - {}^-7.8 = 0$

22. $? + \frac{{}^-93}{10} = 10$

23. Decide whether the statement is always true, sometimes true, or always false. Explain your reasoning.

a. If a positive integer is subtracted from a negative integer, the difference is a negative integer.

b. If a positive integer is subtracted from a positive integer, the difference is a positive integer.

Investigation 4

Use these problems for additional practice after Investigation 4.

1. Last year, the Tri-County Bike Shop had average monthly sales totaling $24,500 and average monthly expenses totaling $18,900.
   a. What were the total sales for the shop last year? Explain how you found your answer.
   b. What were the total expenses of the shop last year?
   c. What was the total profit or loss of the shop last year?
   d. What was the average monthly profit or loss of the shop last year?

In 2–6, use this graph, which shows the monthly profit of a small bike repair shop.

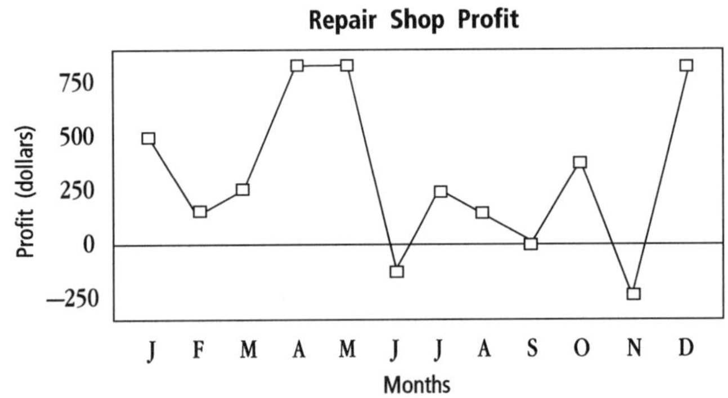

2. For each month, tell whether the repair shop made money, lost money, or broke even.
3. What was the total profit of the repair shop for the year?
4. What was the average monthly profit for the year?
5. In an average week, how much money would you expect the repair shop to make? Explain your reasoning.
6. Assuming that prices remain the same, what total profit would you expect the bike repair shop to make over the next 5 years? Explain your reasoning.

In 7–10, list all the integer factor pairs for the number.

7. 17 8. $^{-}24$ 9. 18 10. $^{-}18$

Additional Practice

In problems 11–25, find the value for "?".

11. $? \times 8 = 56$

12. $12 \times ? = {}^{-}36$

13. $? \times {}^{-}10 = 90$

14. $7 \times ? = {}^{-}147$

15. $? \div 18 = {}^{-}54$

16. $64 \div ? = 8$

17. ${}^{-}192 \div ? = 16$

18. ${}^{-}99.99 \div ? = {}^{-}3.03$

19. $\frac{2}{3} \times ? = \frac{10}{24}$

20. $? \times 13 = {}^{-}169$

21. ${}^{-}234 \div 12.5 = ?$

22. $3\frac{1}{5} \div ? = {}^{-}8$

23. $? \times {}^{-}7.6 = 67.64$

24. $? \div {}^{-}77.8 = 1$

25. $? \div \frac{{}^{-}93}{10} = 10$

Investigation 5

Use these problems for additional practice after Investigation 5.

1. a. Plot the following points on a coordinate grid: (5, 0), (⁻5, 0), (3, 4), (3,⁻4), (4, 3), (⁻3, 4), (0, 5), (0, ⁻5), (⁻4, 3), (4, ⁻3), (⁻3, ⁻4), (⁻4, ⁻3).
   b. Connect the points to form a familiar geometric figure and describe the graph.

2. The graph of the equation $y = 4 - x$ consists of all the points in the coordinate plane that satisfy the equation.
   a. Is the point (6, ⁻2) on the graph of $y = 4 - x$? Explain your reasoning.
   b. Is the point (3, 3) on the graph of $y = 4 - x$? Explain your reasoning.
   c. List four points that satisfy $y = 4 - x$. Plot the points on a coordinate grid. Describe the shape of the graph of $y = 4 - x$.
   d. What do you think is the minimum number of points you need to plot in order to draw the graph of $y = 4 - x$? Explain your reasoning.

3. Use the graph below to answer the following questions.

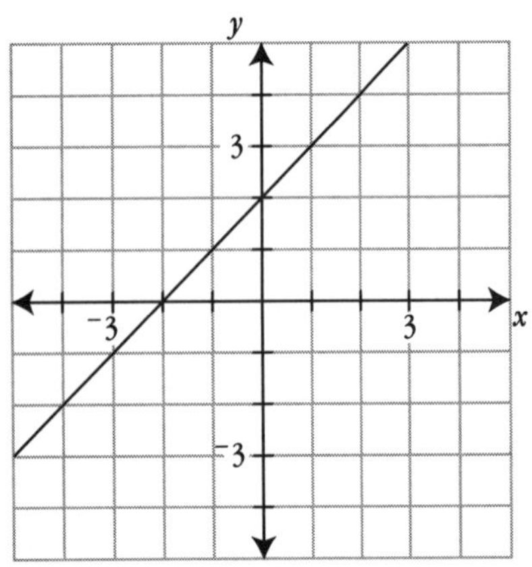

   a. Give the coordinates of six points that lie on the graph.
   b. What is the equation of the graph? Explain how your found your answer.

Investigation 1

1. 200 points; answered correctly
2. 150 points; answered incorrectly
3. 150 points; answered correctly
4. 250 points; answered incorrectly
5. 250 points; answered incorrectly
6. Possible answers: 9 and $^-5$, 4 and $^-10$, 0 and $^-14$, $^-1$ and $^-15$
7. Possible answers: 4 and $^-2$, 3 and $^-3$, 2 and $^-4$, 0 and $^-6$
8. $^-35$ and $^-15$ or $^-35$ and $^-55$
9. $^-9$ and 9
10. 17 and 8
11. $^-2$°F
12. 13°F
13. 0°F
14. $^-26$°F
15. $^-45$°F
16. $^-25$ m
17. 80 m
18. $^-180$ m
19. 110 m
20. The three changes are $^-15$, 55, and $^-75$. The total change is $^-35$. So the submarine ends 35 m lower than its initial position.

Investigation 2

1. 0

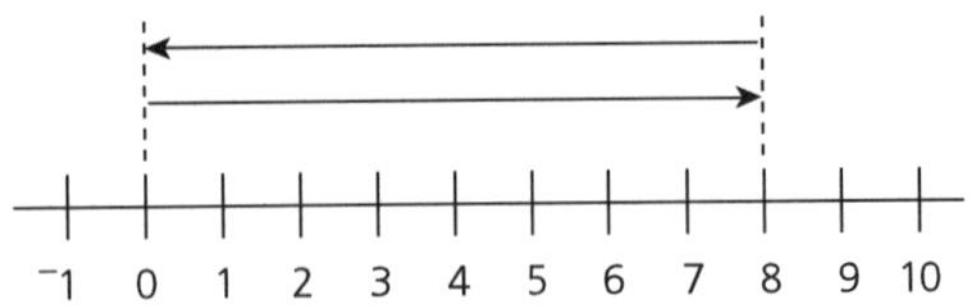

2. $^{-}11$

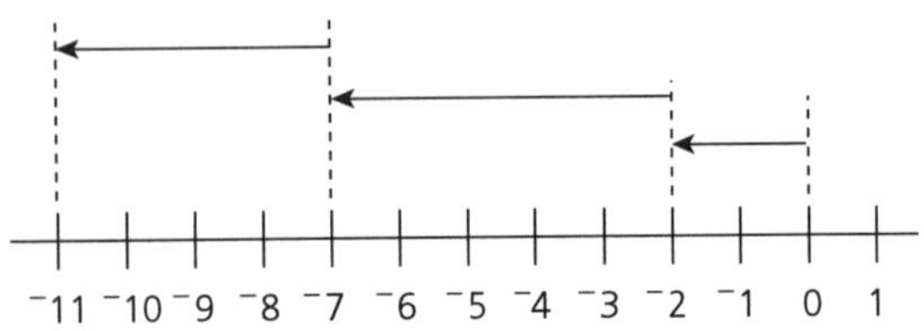

3. $^{-}3$

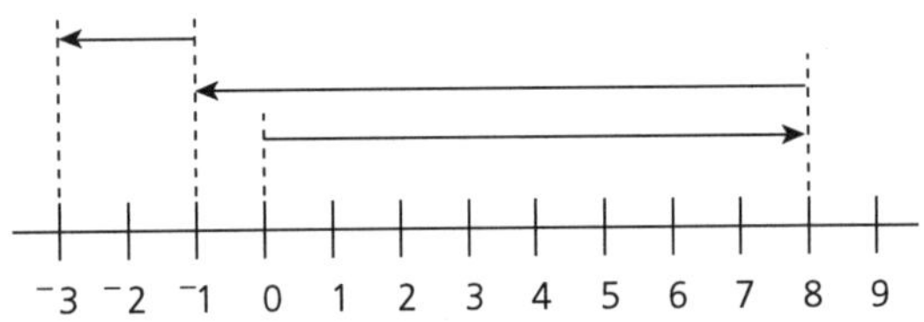

4. $^{-}3$

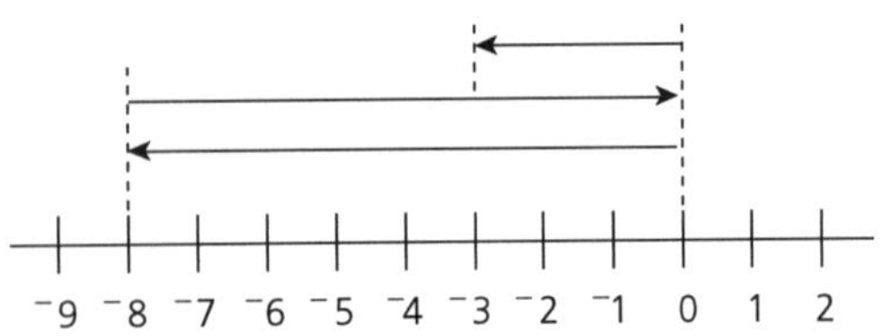

5. 0

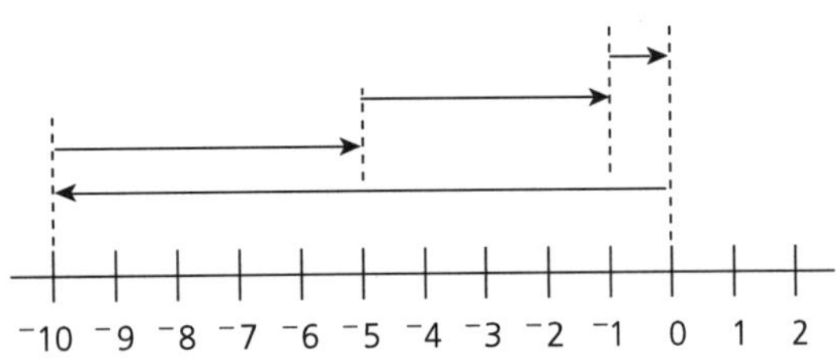

6. $^{-}5 + 8 = 3$

7. $9 + {}^{-}2 = 7$

8. $9 + {}^{-}11 = {}^{-}2$

9. $^{-}6 + {}^{-}3 = {}^{-}9$

10. $^{-}6 + 3 + 4 = 1$

11. The original board had 1 black chip and 3 red chips. The addition sentence would be $^{-}2 + 7 = 5$.

12. The original board had 8 black chips and 7 red chips. The addition sentence would be $1 + {}^{-}5 = {}^{-}4$.

13. The original board had 3 black chips and 1 red chip. The addition sentence would be $2 + 2 + {}^{-}2 = 2$.

14. The original board had 2 black chips and 0 red chips. The addition sentence would be $2 + 5 + {}^{-}8 = {}^{-}1$.

15. The original board had 0 black chips and 3 red chips. The addition sentence would be $^{-}3 + 6 + {}^{-}8 = {}^{-}5$.

16. Answers will vary.

17. **a.** $^{-}7 + 4$ is 7 red chips and 4 black chips.

    $7 + {}^{-}10$ is 7 black chips and 10 red chips.

    b. When simplified, both boards have 3 red chips, so they represent the same number.

18. Possible answer: $^{-}3 + 5$ is 3 red chips and 5 black chips, or 2 black chips; $8 + {}^{-}5$ is 8 black chips and 5 red chips, or 3 black chips; $7 + {}^{-}5$ is 7 black chips and 5 red chips, or 2 black chips; $12 + {}^{-}10$ is 12 black chips and 10 red chips, or 2 black chips; so $8 + {}^{-}5$ is different.

19. \$5.00 – \$0.75 – \$3.50 + \$2.00 – \$1.25 = \$1.50

20. **a.** $^{-}45 + 273 = 228$°K

    b. $71 = C + 273$, so the temperature is $^{-}202$°C.

    c. $^{-}171$°C to $^{-}43$°C

Investigation 3

1. **a.** $90 + 60 + 80 + 40 + 50 + 80 = \$400$

   b. $^{-}50 + {}^{-}40 + {}^{-}60 + {}^{-}90 + {}^{-}10 + {}^{-}20 = {}^{-}\$270$

   c. $\$400 + {}^{-}\$270 = \$130$; The store made money.

   d. By comparing the heights of the bars for credit and debit for each month, it is easy to tell which months had profits and which had losses. December was the only month with a loss. September, October, November, January, and February all showed a profit.

2. Possible answer: Represent $^{-}8$ as 13 red chips and 5 black chips. Remove 5 black chips. The difference is $^{-}13$.

3. Possible answer: Represent 3 as 6 red chips and 9 black chips. Remove 9 black chips. The difference is $^{-}6$.

4. Possible answer: Represent $^{-}6$ as 12 red chips and 6 black chips. Remove 12 red chips. The difference is 6.

5. $^{-}7 + 4 = {}^{-}3$; $^{-}7 - {}^{-}4 = {}^{-}3$

6. $4 + {}^{-}9 = {}^{-}5$; $4 - 9 = {}^{-}5$

7. **a.** 0 **b.** 0 **c.** 0

8. 2
9. $^{-}8$
10. $^{-}6$
11. 4
12. 4
13. $^{-}5$
14. $^{-}13$
15. 2.2
16. $\frac{-1}{3}$
17. 7
18. $^{-}9$
19. $^{-}3$
20. $^{-}4$
21. $^{-}7.8$
22. 19.3

23. **a.** Always true; Subtracting a positive number from a negative number is equivalent to adding a negative number to a negative number. A negative number plus a negative number is always negative.

b. The statement is sometimes true. Here are some examples: $5 - 3 = {}^{+}2$, $5 - 5 = 0$, $5 - 8 = {}^{-}3$

Investigation 4

1. **a.** Multiply the average sales by 12, which is the number of months in the year: $12 \times \$24{,}500 = \$294{,}000$.

b. $12 \times 18{,}900 = \$226{,}800$

c. Profit $= \$294{,}000 - \$226{,}800 = \$67{,}200$

d. $\frac{67{,}200}{12} = \$5600$

2. The shop made money in January, February, March, April, May, July, August, October, and December.
The shop lost money in June and November.
The shop broke even in September.

3. $500 + 125 + 250 + 750 + 750 + {}^{-}125 + 250 + 125 + 0 + 375 + {}^{-}250 + 750 = \$3500$

4. $\frac{3500}{12} = \$291.67$

5. $\frac{3500}{52} = \$67.31$; There are 52 weeks in a year, so the weekly profit is the yearly profit divided by 52.

6. $3500 \times 5 = \$17{,}500$; Multiply the yearly profit by 5.

7. 1×17 and ${}^{-}1 \times {}^{-}17$

8. $1 \times {}^{-}24, {}^{-}1 \times 24, 2 \times {}^{-}12, {}^{-}2 \times 12, 3 \times {}^{-}8, {}^{-}3 \times 8, 4 \times {}^{-}6, {}^{-}6 \times 4$

9. ${}^{-}1 \times {}^{-}18, 1 \times 18, {}^{-}2 \times {}^{-}9, 2 \times 9, {}^{-}3 \times {}^{-}6, 3 \times 6$

10. $1 \times {}^{-}18, {}^{-}1 \times 18, 2 \times {}^{-}9, {}^{-}2 \times 9, 3 \times {}^{-}6, {}^{-}3 \times 6$

11. 7
12. $^{-}3$
13. $^{-}9$
14. $^{-}21$
15. $^{-}972$
16. 8
17. $^{-}12$
18. 33
19. $\frac{5}{8}$
20. $^{-}13$
21. $^{-}18.72$
22. $\frac{-2}{5}$

23. $^-8.9$ **24.** $^-77.8$ **25.** $^-93$

Investigation 5

1. All the points lie on a circle of radius 5 that is centered at the point (0, 0). (Note: Instead of drawing a circle, students may connect the points with straight line segments.)

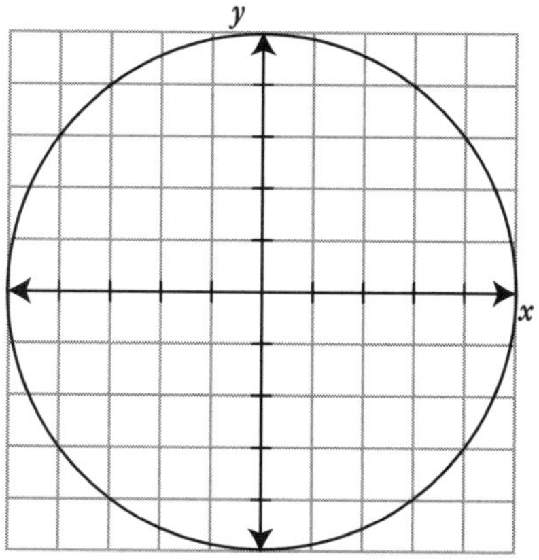

2. a. yes; $^-2 = 4 - 6$

   b. no; $3 \neq 4 - 3$

   c. Students' points will vary, but the graph should look like this:

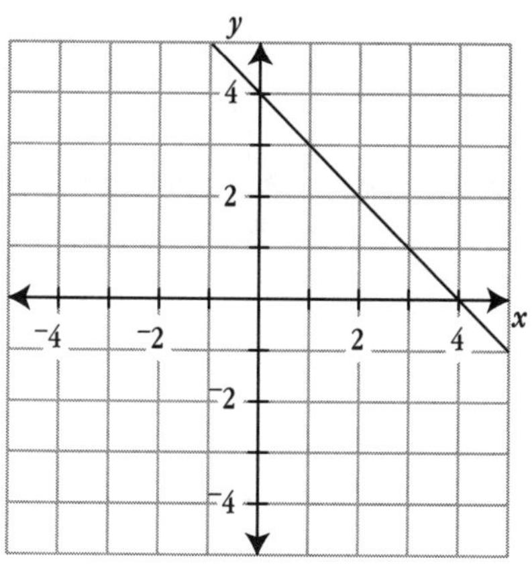

   d. You would need to plot a minimum of two points because the graph is a line, and two points determine a unique line.

3. a. Answers will vary, but all points should be of the form $(x, x + 2)$.

   b. Possible answer: All the points have a y-coordinate that is 2 more than the x-coordinate, so the equation of the graph is $y = x + 2$.

Descriptive Glossary

absolute value The absolute value of a number is its distance from 0 on a number line. It can be thought of as the value of a number when its sign is ignored. For example, $^{-}3$ and 3 both have an absolute value of 3.

expense, loss Expenses are the costs incurred while doing business, including cost of merchandise sold, rent on a building, and wages for employees. Loss is the amount the business is "short" if expenses exceed income.

income, profit Income is the amount of money a business takes in (for example, from sales of merchandise); profit is the amount left over from income after expenses are subtracted.

integer The integers are the whole numbers and their opposites. The integers from $^{-}4$ to 4 are shown on the number line below.

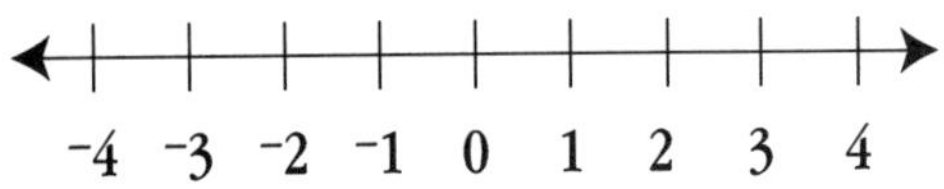

inverse operations Operations that "undo" each other are called inverse, or opposite, operations. Addition and subtraction are inverse operations. For example, the subtraction equation $7 + {}^{-}4 = 3$ is undone by the addition equation $3 - {}^{-}4 = 7$. Multiplication and division are inverse operations. For example, the multiplication equation $2 \times 6 = 12$ is undone by the division equations $12 \div 2 = 6$ and $12 \div 6 = 2$.

negative integer, negative number A negative integer is an integer less than 0. On a number line, negative numbers are located to the left of 0 (on a vertical number line, negative numbers are located below 0).

number sentence A number sentence gives the relationship between two expressions, which are composed of numbers and operation signs. For example, $3 + 2 = 5$ and $6 \times 2 > 10$ are number sentences; $3 + 2$, 5, 6×2, and 10 are expressions.

opposites Two numbers that add to 0 are opposites. For example, $^{-}3$ and 3 are opposites. On a number line, opposites are the same distance from 0 but in different directions from 0. The number 0 is its own opposite.

positive integer, positive number A positive integer is an integer greater than 0. (The number 0 is neither positive nor negative.) On a number line, positive numbers are located to the right of 0 (on a vertical number line, positive numbers are located above 0).

quadrant The quadrants are the four sections into which the coordinate plane is divided. They are labeled as follows:

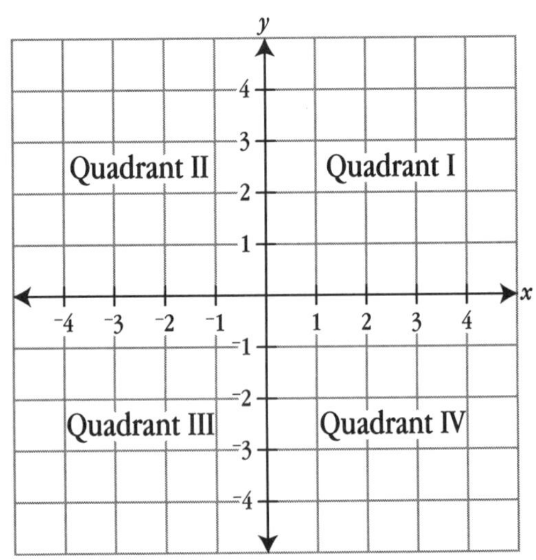

cuadrantes Las cuatro secciones en las que un plano de coordenadas queda dividido por los ejes x e y. Los cuadrantes se identifican de la siguiente manera:

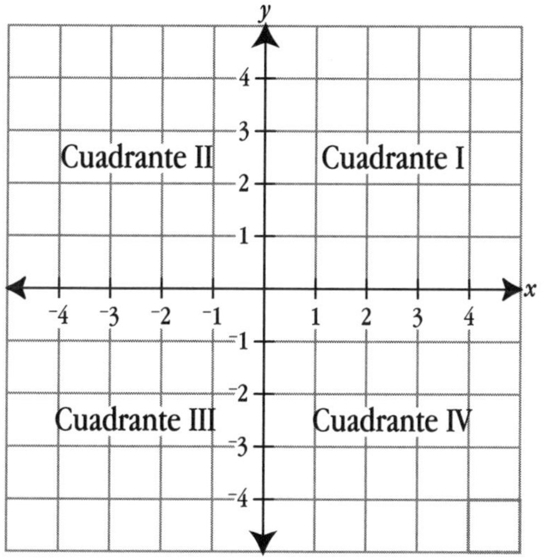

enteros Números enteros positivos y sus opuestos. 0 es un entero, pero no es ni positivo ni negativo. En la siguiente recta numérica figuran los enteros comprendidos entre $^{-}4$ y 4.

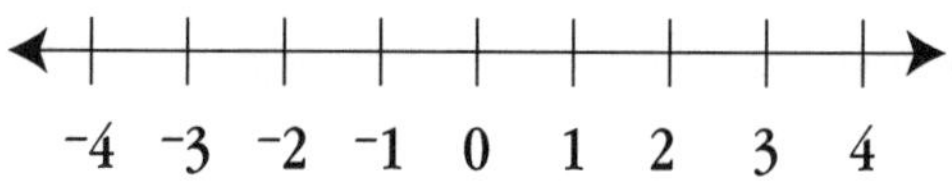

número negativo Un número menor que 0. En una recta numérica, los números negativos están ubicados a la izquierda de 0 (en una recta numérica vertical, los números negativos están ubicados debajo de 0).

número positivo Un número mayor que 0. (El número 0 no es ni positivo ni negativo.) En una recta numérica los números positivos se ubican a la derecha de 0 (en una recta numérica vertical, los números positivos están por encima de 0).

operaciones inversas Operaciones que se "anulan" mutuamente. Por ejemplo, la ecuación de resta $7 - 4 = 3$ queda anulada por la ecuación de suma $3 + 4 = 7$. La multiplicación y la división son operaciones inversas. Por ejemplo, la ecuación de multiplicación $2 \times 6 = 12$ queda anulada por las ecuaciones de división $12 \div 2 = 6$ y $12 \div 6 = 2$.

opuestos Dos números cuya suma da 0. Por ejemplo, $^{-}3$ y 3 son opuestos. En una recta numérica, los opuestos se encuentran a la misma distancia de 0 pero en distintos sentidos. El número 0 es su propio opuesto.

oración numérica Un enunciado matemático que describe la relación entre dos expresiones compuestas por números y signos de operaciones. Por ejemplo, $3 + 2 = 5$ y $6 \times 2 > 10$ son oraciones numéricas. $3 + 2$, 5, 6×2 y 10 son expresiones.

valor absoluto El valor absoluto de un número es su distancia de 0 sobre una recta numérica. Se puede interpretar como el valor de un número cuando no importa su signo. Por ejemplo, tanto $^{-}3$ como 3 tienen un valor absoluto de 3.

Index

Index

Index